Theories of Mood and Cognition

A User's Handbook

Theories of Mood and Cognition
A User's Handbook

Edited by

Leonard L. Martin
University of Georgia

Gerald L. Clore
University of Illinois, Urbana–Champaign

2001

LAWRENCE ERLBAUM ASSOCIATES, PUBLISHERS
Mahwah, New Jersey   London

Lawrence Erlbaum Associates, Inc., Publishers
10 Industrial Avenue
Mahwah, New Jersey 07430

Cover design by Kathryn Houghtaling Lacey

Library of Congress Cataloging-in-Publication Data

Theories of mood and cognition : a users handbook / edited by Leonard L. Martin, Gerald
L. Clore
    p. cm.
    Includes bibliographical references and indexes.
    ISBN 0-8058-2783-8 (cloth : alk. paper) — ISBN 0-8058-2784-6 (pbk. : alk. paper)
    1.   Emotions and cognition. I. Martin, Leonard L. II. Clore, Gerald L.

  BF531 T52 2000
  152.4—dc21

                          00-042191

Contents

Preface

In 1957, Leon Festinger published his now-famous theory of cognitive dissonance. According to the theory, when individuals hold two inconsistent cognitions, they experience an unpleasant affective state that, in turn, motivates them to restore cognitive consistency (e.g., to change one of the cognitions). This theory and its associated experimental paradigms are now well established. In the early days of the theory, however, researchers had a problem. It was difficult for them to know on an a priori basis whether any given manipulation would produce cognitive dissonance. One recommendation apparently followed by many of the early researchers was to "ask Leon." That is, when these early researchers were unsure what cognitive dissonance theory would predict, they simply called up Leon Festinger and asked him. The more general point is that if you want to get a good idea of what a theory would predict in any given situation, you cannot do any better than going directly to the theorist.

That is the spirit behind this volume. But instead of "ask Leon," we are, in essence, giving readers a chance to "ask Duane, Herbert, Jerry, Joe, Klaus, Lenny, Norbert, and Rich." More specifically, this volume offers readers a chance to see how eight investigators address some central questions regarding the effects of affective states on cognition. We invited as contributors researchers who were active in the field and who were associated with sell-specified explanations of mood effects. The goal was to have these investigators lay out their positions as clearly and concisely as possible and then show how they would use their accounts to explain a range of phenomena. The phenomena in this case were four findings that seemed to show up most consistently in affect-cognition research: mood-congruent recall, mood-congruent judgment, negative affect leading to more systematic processing, and positive affect leading to more creative processing.

After the contributors had described their basic theoretical assumptions and had indicated how they used these assumptions to address the four major phenomena, these initial parts of each chapter were circulated among the other contributors for comments. The editors then distilled the comments into three questions for each contributor, and the contributors addressed their respective questions in the final parts of their chapters. In this way, each chapter presents us with a theory, an application of that theory to the four major phenomena in the affect-cognition area, and some answers regarding the basic theory, the applications of that theory, or both.

This volume was truly a collaborative effort. Not only did each contributor have a chance to make suggestions on each of the other chapters, they also had input at each stage of the project. The selection of the four target phenomena, for example, was accomplished by means of a democratic vote. It was hoped that, in this way, the result would be a fair and objective treatment of each position. After all, the goal of this volume was descriptive, not evaluative. We did not want a volume that suggested a contest to choose which theoretical account is the best. What we wanted instead was to see how the theorists actually use their explanations in a variety of situations, so that it would become clearer to those of us who are not the theorists how to use each particular theory.

The initial idea for this volume grew out of a symposium organized by Herbert Bless at the 1994 meeting of the European Association of Experimental Social Psychology in Lisbon. A number of the contributors to this volume participated in that symposium, and a number of mood-related papers by other researchers were presented as well. This arrangement gave us as the editors a chance to listen to a series of talks that addressed affect-cognition interactions. Over the course of these talks, we found ourselves evaluating each set of findings against our own theories. One talk might present data that were perfectly congruent with our theories, another might present data that did not readily fit, and a third might present data that tested hypotheses that were not even considered by our theories. In each case, however, we found ourselves thinking about how we would pull the various findings together. These experiences led us to conjecture that a book that provided a similar opportunity to the major theorists in the area would be an interesting work. This volume represents our attempt to capture that experience.

Although reading this volume is not likely to be as colorful as engaging Leon Festinger in a conversation about cognitive dissonance theory, we hope that it will serve much the same purpose. It is intended to allow readers to get inside the heads of the theorists, and this, in turn, may help readers to apply the various theories, as well as to sharpen their own theoretical ideas.

Leonard L. Martin
Gerald L. Clore

Introduction

Gerald L. Clore
University of Illinois

Leonard L. Martin
University of Georgia

In his classic definition, Allport (1968) described social psychology as the scientific study of the way in which the real, imagined, or implied presence of others influences the thoughts, feelings, and behaviors of individuals. When Allport wrote this definition, however, most of the research addressed thoughts and behaviors rather than feelings. Traditionally, when feelings were studied, they were studied in the form of attitudes, evaluations, or sentiments (e.g., balance theory). That began to change in the early 1970s when researchers began directly manipulating feelings in the laboratory and assessing the effects of these feelings on thoughts and behavior. Gouaux (1971), for example, had participants watch either a happy or a sad film and then evaluate a stimulus person. Griffit and Veitch (1971) had participants evaluate a stimulus person while working either in an unpleasantly hot and crowded room or in a pleasant, uncrowded room. Both of these experiments showed that participants' affective experiences could influence their attraction toward a stimulus person over and above their evaluative beliefs about the person. Because much of this initial work was couched in conditioning terms (e.g., Clore & Byrne, 1974), however, it did not directly address the effects of feelings on cognition.

Interest in the relation between feelings and cognition was sparked when G. H. Bower and A. M. Isen published, each in the same year, research showing mood-dependent recall (Bower, Montiero, & Gilligan, 1978) and mood-congruent evaluation, explained in terms of mood-congruent memory (Isen, Shalker, Clark, & Karp, 1978). Bower and col-

1

leagues induced mood through hypnosis, whereas Isen and colleagues handed out free gifts at a shopping mall. More important, though, was the fact that these researchers explained their findings in purely cognitive terms (i.e., spreading activation, mood as a memory cue). As much as anything else, this theoretical move brought the study of emotion and mood into the purview of mainstream experimental psychology.

In the late 1980s and early 1990s, it became clear that moods did more than affect the outcome of processing (e.g., memory, evaluation); they also affected the nature of the processing. Worth and Mackie (1987), for example, presented participants in neutral or positive moods with either a strong or a weak persuasive message and found that those in neutral moods were more persuaded by the strong than the weak argument, whereas those in positive moods were equally persuaded by the strong and weak arguments. These results suggested that the positive mood led participants to exert little effort in processing the persuasive messages.

More recent research (summarized in this volume) has replicated the aforementioned findings and has also provided qualifications of these findings. For example, recent research has shown that the effects of mood on cognitive processing are dependent on a number of moderating variables (e.g., familiarity of target, attribution of source of mood). Despite the increasing complexity of the findings, there are some consistencies. More often than not, being in a mood leads to mood-congruent recall, as well as mood-congruent evaluation. Similarly, individuals in negative moods typically process more systematically than individuals in positive moods, whereas individuals in positive moods typically process more flexibly and creatively than individuals in negative moods. To account for these consistencies, as well as their qualifications, a new set of theoretical conceptualizations has been developed. This volume presents some of these conceptualizations.

To make the presentation of these conceptualizations as clear as possible, the contributors have attempted to describe their theoretical models briefly and simply. Moreover, to facilitate comparisons among the models, the contributors described how their models addressed four of the most commonly reported phenomena in the mood literature (i.e., the effects of mood on memory, judgment, processing, and creativity). It is hoped that this format will allow readers to discern the basic assumptions of each model and the way in which the theorists use these assumptions to address the major findings and their qualifications.

Throughout the various chapters, readers may note that beyond the differences in assumptions and proposed theoretical mechanisms, there is a considerable degree of similarity. There are two reasons for this: (a) The models address the same target phenomena. It is not surprising, therefore, that they have converged on some common answers. (b) Perhaps even more important, is the considerable amount of collaboration and cross-fertilization that has occurred among the contributors. Frequent and open patterns of communication have led to some common ideas, and there is a good deal of tolerance on the part of each theorist for the ideas proposed by the others. Each of the chapters is laid out independently, however, and it is up to the reader to extract the commonalities and differences.

Herbert Bless presents an account of affect and cognition that depends on an association between positive affect and the use of general knowledge structures (e.g., schemas, scripts). In agreement with Fiedler, he says that negative affect (and unsuccessful attempts to apply general knowledge) should lead to stimulus-specific processing. As a whole, Bless' position is a variation on the general affect-as-information approach. His model, however, focuses mainly on the problem of mood and processing. Bless suggests that the effects of mood on processing do not depend on mood-elicited procedural knowledge, as suggested by Norbert Schwarz, but rather that mood acts directly to elicit a focus on different kinds of cognitive content, that is, on general knowledge versus situational detail. Also, he rejects implications that positive mood reduces the capacity or motivation to process. His experiments suggest that any association between positive mood and reduced processing does not mean that positive mood leads to diminished capacity, as is often assumed, but that the reliance on general knowledge structures by individuals in positive moods simply makes extensive processing unnecessary.

Clore, Wyer, Dienes, Gasper, Gohm, and Isbell propose nine principles intended to capture the processes underlying the affect-as-information approach (Schwarz & Clore, 1983). For example, the immediacy principle indicates that affect tends to be experienced as relevant to whatever is currently in consciousness. The informational value of feelings depends on the focus of the individual and his or her goals in the situation in which the feelings are experienced. Thus positive affective feelings may be experienced as liking when an individual's focus is on the goal of evaluating objects, but the same feelings may be experienced as confidence in accessible beliefs and inclinations when he or she focuses on tasks with the goal of performance. Similarly, the feelings may be perceived as feedback about affect when the goal is affect regulation. The model accounts for mood-related phenomena without assuming that feelings of mood influence memory. Thus it departs from traditional judgment theory, which holds that liking depends on the attributes and memories retrieved about an object of judgment. The affect-as-information hypothesis says that feelings may directly affect either judgment (when experienced as liking) or information processing (when experienced as feedback about accessible information).

Ralph and Maureen Erber's self-regulation perspective represents a departure from the other approaches to mood and cognition. They suggest that some of the more problematic phenomena observed in the mood literature may actually reflect efforts at affect regulation. They discuss intriguing experiments showing that the anticipation of social interaction, as well as effortful demands of particular tasks, often stimulate people to regulate their feeling states and that it is this regulation that leads to surprising effects. For example, in a study of recall, Erber and Erber found the usual evidence of mood congruency when they asked students to recall events at the end of class. However, they found mood incongruency on the same task when they obtained recall data at the beginning of class. They inferred that students engaged in mood regulation at the beginning but not at the end of class in order to process the upcoming lecture. They thus agree with Martin that moods are not tightly linked to particular processing styles. Their model predicts that many mood effects may be altered or reduced by the presence of social or task constraints and that processing is ultimately governed by such constraints.

In his chapter, Klaus Fiedler presents the "dual force" model. He argues that all cognitive tasks require the dual processes of conserving input information (accommodation) and transforming it on the basis of knowledge (assimilation). He suggests that positive and negative moods influence such processing as instances of appetitive and aversive motivation more generally. Specifically, appetitive motivation encourages exploration and creativity, whereas aversive situations motivate one to avoid mistakes. He predicts that the effect of mood on performance depends on a match between the requirements of particular cognitive tasks and the processes that follow from appetitive and aversive motivation. Fiedler proposes that mood influences occur mainly on generative tasks because mood effects are knowledge based rather than based on capacity or motivation. Mood is assumed to be an associative cue for material in memory, so that the more generative the task, the more mood has a chance to cue mood-congruent material in memory. For example, positive mood enhances the "generation effect," in which memory is superior for generated rather than merely reproduced material.

In chapter 5, Joseph Forgas outlines his affect infusion model (AIM). This model was developed to explain why affect sometimes influences (i.e., infuses) judgments and sometimes does not. The model's starting assumption is that affect is most likely to influence judgments that involve constructive processing (i.e., substantial transformation of the input) rather than mere reproduction of existing cognitive representations (cf. Fiedler). This means that affect is likely to influence the impression one forms of a stranger, for example, but not the impression one forms of a good friend for whom one can directly retrieve a previously stored evaluation. Whether or not individuals engage in the type of processing that allows for affect infusion is determined by variables such as target familiarity, target complexity, personal relevance, specific motivation, cognitive capacity, and situational pragmatics. The AIM is also explicit in suggesting that there may be more than one process by which affect can infuse judgments. Specifically, the model assumes that affect can infuse judgments either directly, through the "How do I feel about it?" heuristic, or indirectly, by priming affect-related cognitive categories.

In chapter 6, Leonard Martin presents his mood-as-input model. This model is a variant of the informational views taken by others (e.g., Bless, Clore, Schwarz). The model, however, argues for a distinction between the information conveyed by one's subjective experiences and the implications of that information. This distinction allows positive moods to convey negative implications and negative moods to convey positive implications. For example, if an individual feels sad after hearing of an unfortunate event in the life of a friend, the individual might infer that he or she is empathetic, a socially desirable trait. In this way, a negative feeling can give rise to a positive evaluation. More generally, the mood-as-input model suggests that individuals evaluate a target by asking themselves (hypothetically), "What would I feel if the target fulfilled the role for which I am evaluating it?" Favorable evaluations arise to the extent that the person's feelings (positive or negative) are congruent with what would be expected if the target had fulfilled a positive role. Negative evaluations arise to the extent that the person's feelings are incongruent with what would be expected if the target had fulfilled a positive role. This role-fulfillment mechanism allows the mood-as-input model to account for both mood-congruent and mood-incongruent judgments without recourse to an outside influence (e.g., mood- repair motivations). The model also suggests that there are no inherent associations between specific feelings and specific motivations (e.g., to repair mood, to process systematically)

In chapter 7, Norbert Schwarz summarizes his feelings-as-information model, as well as the cognitive-tuning derivative of that model. The former focuses on the heuristic processes through which individuals' subjective experiences (e.g., mood, boredom, ease of retrieval) can influence their evaluations. Specifically, Schwarz suggests that in many situations individuals avoid making judgments that entail an effortful, detailed review and integration of the relevant information. What they do instead is hold the target of judgment in mind and ask themselves, "How do I feel about it?" If they feel good, then they render a positive evaluation. If they feel bad, then they render a negative evaluation. These mood-congruent judgments occur, according to Schwarz, because individuals interpret their affective reactions as aspects of their evaluation of the target. If individuals become aware that their affective reactions are not due to the target, however, then their reactions do not influence their judgments of the target. Schwarz also notes that affective states can inform individuals about their current situation. Being in a negative mood signals a problematic situation, whereas being in a positive mood signals a benign situation. Then, because individuals' cognitive processes are tuned to meet these perceived situational demands, negative moods engender careful, conservative, effortful processing, whereas positive moods allow individuals the freedom to take risks, explore new associations, and engage in heuristic, as opposed to effortful, processing.

In chapter 8, Duane Wegener and Richard Petty address affective influences by using a combination of the elaboration likelihood model and the flexible correction model. The former emphasizes differences in the extent to which individuals are willing and able to exert a high level of cognitive effort in forming their evaluations. The more highly motivated individuals are, the more likely it is that they will engage in careful scrutiny of the information they perceive to be central to forming their evaluations. Conversely, the lower their motivation, the more likely it is that individuals will base their evaluations on low-effort shortcuts. Wegener and Petty note that the amount of effort one exerts can determine the process through which one's affective state can influence one's judgment. For example, an individual's mood can influence judgments by serving as a central feature of a target, by biasing processing of judgment-relevant information, by serving as a peripheral cue to judging the target, and by itself affecting the level of scrutiny given to judgment-relevant information. To account for those times when individuals become aware that some factor (e.g., their mood) might be inappropriately influencing their judgments, Wegener and Petty discuss their flexible correction model. This model assumes that identification of potential biases in one's judgments and one's efforts to correct for those biases are guided by individuals' naive theories. Wegener and Petty also address the motivational consequences of pressures toward mood management.

For the contributors, each chapter was not so much an attempt to persuade (i.e., "my theory is better than the others") as it was an attempt to be clear. Our goal was to present the important assumptions of each theoretical model in a concise, understandable way and then show how these assumptions could be used to address some central mood-related phenomena. If we have done our job well, then readers will be able not only to understand each theoretical position but also to extract the larger theoretical commonalities and differences. They might note, for example, that all of the models assume that the effects of feelings on cognitive processing are context dependent. The reasons for this context dependence range from the effect of overriding goals to the availability of more diagnostic information (e.g., a prior evaluation) to the meaning of mood in the particular judgment context and more. Many of the models also incorporate the assumption that feelings have different effects depending on the amount of cognitive effort individuals exert while forming their judgments. In terms of differences, some theorists assume that moods have their effects primarily through the activation of mood-congruent memories and concepts, whereas others assume that moods convey information more directly through subjective experience.

We recommend that readers approach this volume not by trying to see which theoretical approach is right but by trying to appreciate each model's "range and focus of convenience" (Kelly, 1955). No one theory can presume to explain it all. Each, however, may point the way to some useful ideas, and subsequent researchers may be able to work through the strengths and weaknesses of our current attempts to forge a more complete explanation of mood and cognitive processing.

REFERENCES

Allport, G. W. (1968). The historical background of modern social psychology. In G. Lindzey & E. Aronson (Ed.), *The handbook of social psychology* (2nd ed., pp. 3–56). Reading, MA: Addison-Wesley.

Bower, G. H., Montiero, K. P., & Gilligan, S. G. (1978). Emotional mood as a context for learning and recall. *Journal of Verbal Learning and Verbal Behavior, 17,* 573–585.

Clore, G. L., & Byrne, D. (1974). A reinforcement-affect model of attraction. In T. L. Houston (Ed.), *Foundations of interpersonal attraction* (pp. 143–170). New York: Academic Press.

Gouaux, C. (1971). Induced affective states and interpersonal attraction. *Journal of Personality and Social Psychology, 20,* 37–43.

Griffit, W., & Veitch, R. (1971). Hot and crowded: Influence of population density and temperature on interpersonal affective behavior. *Journal of Personality and Social Psychology, 17,* 92–98.

Isen, A.. M., Shalker, T. E., Clark, M., & Karp, L. (1978). Affect, accessibility of material in memory, and behavior: A cognitive loop? *Journal of Personality and Social Psychology, 36,* 1–12.

Kelly, G. A. (1955). *The psychology of personal constructs.* New York: Norton.

Schwarz, N., & Clore, G. L. (1983). Mood, misattribution, and judgments of well-being: Informative and directive functions of affective states. *Journal of Personality and Social Psychology, 45,* 513–523.

Worth, L. T., & Mackie, D. M. (1987). Cognitive mediation of positive affect in persuasion. *Social Cognition, 5,* 76–94.

Chapter 1

Mood and the Use of General Knowledge Structures

Herbert Bless
University of Heidelberg

Research into the interplay of affect and cognition documents that minor differences in affective states may have a pronounced impact on cognitive processes (for overviews, see Clore, Schwarz, & Conway, 1994; Fiedler, 1991; Forgas, 1992; Isen, 1987; Schwarz, 1990; Schwarz & Bless, 1991). Among the various effects of affect on information processing, researchers have been particularly interested in how different affective states are linked to different styles of information processing. In general, the empirical evidence suggests that information processing in positive affective states is strongly influenced by heuristics, stereotypes, or scripts. In contrast, individuals in negative affective states seem more likely to be affected by the implications of specific information provided in the situation.

Various models that have been proposed to account for these findings emphasize the impact of affective states on the amount of processing. Specifically, it has been suggested that positive but not negative affective states decrease individuals' processing motivation (e.g., Schwarz, 1990) or capacity (e.g., Mackie & Worth, 1989) and that these motivational or capacity deficits in turn mediate the increased reliance on heuristics under positive affective states. In contrast, the present mood-and-general-knowledge model accounts for the available evidence without entailing assumptions about affect influencing individuals' processing motivation or capacity.

THE MOOD-AND-GENERAL-KNOWLEDGE ASSUMPTION

The present model can be separated into two parts: (a) Building on previous theorizing (Frijda, 1988; Schwarz, 1990), it is assumed that individuals' affective states inform the individual about the psychological nature of the current situation; and (b) departing from previous theorizing, it is assumed that, based on affect influencing their interpretation of the current situation as benign or problematic, individuals in positive affective states are more likely to rely on activated general knowledge structures, whereas individuals in negative affective states are more likely to focus on the data at hand.

Affective States Provide Information About the Current Situation. The notion that affective states provide a useful source of information has been incorporated in rather divergent theoretical approaches. In this respect, individuals' affective states have been conceptualized, for example, as "barometers of the ego" (Jacobsen, 1957), as a "source of information" (Nowlis & Nowlis, 1956), or as "monitors" (Pribram, 1970). The present approach builds primarily on the theorizing offered by Schwarz (1990; Schwarz & Bless, 1991). It is assumed that individuals usually feel good in situations that are characterized by positive outcomes, in situations that do not threaten their current goals, or both. In contrast, individuals usually feel bad in situations that threaten their current goals either because of the presence of negative outcomes or because of the lack of positive outcomes. If different situations result in different affective states, individuals may consult their affect as a usually valid and quick indicator of the nature of the current psychological situation. Specifically, positive affective states may inform the individual that the current situation poses no problem, whereas negative affective states may signal that the current situation is problematic. (For a more detailed discussion see Schwarz, 1990.)

The Nature of a Situation and the Use of General Knowledge Structures. The general notion that affective states inform the individual about the nature of the current situation has implicitly or explicitly been entailed in various approaches. The present position departs from previous theorizing, however, with respect to what follows from the information provided by the individual's affective state. Presumably, rather different implications may potentially result from interpreting the current situation as problematic or benign. Evidence for the diversity of the possible implications has been reported by Martin and colleagues (Martin, Ward, Achee, & Wyer, 1993). Their findings suggest that although individuals rely on their affective states as a source of information, this reliance may imply either less or more processing, depending on the nature of the inference task activated in a specific situation.

Accepting the diversity of possible implications, research needs to address (a) the relation between specific situational aspects and different implications for individuals' information processing, and (b) what implications would be functional and adaptive for the individual in general. Pursuing the latter aspect, I have proposed that in general it would be highly adaptive for individuals to differentially rely on their general knowledge structures as a function of the current psychological situation (Bless, Clore, et al., 1999).

Specifically, individuals in benign situations may rely on their general knowledge structures, which usually serve them well. In contrast, in problematic situations reliance on general knowledge structures is risky. This reflects the fact that successfully dealing with problematic situations usually requires considerable attention to the specific details. If so, individuals' current affective states may influence the interpretation of the current situation, and this may in turn influence the degree to which individuals rely on their general knowledge structures. Specifically, individuals in positive affective states may feel more confident about relying on activated general knowledge structures that are potentially applicable to the situation. In contrast, individuals in negative affective states may feel less confident about relying on general knowledge structures and about focusing on the data at hand.

In sum, the proposed account shares the general notion of previous theorizing that affective states inform the individual about the current situation. It departs, however, from previous theorizing in what follows from this information. Most important, the approach neither implies a mood-dependent motivation to engage in more or less processing nor requires the assumption that different procedural knowledge is activated as a function of mood.

In the remainder of this chapter I address a number of aspects that arise from this mood-and-general-knowledge assumption: (a) the potential advantages for happy individuals relying on general knowledge structures, (b) reduced processing as an antecedent versus a consequence of relying on general knowledge structures, (c) specific hypotheses that can be derived from the current approach, (d) limitations, overriding effects, and the impact of specific affective states, and (e) how the proposed model can account for available evidence on mood and processing style.

WHY SHOULD HAPPY INDIVIDUALS RELY ON GENERAL KNOWLEDGE STRUCTURES?

For a number of reasons it would be highly adaptive for individuals to rely on general knowledge structures in benign situations, that is, when they are in a positive affective state, and to focus on the data at hand in problematic situations, that is, when they are in a negative affective state. As discussed previously, the two different processing perspectives direct individuals' attention toward the information that is presumably most useful in the current situation. Problematic situations are usually deviations from normal, routine situations. If so, individuals would be poorly advised to rely on the knowledge they usually apply. Rather, successfully dealing with problematic situations requires one to focus on the specifics of the current situation. In contrast, situations that are not problematic require less attention to the specifics. In this case it would be highly adaptive to save processing resources allocated to the specifics of the situation and to direct the spared resources toward other tasks. Such a mechanism would be particularly beneficial if it allowed one to redirect processing attention when certain aspects of the situation require additional attention. Finally, individuals would be well advised to generate and test new, creative inferences beyond the information given in safe rather than problematic situations. The reliance on general structures may support individuals with these requirements.

1. General knowledge structures serve as energy-saving devices (e.g., Macrae, Milne, & Bodenhausen, 1994; cf. Fiske & Taylor, 1991). Thus they enable the individual to reduce the attention allocated to those aspects of the situation that match the general knowledge structure. The present approach holds that the spared resources are allocated to other aspects of the situation or to other tasks. This "transfer" of resources would be a highly adaptive mechanism, as it directs the attention to those aspects for which additional processing is potentially more beneficial and effective. Note that according to this assumption individuals in positive versus negative affective states are not differentially decreasing their amount of processing but differentially allocating their processing attention.

2. General knowledge structures enable a parsimonious processing of information that is consistent with the knowledge structure. However, inconsistent information will not go unnoticed. To the contrary, given sufficient processing motivation and capacity, inconsistent information receives additional processing attention (Fiske & Taylor, 1991): Because of the attempt to apply general knowledge structures, more resources are allocated to schema-inconsistent information. Thus the reliance on general knowledge structures has a built-in mechanism; that is, the same process that allows one to allocate resources to other tasks will quasi-automatically redirect attention to the data at hand if necessary. Note that this reallocation requires that happy individuals are willing and able to engage in additional processing.

The advantage of this redirection of attention rests on the assumption that the important and adaptive additional attention is not a function of mood. Once happy individuals rely on a general knowledge structure, the additional processing is a function of the match between the knowledge structure and the information at hand, with the inconsistent information itself triggering the additional processing. Therefore, this mechanism allows for a flexibility in attention to the specifics of a situation without a previous change of individuals' affective states. As a consequence, individuals in not only negative but also positive affective states may elaborate on the data at hand if the specific information does not match the general knowledge structure.

3. General knowledge structures can serve to enrich the stimulus information at hand and provide a basis for making inferences beyond the information given (Bruner, 1957). This going beyond the information given may sometimes lead individuals to new, creative inferences. Given the risky nature of new solutions, it seems highly adaptive to rely on general knowledge structures as a basis for inferences, particularly if the situation is safe rather than already problematic (see also Schwartz, 1990).

The general assumption that individuals in problematic situations more strongly attend to the data at hand whereas individuals in less problematic situations more strongly rely on preexisting knowledge is shared by other theorists. Although coming from a different starting point, Gray (1971) has made analogous suggestions with respect to the role of positive and negative affect. According to his position, positive affect leads organisms to behave on the basis of habits, and negative affect leads them to engage in learning. In a related vein, Piaget (1955) differentiated between processes of assimilation, that is, applying general structures to the current situation, and accommodation, that is, adapting general knowledge structures to fit the data at hand. Interestingly, Piaget assumed that accommodation results from unsuccessful assimilation attempts that are often associated with negative affect. In other words, individuals in negative affective states are less likely to rely on general knowledge structures. The notion that negative situations are associated with more specific representations is also part of action identification theory (Vallacher & Wegner, 1986), which assumes that successful actions are represented on a more general level, whereas unsuccessful actions are represented on more specific levels. Finally, Fiedler's "dual-force" model (1991; see also Fiedler, chapter 4, this volume) incorporates similar assumptions, holding that positive moods encourage individuals not to stick to the external data but to rely more on top-down processes, whereas the reverse is assumed for negative moods.

THE DIFFERENCE BETWEEN RELYING
ON GENERAL KNOWLEDGE STRUCTURES
AND REDUCED PROCESSING MOTIVATION

Because general knowledge structures often allow efficient and parsimonious processing, my approach may at first glance seem equivalent to the assumption that happy mood reduces processing motivation (Schwarz, 1990) or processing capacity (Mackie & Worth, 1989). In other words, happy individuals rely on general knowledge structures due to their reduced capacity or motivation. A closer look, however, reveals that my perspective does not share this assumption. My approach explicitly refrains from assumptions about a mood-dependent amount of processing. From this perspective, reliance on general knowledge structure is considered an antecedent, not a consequence, of simplified processing. For example, it has been observed that happy individuals are more likely to rely on their stereotypes than are emotionally neutral (Bodenhausen, Kramer, & Süsser, 1994) or sad (Bless, Schwarz, & Wieland, 1996) individuals. From a re-duced-capacity or a reduced-motivation perspective it is argued that happy individuals' reliance on stereotypes is a consequence of their need or their motivation to simplify processing. According to the proposed mood-and-general-knowledge assumption, the increased impact of stereotypes under happy mood does not reflect different processing motivation or ca-pacity but the different reliance on general knowledge structures. As a re-sult of this reliance, happy individuals' processing is parsimonious. This parsimony is, however, not caused by processing deficits. I will return to different empirical implications of the two perspectives in the discussion of the available evidence.

LIMITATIONS AND OVERRIDING EFFECTS

A number of limitations should be mentioned:

1. The proposed model focuses on mood and processing style, but it does not directly address the issues of mood-congruent recall (Bower, 1981; Forgas, 1992) and mood-congruent judgment (Schwarz & Clore, 1983).

2. The approach discussed here is restricted to situations in which a po-tentially applicable general knowledge structure has been activated or is otherwise easily accessible. Thus the mood-and-general-knowledge as-sumption does not entail any direct implications for tasks in which this an-tecedent is not given. What, however, are the consequences if a general knowledge structure is applied? The answer is obviously not included in the proposed model itself but must rest on other theories and models ad-dressing how different forms of general knowledge structures influence processing, social judgment, and behavior. The exact consequences are of course not just mood dependent but result from an interaction of mood and the nature of the task. For example, in most cases general knowledge structures may structure the social situation and are very useful. In these cases, happy mood facilitates better performance. Under some conditions, however, due to the nature of the situation, applying a seemingly applica-ble general knowledge structure may perhaps result in poorer perfor-mance. Given that this issue presumably applies to several models, such as those discussed in this volume, it seems particularly important to investigate the impact of mood on tasks that are well conceptualized within existing theories.

3. A related limitation is that at the current stage the proposed model itself does not provide an exact definition of general knowledge struc-

tures. According to the model, general knowledge structures may comprise different forms, such as scripts, stereotypes, schemas, or other forms of generic knowledge. Different situations and tasks require the application of these knowledge structures to a different degree (for a discussion of this issue, see Bless & Fiedler, 1995; Fiedler, chap. 4, this volume). For example, the dual process models in person perception (e.g., Fiske & Neuberg, 1990) and persuasion (e.g., Petty & Cacioppo, 1986) differentiate situations characterized by a strong emphasis on prior knowledge, for example, in the form of stereotypes or in form of knowledge related to peripheral cues, from situations characterized by a focus on externally provided information. Note that in contrast to other accounts (e.g., Schwarz, 1990) the model does not explicitly entail assumptions about different forms of procedural knowledge that is activated or relied on as a function of mood but rather focuses on content-related general knowledge structures.

4. The proposed model rests in part on an assumed link between problematic situations and deviations from normal. Although problematic situations usually reflect a deviation from the normal, this may not necessarily always be the case. For example, individuals may repetitively face the same problematic situation. Thus the problem may appear as normal rather than a deviation from normal. Presumably, individuals will develop a standard routine to deal with the problematic situation. In these cases mood per se will have little impact because of the overriding effect of the routine.

5. The mood-and-general-knowledge assumption generally implies that positive affective states should increase, and negative affective states should decrease, reliance on general knowledge structures. Given that not only mood but also other factors influence the reliance on general knowledge structures (see Fiske & Neuberg, 1990; Kruglanski, 1989, for overviews), the impact of mood may co-occur and compete with the impact of these factors. Depending on the relative contributions of the affective state and these other factors, mood effects can be overridden and might not be observable.

6. The proposed model does not exclude the possibility that other processes may be operating. It may therefore be the case that individuals base their judgments on a "how do I feel about it?" heuristic or that being in a positive or negative affective state increases the accessibility of mood-congruent material (Bower, 1981; Forgas, 1992). Specifically with respect to mood and processing style, I do not deny that other mood-as-information-based processes may mediate individuals' processing style (see Martin et al., 1993; Schwarz, 1990), nor do I want to exclude the possibility that happy moods can influence processing motivation (Wegener, Petty, & Smith, 1995) or processing capacity (Worth & Mackie, 1987). In particular, however, in light of the available evidence discussed subsequently, I believe that the discussion about mood and processing styles

could benefit from a perspective that does not focus primarily on the amount of processing per se. Without assuming different processing motivation or capacity, the presented mood-and-general-knowledge hypothesis may provide an integrative explanation for a wide spectrum of findings in the domain of affective influences on the style of information processing.

ADDRESSING THE AVAILABLE EMPIRICAL EVIDENCE

Numerous studies have addressed the interplay of affective states and cognitive processes in various domains. This research has documented a number of consistent findings: (a) mood-congruent recall, (b) mood-congruent judgment, (c) happy mood leads to a more heuristic and sad mood leads to a more systematic processing of new information, and (d) happy mood enhances creative solutions in association tasks and problem solving (for an overview, see Clore et al., 1994). As stated previously, the mood-and-general-knowledge assumption was not proposed to account for all of these findings. As its implications are restricted to the impact of mood on processing styles and indirectly to the relation between affective states and creativity, the following section will primarily focus on these two aspects.

Mood and Processing Style

Evidence Part I: Increased Reliance on Heuristics Under Happy Mood. Recent research suggests that happy moods are associated with heuristic processing strategies, whereas sad moods are associated with systematic elaboration of information (for an overview, see Clore et al., 1994). These mood-induced differences in processing strategy have been most reliably observed in research on mood and persuasion (e.g., Bless, Mackie, & Schwarz, 1992; Mackie & Worth, 1989; for an overview, see Schwarz, Bless, & Bohner, 1991) and person perception (e.g., Bodenhausen, Kramer, & Süsser, 1994). For example, in the domain of persuasion, happy individuals were less influenced by the quality of the arguments in a persuasive message than emotionally neutral (Worth & Mackie, 1987) or sad (Bless, Bohner, Schwarz, & Strack, 1990) individuals, whereas happy individuals were found to be more strongly influenced by a peripheral cue (Mackie & Worth, 1989). These findings converge with findings obtained in person perception research if we equate reliance on peripheral cues with reliance on stereotypes and reliance on presented arguments with reliance on individuating information. This research suggests that activated stereotypes have more impact on the processing of happy than of sad individuals (Bless, Schwarz, & Wieland, 1996; Bodenhausen, Kramer, & Süsser, 1994; Bodenhausen, Sheppard, & Kramer, 1994), whereas individuating information about a target showed more impact on sad individuals' judgments. In combination, happy individuals have been found more likely to rely on heuristics and stereotypes, whereas sad individuals are more likely to attend to the specific information provided.

How can the proposed mood-and-general-knowledge assumption account for these findings? Most obviously, the increased reliance of happy individuals on stereotypes as one form of general knowledge structure follows directly from the assumption that the processing of individuals in positive affective states is more strongly influenced by general knowledge structures. In addition to the evidence from person perception research, there is evidence that other general knowledge structures are more influential on happy than on sad individuals—for example, global representations of persuasive messages (Bless, Mackie, & Schwarz, 1992), general trait judgments (Bless & Fiedler, 1995), or scripts (Bless, Clore, et al., 1996).

Moreover, we may consider heuristic processing as the application of general knowledge structures to specific information (Nisbett & Ross, 1980). If so, the mood-and-general-knowledge assumption can account for a large variety of findings in various domains that suggest a higher reliance on heuristics (general knowledge structures) under happy moods (for examples and overviews, see Clore et al., 1994; Isen, 1987). For example, with respect to the persuasion domain, one may conceptualize the reliance on peripheral cues (e.g., source expertise) as the application of general knowledge (e.g., arguments by experts are usually better). If so, the finding that happy individuals are more likely to rely on their heuristics in a persuasive setting (Mackie & Worth, 1989) is nicely compatible with the proposed model. In contrast, individuals who are less likely to rely on their prior knowledge in the form of heuristics will be more likely to attend to the information provided in the respective situation. Again, this conclusion is in line with numerous research findings suggesting that individuals in a sad mood are more strongly influenced by the information at hand (see Clore et al., 1994) than individuals in a happy mood.

Obviously, the evidence pertaining to the impact of general knowledge structures or heuristics per se does not allow one to distinguish the proposed model from other accounts focusing on motivational or capacity deficits under happy moods that in turn increase heuristic processing. However, as the general finding of increased reliance on heuristics under happy moods is accompanied by a number of additional findings, one may take a closer look at the variety of the accumulated evidence to evaluate the advantages and disadvantages of the proposed account.

Evidence Part II: The Lack of Direct Evidence for Reduced Processing. Despite empirical support for an association between heuristic processing and happy moods, the evidence that heuristic processing is due to hypothesized motivational or capacity deficits is less conclusive than is often assumed.

1. The amount of processing, the crucial mediating variable, has rarely been directly assessed. Most often it has only been inferred that increased use of heuristics must result from some motivational or capacity deficit; therefore researchers do not attend to the difference between sufficient and necessary conditions of systematic and heuristic processing. For example, dual processing models propose sufficient conditions in the form of "if p then q"; for example, if processing motivation or capacity is low, then the impact of heuristic cues increases. However, the reverse logic is often applied when investigating the impact of mood. Following the logic "if q then p," researchers infer, for example, that an observed impact of heuristic cues must reflect that processing motivation or capacity is deficient. To the extent that other variables, unrelated to processing motivation or capacity, may foster heuristic processing, the inference from heuristic processing to deficient capacity or motivation may be unwarranted (for a more extended discussion of this issue, see Bless & Schwarz, 1999).

2. A closer look at the evidence indirectly supporting reduced processing reveals some additional ambiguities. In the persuasion domain, it has been argued that happy participants do not elaborate on the content of the message and miss differences in message quality. Yet the number of cognitive responses reported by happy and sad participants is typically the same (e.g., Bless et al., 1990), although the valence of these responses—and the attitude judgments—reflects message quality for sad recipients but not for happy recipients. More important, the very same happy recipients have been found to differentiate between strong and weak messages (as much as do participants in neutral or sad moods) when asked to rate the quality of the message (e.g., Bless et al., 1990; Worth & Mackie, 1987). Hence happy recipients processed message content in sufficient detail to notice differences in message quality but apparently did not draw on these differential implications in forming a judgment. These findings suggest that processing motivation or capacity were sufficiently allocated while the message was being encoded.

3. In several studies (e.g., Bless et al., 1990) participants in happy, neutral, and sad moods did not differ in their ability to recall the content of a persuasive message, despite the usual differences in attitude judgments. Similarly, in person perception studies, happy and sad participants' recall for stereotype individuating information did not differ, although happy participants showed an increased reliance on stereotypes in their judgments (Bless, Schwarz, & Wieland, 1996). If being in a happy mood decreases the amount of processing, however, we should expect that it also affects the amount and quality of recall.

In sum, the lack of direct evidence that happy moods decrease the amount of processing due to motivation or capacity fits nicely with the proposed mood-and-general-knowledge hypothesis. From this perspective happy individuals' reliance on general knowledge structures is not mediated by motivational or capacity deficits.

Evidence Part III: The Processing of Inconsistent Information and Secondary Tasks. Individuals in a happy mood have consistently been found to be more likely to rely on stereotypes (e.g., Bless, Schwarz, & Wieland, 1996; Bodenhausen, Kramer, & Süsser, 1994). The reliance on general knowledge structures, however, does not exclude the possibility that individuals attend to inconsistent behavioral information. In contrary, inconsistent information often exerts a particular impact just because individuals try to apply their general knowledge structures (Fiske & Taylor, 1991). However, dealing with stereotype-inconsistent information requires considerable cognitive resources (e.g., Macrae, Hewstone, & Griffith, 1993; Stangor & Duan, 1991). From this perspective, it is interesting that we have observed that stereotype-inconsistent information had a specifically pronounced impact on judgments when individuals were in positive rather than negative affective states (Bless, Schwarz, & Wieland, 1996; for similar evidence pertaining to the recall of stereotype inconsistent information see Dovidio, Gaertner, & Loux, 2000).[1] If happy moods reduce processing motivation or capacity, any inconsistencies should be less likely to be noted. Thus the findings suggest that happy moods elicit reliance on general knowledge structures independent of reduced processing motivation or capacity as suggested by the proposed mood-and-general-knowledge assumption.

In a series of studies, the relation between mood and the use of scripts has been investigated (Bless, Clore, et al., 1996). Happy participants were more likely than sad participants to rely on an activated script while encoding tape-recorded information. More important, however, happy participants, while working simultaneously on a secondary task, showed better performance on that task than sad participants. Presumably by relying on a script, happy participants freed up resources that could be applied to the secondary task, which resulted in their improved performance. This observation was predicted by my approach, which holds that the resources saved by relying on general knowledge structures will be reallocated if individuals are confronted with other, secondary tasks in the same situation. Again, this implication allows a differentiation from accounts that emphasize the impact of mood processing motivation or capacity: If happy moods elicit processing constraints, they should impair not only performance on the primary task but also performance on a secondary task.

Evidence Part IV: The Relative Contribution of Mood—or the Overriding Effect of Increasing Processing Motivation and Capacity. The mood-and-

---

[1]Note that information that is only marginally inconsistent should be assimilated toward the activated knowledge structure.

general-knowledge assumption generally implies that positive affective states should increase, and negative affective states should decrease, reliance on general knowledge structures. However, in addition to mood, other factors may influence individuals' reliance on general knowledge structures. For example, increasing individuals' processing motivation or increasing processing capacity will generally decrease reliance on general knowledge structures (see Fiske & Neuberg, 1990; Kruglanski, 1989, for overviews). Depending on the relative contributions of the affective state and the often very pronounced additional manipulations, the effects elicited by the valence of mood can be overridden by these other factors. In line with these considerations, the effects of happy versus sad mood could be eliminated by additional manipulations. Specifically, these findings suggest that individuals' reliance on heuristics and stereotypes decreases as processing motivation (Bless et al., 1990; Bodenhausen, Kramer, & Süsser, 1994) or processing capacity (Mackie & Worth, 1989) increases.

Evidence Part V: The Impact of Different Negative Affective States. Besides variables influencing processing motivation or capacity, additional factors may have impact on individuals' reliance on heuristics and general knowledge structures. For example, an increased reliance on general knowledge structures can also result from individuals' arousal levels being either very low (e.g., Bodenhausen, 1990) or very high (Kim & Baron, 1988; see also Broadbent, 1971; Hasher & Zacks, 1979). As affective states may differ with respect to the associated level of arousal, the valence of the affective state may not be the only determinant of the use of general knowledge structures. Hence the impact of the valence of individuals' mood may be overridden by the arousal level associated with particular mood states. For example, evidence by Bodenhausen and colleagues (Bodenhausen, Sheppard, & Kramer, 1994) suggests that sad participants were less influenced and angry participants were more influenced by an activated stereotype compared with participants in neutral moods (for converging evidence in the persuasion domain, see Bohner, Hauschildt, & Knäuper, 1993).

Evidence Part VI: The Informative Function of Individuals' Mood. The mood-and-general-knowledge assumption holds as a precondition for the emergence of the predicted effects that individuals use their mood state for an interpretation of the nature of the current situation. Accordingly, mood effects on processing style should not be observed when the informational value of one's mood is called into question, for example, because one attributes one's current feelings to an influence that is unrelated to the task at hand. Consistent with this prediction, Sinclair, Mark, and Clore (1994) observed that moods did not influence the processing of a persuasive message when recipients attributed their mood to the weather, much as Schwarz and Clore (1983) had observed that moods did not influence evaluative judgments under these conditions. The emergence of these discounting effects is consistent with those models that emphasize the informational value of individuals' mood, whereas it may be more difficult to reconcile with other accounts.

Similarly, individuals may use their moods for more specific interpretation tasks required in the situation rather than for a global evaluation of the current situation as problematic or unproblematic. Martin and colleagues (Martin, chap. 6, this volume; Martin et al., 1993) demonstrated that individuals can use their affective state as an input for different judgmental task. With respect to the impact of mood on processing style, they found, for example, that happy mood could decrease as well as increase processing, depending on whether individuals used their mood as an input for interpreting their enjoyment of the task, or for interpreting their performance at the task (Martin et al., 1993). In situations such as these—in particular when no activated general knowledge structure can be applied to the task at hand—the precondition for applying the proposed model is no longer given, and consequently no direct implications can be derived from the proposed model.

Mood and Creativity

In various studies, happy participants have been found to outperform sad or emotionally neutral participants in problem solving (e.g., Isen, Daubman, & Nowicki, 1987) and association tasks (e.g., Isen, Johnson, Mertz, & Robinson, 1985; for an overview, see Isen, 1987). Happy individuals' increased reliance on general knowledge structures may support creative solutions in various aspects.

1. New creative solutions require one to go beyond the information given. When a new specific situation is encountered, general knowledge structures can enrich the stimulus information at hand and provide a basis for making new and creative inferences (Bruner, 1957). Happy individuals' increased reliance on general knowledge structures may thus, in many cases, provide a wider basis for going beyond the information given than does sad individuals' sticking to the data at hand.

2. In a related vein, good problem solving often requires one to overcome the problem of functional fixedness. For example, in Duncker's (1945) candle task, the solution requires one to perceive the box of matches not as a container but as a potential platform. Presumably, a global representation of an object (or situation) may foster the chances of thinking of other functions for an object or of allowing for a transfer of knowledge about other, more remote, situations to the present task.

3. Often good problem solving requires one to reduce the complexity of the situation or problem. In many situations, this requirement can be supported by the application of general knowledge structures.

In sum, happy individuals' reliance on general knowledge structures may support problem solving and creative associations. Note, however, that whether happy or sad mood supports problem solving will largely depend on the nature of the problem. In particular, if the solution requires careful attention to the details of the situation and if an activated knowledge structure leads in the wrong direction, happy individuals are expected to be less likely to detect the correct solution. Again, a rather exact specification of the underlying processes is required. Given the lack of these specifications, the domain of creativity may at the moment not be the ideal domain in which to investigate the impact of mood on cognitive processes.

Mood and Recall

Although the proposed model does not directly address the issue of mood-congruent recall (Bower, 1981; Forgas, 1992), it has direct implications for other forms of memory performance. In general, if happy individuals are more likely to rely on general knowledge structures, we should observe that the effects of schemas on memory are more pronounced under happy moods. We have confirmed this prediction in a series of studies investigating the relation between mood and the use of scripts (Bless, Clore, et al., 1996). Specifically, happy participants were more likely than sad individuals to recognize presented schema-consistent information but at the cost of a higher intrusion rate for consistent information that was not presented. Given that happy individuals have no motivational or capacity deficits, schema-inconsistent information should receive additional attention and should be recalled rather accurately. Our findings reflect this high accuracy for the recognition of inconsistent information. Note that in case of a processing deficit, happy individuals' recall should have been impaired, as the recall of inconsistent information requires the allocation of additional processing attention (see also Dovidio et al., 2000, for similar evidence in the stereotyping domain).

Although not directly predicted by the proposed model, another related aspect of the influence of mood on recall seems worth mentioning. Happy individuals may be not only more likely to rely on activated knowledge structures but may be also more likely than sad individuals to cluster specific information into larger chunks of information, although the chunks were not previously activated in the situation. This clustering in turn can facilitate recall. For example, Isen and colleagues (Isen, Daubman, & Gorgoglione, 1987) provided participants with a list of words. One third of these words could be organized around a shared theme ("American Revolution"), whereas the remaining words could not. Happy participants showed better recall for the theme-related words than did control participants, presumably because they clustered the information in this "American Revolution" category, which in turn facilitated later recall. (For additional supporting evidence on mood and clustering, see Bless, Hamilton, & Mackie, 1992.)

OPEN QUESTIONS AND OUTLOOK

I proposed the mood-and-general-knowledge assumption for a specified range of antecedent conditions. Specifically, if an activated general knowledge structure is applicable and if individuals do not call the informative function of their mood into question, happy individuals are expected to be more likely to rely on general knowledge structures than sad individuals. This increased reliance will in turn influence individuals' processing and judgments, depending, in particular, on the degree to which the specific situation matches implications of the general knowledge structure. As discussed herein, the model may account for a variety of phenomena on how mood influences processing style, yet a number of issues and questions need to be addressed by future research. Three of these have been raised by contributors to this volume.

1. *What exactly are general knowledge structures? Do they have to be preexisting or can they be generated in the course of processing?*
The model itself currently does not provide an exact definition of general knowledge structures, but refers to other approaches that have addressed the role of generic knowledge in form of scripts, schemas, or stereotypes. The model thus buys into all the advantages and disadvantages of these conceptualizations. It seems important to point out that most, if not all, tasks do involve the application of such knowledge structures. Different situations and tasks, however, require the application of these knowledge structures to a different degree and situations can be classified according to this aspect (see Bless & Fiedler, 1995; Fiedler, this volume). In its current form, the model addresses only the reliance on existing knowledge structures. However, based on the research briefly reported above (Bless et al., 1992; Isen et al., 1987) one may speculate whether happy moods also facilitate the generation of more general knowledge structures.

2. *The model describes reliance on general knowledge structures as adaptive, but the model does not describe the proximate mechanism by which knowledge structures get activated. What is the proximate mechanism by which positive affect activates a general knowledge structure?*
At present the model does not entail any assumptions that influence the activation of general knowledge structures. It is therefore only applicable to situations in which general knowledge structures have already been made accessible. In these situations, affect influences the degree to which individuals rely on this knowledge structure. It seems, however, worthwhile to investigate the possibility that positive affect not only increases the reliance on but also facilitates the activation of general knowledge structures.

3. *The model seems to suggest that the effect of mood on processing motivation will be global. How does the model account for context dependent mood effects?* The situational context may influence the impact of mood in several ways. If the situational context renders individuals' mood as uninformative for interpreting the psychological nature of the current situation, the proposed mood effects should no longer be obtained (see Sinclair et al., 1994). Moreover, strong situational constraints, for example, direct instructions, may override more subtle mood effects. Finally, a happy or a sad mood may have different implications for different judgmental tasks (Martin, this volume). Although the proposed model does not deny this possibility, it refers primarily to situations in which individuals use their affective state to interpret the current situation as problematic or benign, rather than to situations in which mood serves as information for other judgments.

It should have become obvious that the proposed model is not applicable to all situations and phenomena. This limited range is perhaps rather an asset than a handicap. The model's particular advantage is its ability to predict the increased impact of general knowledge structures and heuristics under happy mood without having to assume different processing motivation or capacity. The general-knowledge-assumption may thus be one possible way of bridging the gap between the strong evidence for heuristic processing under happy moods, on the one hand, and the rather limited direct evidence for motivational or capacity deficits mediating the use of heuristics, on the other hand.

ACKNOWLEDGMENTS

Research was supported by grants from the Deutsche Forschungsgemeinschaft (Bl 286/5 to H. Bless, N. Schwarz, & M. Wänke). Thanks are due to Gerald L. Clore, Klaus Fiedler, Leonard L. Martin, Norbert Schwarz, and Michaela Wänke for stimulating discussions and comments on a previous draft.

REFERENCES

Bless, H. (1994). *Stimmung und die Nutzung allgemeiner Wissensstrukturen: Ein Modell zum Einfluß von Stimmungen auf Denkprozesse* [Mood and the use of general knowledge structures]. Habilitationsschrift, Universität Heidelberg.

Bless, H., Bohner, G., Schwarz, N., & Strack, F. (1990). Mood and persuasion: A cognitive response analysis. *Personality and Social Psychology Bulletin, 16,* 331–345.

Bless, H., Clore, G., Schwarz, N., Golisano, V., Rabe, C., & Wölk, M. (1996). Mood and the use of scripts: Does happy mood make people really mindless? *Journal of Personality and Social Psychology, 71,* 665–679.

Bless, H., & Fiedler, K. (1995). Affective states and the influence of activated general knowledge. *Personality and Social Psychology Bulletin, 21,* 766–778.

Bless, H., Hamilton, D. L., & Mackie, D. M. (1992). Mood effects on the organization of person information. *European Journal of Social Psychology, 22*, 497–509.

Bless, H., Mackie, D. M., & Schwarz, N. (1992). Mood effects on encoding and judgmental processes in persuasion. *Journal of Personality and Social Psychology, 63*, 585–595.

Bless, H., & Schwarz, N. (1999). Sufficient and necessary conditions in dual process models: The case of mood and information processing. In S. Chaiken & Y. Trope (Eds.), *Dual process theories in social psychology* (pp. 423–440). New York: Guilford Press.

Bless, H., Schwarz, N., & Wieland, R. (1996). Mood and the impact of category membership and individuating information. *European Journal of Social Psychology, 26*, 935–959.

Bodenhausen, G. V. (1990). Stereotypes as judgmental heuristics: Evidence of circadian variations in discrimination. *Psychological Science, 1*, 319–322.

Bodenhausen, G. V., Kramer, G. P., & Süsser, K. (1994). Happiness and stereotypic thinking in social judgment. *Journal of Personality and Social Psychology, 66*, 621–632.

Bodenhausen, G. V., Sheppard, L. A., & Kramer, G. P. (1994). Negative affect and social judgment: The differential impact of anger and sadness. *European Journal of Social Psychology, 24*, 45–62.

Bohner, G., Hauschildt, A., & Knäuper, B. (1993). Einflüsse freudiger, trauriger und ärgerlicher Stimmung auf die Verarbeitung persuasiver Kommunikation [The impact of happy, sad, and angry moods on the processing of persuasive communications]. *Zeitschrift für Sozialpsychologie, 24*, 103–116.

Bower, G. H. (1981). Mood and memory. *American Psychologist, 36*, 129–148.

Broadbent, D. E. (1971). *Decision and stress*. London: Academic Press.

Bruner, J. S. (1957). On perceptual readiness. *Psychological Review, 64*, 123–152.

Clore, G. L., Schwarz, N., & Conway, M. (1994). Cognitive causes and consequences of emotion. In R. S. Wyer & T. K. Srull (Eds.), *Handbook of social cognition* (2nd ed., pp. 323–417). Hillsdale, NJ: Lawrence Erlbaum Associates.

Dovidio, J. F., Gaertner, S. L., & Loux, S. (1998). Subjective experiences and intergroup relations: The role of positive affect. In H. Bless & J. P. Forgas (Eds.), *The message within: The role of subjective experience in social cognition and behavior* (pp. 340–371). Philadelphia: Psychology Press.

Duncker, K. (1945). On problem solving. *Psychological Monographs, 58*(5, Whole No. 270).

Fiedler, K. (1991). On the task, the measures and the mood in research on affect and cognition. In J. Forgas (Ed.), *Emotion and social judgments* (pp. 83–104). Oxford, England: Pergamon.

Fiske, S. T., & Neuberg, S. L. (1990). A continuum of impression formation from category-based to individuating processing: Influences of information and motivation on attention and interpretation. In M. P. Zanna (Ed.), *Advances in experimental social psychology* (Vol. 23, pp. 1–74). Orlando, FL: Academic Press.

Fiske, S. T., & Taylor, S. E. (1991). *Social cognition*. New York: McGraw-Hill.

Forgas, J. P. (1992). Affect in social judgments and decisions: A multi-process model. In M. P. Zanna (Ed.), *Advances in experimental social psychology* (Vol. 25, pp. 227–275). San Diego, CA: Academic Press.

Frijda, N. H. (1988). The laws of emotion. *American Psychologist, 43*, 349–358.

Gray, J. A. (1971). *The psychology of fear and stress*. Cambridge, England: Cambridge University Press.

Hasher, L., & Zacks, R. T. (1979). Automatic and effortful processes in memory. *Journal of Experimental Psychology: General, 108*, 356–388.

Isen, A. M. (1987). Positive affect, cognitive processes, and social behavior. In L. Berkowitz (Ed.), *Advances in experimental social psychology* (Vol. 20, pp. 203–253). San Diego, CA: Academic Press.

Isen, A. M., Daubman, K. A., & Gorgolione, J. M. (1987). The influence of positive affect on cognitive organization. In R. Snow & M. Farr (Eds.), *Aptitude, learning, and instruction: Af-*

fective and conative processes (Vol. 3, pp. 143–164). Hillsdale, NJ: Lawrence Erlbaum Associates.

Isen, A. M., Daubman, K. A., & Nowicki, G. P. (1987). Positive affect facilitates creative problem solving. *Journal of Personality and Social Psychology, 52,* 1122–1131.

Isen, A. M., Johnson, M. M. S., Mertz, E., & Robinson, G. (1985). The influence of positive affect on the unusualness of word association. *Journal of Personality and Social Psychology, 48,* 1413–1426.

Jacobsen, E. (1957). Normal and pathological moods: Their nature and function. In R. S. Eisler, A. F. Freud, H. Hartman, & E. Kris (Eds.), *The psychoanalytic study of the child* (pp. 73–113). New York: International University Press.

Kim, H.-S., & Baron, R. S. (1988). Exercise and illusory correlation: Does arousal heighten stereotypic processing? *Journal of Experimental Social Psychology, 24,* 366–380.

Kruglanski, A. W. (1989). The psychology of being "right": On the problem of accuracy in social perception and cognition. *Psychological Bulletin, 106,* 395–409.

Mackie, D. M., & Worth, L. T. (1989). Cognitive deficits and the mediation of positive affect in persuasion. *Journal of Personality and Social Psychology, 57,* 27–40.

Macrae, C. N., Hewstone, M., Griffith, R. J. (1993). Processing load and memory for stereotype-based information. *European Journal of Social Psychology, 23,* 77–87.

Macrae, C. N., Milne, A. B., & Bodenhausen, G. V. (1994). Stereotypes as energy-saving devices: A peek inside the toolbox. *Journal of Personality and Social Psychology, 66,* 37–47.

Martin, L. M., Ward, D. W., Achee, J. W., & Wyer, R. S. (1993). Mood as input: People have to interpret the motivational implications of their moods. *Journal of Personality and Social Psychology, 64,* 317–326.

Nisbett, R. E., & Ross, L. (1980). *Human inference: Strategies and shortcomings of social judgment.* Englewood Cliffs, NJ: Prentice-Hall.

Nowlis, V., & Nowlis, H. H. (1956). The description and analysis of mood. *Annals of the New York Academy of Sciences, 65,* 345–355.

Piaget, J. (1955). *The child's construction of reality.* London: Routledge.

Pribram, H. H. (1970). Feelings as monitors. In M. Arnold (Ed.), *Feelings and emotions* (pp. 41–53). New York: Academic Press.

Schwarz, N. (1990). Feelings as information: Informational and motivational functions of affective states. In R. M. Sorrentino & E. T. Higgins (Eds.), *Handbook of motivation and cognition: Foundations of social behavior* (Vol. 2, pp. 527–561). New York: Guilford.

Schwarz, N., & Bless, H. (1991). Happy and mindless, but sad and smart? The impact of affective states on analytic reasoning. In J. Forgas (Ed.), *Emotion and social judgments* (pp. 55–71). Oxford, England: Pergamon.

Schwarz, N., Bless, H., & Bohner, G. (1991). Mood and persuasion: Affective states influence the processing of persuasive communications. In M. Zanna (Ed.), *Advances in experimental social psychology* (Vol. 24, pp. 161–197). New York: Academic Press.

Schwarz, N., & Clore, G. L. (1983). Mood, misattribution, and judgments of well-being: Informative and directive functions of affective states. *Journal of Personality and Social Psychology, 45,* 513–523.

Sinclair, R. C., Mark, M. M., & Clore, G. L. (1994). Mood-related persuasion depends on misattributions. *Social Cognition, 12,* 309–326.

Stangor, C., & Duan, C. (1991). Effects of multiple task demands upon memory for information about social groups. *Journal of Experimental Social Psychology, 27,* 357–378.

Vallacher, R. R., & Wegner, D. M. (1986). What do people think they're doing? Action identification theory and human information processing. *Psychological Review, 94,* 3–15.

Wegener, D. T., Petty, R. E., & Smith, S. M. (1995). Positive mood can increase or decrease message scrunity: The hedonic contingency view of mood and message processing. *Journal of Personality and Social Psychology, 69,* 5–15.

Worth, L. T., & Mackie, D. M. (1987). Cognitive mediation of positive affect in persuasion. *Social Cognition, 5,* 76–94.

Chapter 2

Affective Feelings as Feedback: Some Cognitive Consequences

Gerald L. Clore
Robert S. Wyer, Jr.
Bruce Dienes
Karen Gasper
Carol Gohm
Linda Isbell
University of Illinois, Urbana-Champaign

We are attracted to people we believe to be friendly, we favor policies we believe to be fair, and we prefer products we believe to be reliable. Indeed, we evaluate positively anything about which we have positive information. This fact illustrates a basic principle of human judgment—that evaluative judgments depend on evaluative information. But the process is more interesting than such a prosaic statement suggests, because an important kind of information used for judgment and decision making turns out to be information gained from our own feelings. This extension of the basic principle of evaluative judgment is the affect-as-information hypothesis (Clore, 1992; 1994; Clore, Schwarz, & Conway, 1994; Schwarz & Clore, 1983; 1988; 1996). Before we describe that approach in detail, a bit of background is in order.

BACKGROUND

In the 1960s and 1970s, social psychologists were interested in formalizing the process whereby evaluative beliefs influence evaluative judgments, impressions, or attitudes. For example, Anderson (1971) assumed that overall liking for anything equals the average of evaluative beliefs about its attributes. In contrast, Fishbein and Ajzen (1975) assumed that an attitude equals the sum of evaluative beliefs about an object, and Byrne and Clore

27

(1966) assumed that attraction to a person equals the proportion of information associated with the person that is positive.

By the late 1970s, research on social cognition had gradually supplanted work on impression formation (e.g., compare Srull & Wyer, 1979, with Wyer, 1974). In place of mathematical models of information combination, investigators began developing conceptual models of the encoding, storage, and retrieval of information. This social cognition research emphasized how the cognitive accessibility of concepts and beliefs influenced judgment, often using subtle priming techniques to increase accessibility (e.g., Higgins, Rholes, & Jones, 1977).

Paralleling the research on impression formation was work on interpersonal attraction, which was focused not on concepts and beliefs but on the role of experienced affect. The "reinforcement-affect model of attraction" proposed that attraction toward another person depends on one's own affective reactions (Byrne & Clore, 1970; Clore, 1966; Clore & Byrne, 1974).

The proposed process is illustrated in an experiment to determine the kinds of conversational behaviors that make people attractive. A variety of behaviors were coded from transcriptions of conversations under several instructional conditions. Surprisingly, ratings of liking for conversational partners turned out to depend as much on what raters themselves did as on what their partners did. Raters liked partners when they got a chance to talk about themselves and when they found the conversations rewarding (Clore & Itkin, 1982). Similar observations emerged from a related study of attraction toward conversational partners who had voiced opinions that agreed or disagreed with those of the rater. The researchers measured skin conductance during the interaction, and results showed that similarity of opinion was related to attraction if and only if raters responded affectively to what they heard, as evidenced by changes in skin conductance (Clore & Gormly, 1974).

There is nothing surprising about the fact that people like those who reward them, but the reinforcement-affect model (Clore, 1966) maintained that the key ingredient is the subjective experience of reward and that merely associating positive feelings with others is sufficient to generate liking for them, regardless of whether they are actually the source of the affect. To test this hypothesis, Charles Gouaux and William Griffitt developed clever paradigms in which they induced affect from various irrelevant sources, such as having participants watch happy or sad films (Gouaux, 1971) or work in a hot and crowded room (Griffitt & Veitch, 1971). The experiments confirmed that attraction to another depends on how raters feel in addition to but independently of evaluative beliefs about the person.

Years later, Schwarz and Clore returned to this idea, examining the influence of affect from extraneous sources on judgments of life satisfaction

(Schwarz & Clore, 1983). In one experiment, affect was induced by asking participants to describe happy or sad events from their recent past, and in another warm and sunny versus cold and rainy spring weather was relied on to induce mood. As in the reinforcement-affect model (Clore & Byrne, 1974), mood-congruent judgments were explained by saying that affective reactions can influence judgments directly without being mediated by beliefs about the object of judgment. As before, a mere association with positive affect yielded positive judgments. Now, however, the "affect-as-information" account was framed in the language of attribution rather than of conditioning. Wyer and Carlston (1979) had also entertained the hypothesis that positive and negative affect might be experienced directly as liking or disliking, but at the time they favored an alternative hypothesis that the influence of mood manipulations was only indirect. They proposed that it was the cognitive rather than the affective content of mood manipulations that explained mood effects on judgment.

THE AFFECT-AS-INFORMATION HYPOTHESIS

The affect-as-information hypothesis (Schwarz & Clore, 1983) states that affective feelings influence judgments when they are experienced as reactions to what is being judged. This process is seen as a normal and adaptive role for feelings that represent emotional appraisals. Feelings due to mood, however, do not necessarily reflect such appraisals, although they have similar effects when the feelings are experienced as a reaction to (i.e., misattributed to) what is being judged. Although the affect-as-information hypothesis can be easily summarized in this way, it is based on propositions and concepts about affective and cognitive processes that we have explicated in this chapter as nine principles. The first five are: (a) the experience principle, (b) the information principle, (c) the attribution principle, (d) the attribution constraint principle, and (e) the immediacy principle. Four more are presented as applications: (f) the memory principle, (g) the processing principle, (h) the enjoyment principle, and (i) the levels-of-focus principle. Before elaborating these, however, we clarify our usage of six key terms.

Definitions

1. *Affect*: Analogous to the term *cognitive*, which refers to representations of knowledge (truth and falsity), the term *affective* refers to representations of value (goodness and badness). *Affective* thus designates a broad category of things with positive or negative personal value. These include

preferences and attitudes, which are affective dispositions, and emotions and moods, which are affective states.

2. *State*: *States* are temporary conditions of an organism reflected in multiple systems. Thus a comment such as, "He was in quite a state," suggests that many aspects of the person (e.g., words, facial expressions, actions) all reflect the same condition (e.g., frustration, exhaustion). Because emotions and moods are states, they also typically involve multiple systems (e.g., cognitive, physiological, experiential, expressive).

3. *Emotion*: We reserve the term *emotion* for affective states that represent appraisals of something as good or bad. Appraisals are perceptions of situations as being either positive or negative for one's goals and concerns (Clore & Ortony, in press). Emotions consist of the simultaneous representation of appraisals in multiple systems that often include feelings, physiology, facial expressions, thoughts, and so on. Representing appraisals as they do, emotions are not just states of feeling, but feelings about something, as when one is angry at someone or happy about something. More formally, emotions are psychological states focused on the goodness or badness of events, actions, or objects appraised for their relevance to one's goals, standards, and attitudes/tastes (Ortony, Clore, & Collins, 1988).

4. *Mood*: It is useful to think of emotions as affective states with objects and of moods as affective states without objects. But it is important to recognize that emotions act like moods when their objects are not focal. Affective states lie on a continuum with respect to the degree to which their effects are constrained by their objects. Thus we generally use the term *mood* to refer to a state of feeling that may or may not be appraisal-based but for which the object is not salient or has become diffuse and nonspecific. In this sense, moodlike conditions are state-focused, whereas emotionlike conditions are object-focused. "Emotional feelings," therefore, are experiential representations of the goodness or badness of something, whereas "affective feelings" (or "affect" for short) refer to the experience of goodness or badness itself, whether or not they have an object.

5. *Feeling*: Affective feelings are experiential representations of value. Feelings of a specific emotion (e.g., fear) are an experiential representation of the eliciting conditions for that emotion (e.g., perceived threat). But we use the term *feeling* as a generic designation for all kinds of internal signals that provide consciously available feedback from nonconscious affective, bodily, or cognitive processes (Clore, 1992). These include bodily aches and pains, cognitive experiences of insight, surprise, or confusion, and affective feelings of happiness, embarrassment, or preference.

Affective feelings vary in valence and intensity (Russell, 1980). Intensity includes both the magnitude and duration of feeling, where magnitude reflects the urgency of situations and duration reflects their importance

(Frijda, Ortony, Sonnemans, & Clore, 1992). To the extent that these feelings are arousing, they command attention, and to the extent that they are pleasant or unpleasant, they provide motivation. Although high-magnitude feelings commandeer attention automatically, more subtle feelings from ongoing appraisals (e.g., how one is doing at a task) convey less urgent information that can be attended to as judgments and decisions require. Affective feelings, then, can vary from the heart-pounding intensity of terror to the vague inclination to eat Chinese food. Although some feelings are located in particular parts of the body (e.g., having a pit in one's stomach when anxious, feeling flushed in the face when embarrassed), many feelings have no such location (e.g., aesthetic appeal, surprise).

6. *Information*: The information provided by affect is conveyed in feelings rather than words (Clore, 1992). Feelings must be conscious to be felt, of course, but in this affect-as-feedback model, those feelings are experienced directly, for example, as liking. However, the apparent meaning or significance of the experience depends on what else is in consciousness at the time. Thus, when a person is engaged in a task, positive affect might be experienced as information about the task ("This is fun"), as information about oneself ("I'm really good at this"), or as information about one's strategy ("I'm doing this right"), depending on what is in focus. It is easy to misunderstand the informational model by assuming that attribution involves decision making and that information is about concepts. That approach yields an awkward and unnatural account of such fluid and seamless phenomena as liking what we enjoy. Affective feelings are an experiential representation of the information about goodness and badness that they convey. The feelings may often be accompanied by a conceptual representation of the same information, but that is not the form of the information to which this affect-as-information model refers.

We turn now to five principles that rely on these terms and that constitute the affect-as-information approach.

Principles

1. *The experience principle: The cognitive consequences of affective states may be mediated by the subjective experience of affect.* In contrast to the recent emphasis on unconscious aspects of affect (e.g., Bargh, 1997; LeDoux, 1996), our own focus has been on the role of conscious feelings in information processing. One of the most distinctive aspects of emotions is that they are felt, and if there is a necessary ingredient in emotion, it is surely experience. One can have an emotion without doing anything or saying anything, but not without feeling anything.

One way we have examined the experience principle is by looking at the individual differences and situational factors that make feelings more or less salient. We have found that mood effects are most pronounced among individuals who routinely focus on their emotions (Gasper & Clore, 2000) and who are especially clear about what their feelings mean (Gohm & Clore, 2000) and also among those whose attention has been drawn to experiential factors through instructions (Gasper & Clore, 2000) or through exposure to pleasant odors (Clore, Wong, Isbell, & Gasper, 1994). We hypothesize that the lion's share of the influences of affect on judgment and processing are mediated by how individuals experience such affect. More particularly, Schwarz and Clore (1983) proposed that the important aspect of affective experience in these effects is its information value, which brings us to the second principle.

2. *The information principle: Emotional feelings provide information about the appraised relevance of situations for one's goals and concerns.* Like most cognitive processes, the appraisal process is largely unconscious, but conscious feedback from this process is available in the form of emotional feelings. Just as facial expressions provide externally available information about appraisals to others (Ekman, 1984), feelings provide such information internally to oneself. How one feels about something acts as an affective bottom line representing the overall personal significance of an object or situation. Any information that is felt may be experienced as especially credible, as when one says, "He had a heartfelt conviction that he was right." Studies of brain-damaged patients suggest also that the ability to detect and use such affective feedback is essential for engaging in even the most routine goal-directed activity (Damasio, 1994). In addition, what has been called "emotional intelligence" appears to involve the ability not only to read the emotions of others but also to read one's own feelings (Salovey & Mayer, 1990). The apparent meaning of affective cues depends on processes that we refer to in the attribution principle.

3. *The attribution principle: The information value of affect and its cognitive consequences depends on how the experience of affect is attributed.* Attributions are implicit perceptions of the causes of events. In our view, the influence of affect on judgment depends on attributions of one's subjective experience as a reaction to the object of judgment. It is important to realize that perceptions of events always occur within a network of causal beliefs, so that such causal attributions are normal parts of perception, not separable cognitive acts. Thus we automatically perceive the movement of one billiard ball that is struck by another as caused by that action without thinking about it. Similarly, we experience affective feelings as caused by whatever is currently in our focus of attention (see the immediacy principle, discussed later). Attribution theory provides a powerful framework for the analysis of affect and perception, but somewhere on the way from Heider's

(1958) brilliant exposition to the present, social psychologists began to think of attributions as optional, deliberative acts. Making ratings on attribution questionnaires is, of course, an optional, deliberative act, but attributions themselves are an inherent part of perceiving. The apparent information provided by affect is constrained in important ways by the nature of the affective condition, as indicated by the attributional constraint principle.

4. *The attributional constraint principle: Attributions for affect are constrained by the duration of the affect and the salience of its object.* We propose that affective conditions can be distinguished by their relative duration and by the specificity of their objects. Making these distinctions allows us to predict which affective conditions should be more and less easily misattributed to a substitute source. A primary constraint on attributions for affective conditions is whether they already have a salient object. In addition, whether the condition is a momentary state or an enduring disposition governs the availability of feelings to be attributed at any given time. Emotions, moods, attitudes, and temperaments can be distinguished in these terms, as seen in Table 2.1.

The fact that their objects are salient means that emotions and attitudes are the least likely to be misattributed to substitute objects, whereas the relative nonsalience of their objects should make moods and temperaments the most likely to be misattributed. In addition, the fact that attitudes and temperaments are enduring dispositions means that they are always potentially accessible to be misattributed. Conversely, the fact that emotions and moods are both temporary states means that opportunities for misattribution are temporally limited.

In the case of emotions, particular appraisals of situations may automatically trigger biochemical reactions that are then experienced as distinctive feelings. But such biochemical reactions can also be produced by endogenous causes, by drugs, or simply by "waking up on the wrong side of the bed." As a result, affect can occur that feels like emotion but that does not reflect appraisals. Thus having a sad emotion and being in a sad mood may produce the same feeling, both being experienced as a sense of loss. But in the case of sad mood, no actual loss may be involved, so the

TABLE 2.1
Object Salience and Duration as Factors
That Distinguish Affective Conditions

	Duration of Affect	
Object Salience	*Temporary State*	*Enduring Disposition*
Object Salient	Emotion	Attitude
Object Not Salient	Mood	Temperament

feelings of loss have no real object. As a result they may be experienced as a reaction to a substitute object. When they are, the feelings will appear to provide information about that object and hence govern reactions to it. The dynamics of affective dispositions can be seen in cases of depression and trait anxiety, in which objectless negative affect is chronically accessible (Gasper & Clore, 1998). Because everyone engages in frequent self-monitoring, the self is especially likely to become an object of chronically accessible affect.

Plausible as this account is, a question that remains unanswered is exactly how feelings arising from one cause (e.g., experiencing the first days of spring) can so readily be attributed to different objects (e.g., satisfaction with one's life). This phenomenon implicates what might be called the immediacy principle.

5. *The immediacy principle: Affective feelings tend to be experienced as reactions to current mental content.* Emotional feelings follow emotional appraisals instantly, so that the causes of one's emotional feelings are almost always whatever is in focus at the time. By contrast, feelings of indigestion may occur hours after eating certain foods, and feelings of illness may occur days or weeks after exposure to relevant pathogens. This immediacy of emotional reactions is presumably responsible for the more or less automatic tendency for people to experience emotional feelings as reactions to their current mental content.

From a gestalt point of view, this might be called the "montage effect." Early filmmakers learned what gestalt psychologists had figured out in the nineteenth century—that people automatically perceive things associated in time and space as being grouped together. Thus in a silent film the meaning of an image of the heroine shrinking in fear depends on what is shown in immediately preceding or succeeding frames. If the image is preceded by a picture of a tiger, then she is seen as fearing the tiger. If preceded by a picture of an onrushing locomotive, then she is seen as fearing the locomotive, and so on. Indeed, the effect is sufficiently powerful and reliable that, when it was not desired, filmmakers often had to include a brief delay between scenes or use a slow dissolve of one image into another as a form of punctuation.

The problem with mood and more chronic affective states is that to the extent that the affect intrudes on consciousness, it will tend to be involved in montage effects that influence the apparent meaning and significance of everything else that is experienced. In mood, the feelings persevere, so that their true cause may not only be ambiguous but also remote in time. Consistent with the immediacy principle, feelings that are not already linked to a particular cause may be experienced as appraisals of whatever is in one's focus at that moment. These considerations highlight the importance of the attributional constraint principle discussed earlier.

To summarize, we have now elaborated the affect-as-information hypothesis in three different ways: (a) by sketching the background for the hypothesis; (b) by defining six terms basic to the hypothesis, including the terms *affect, state, emotion, mood, feeling*, and *information*; and (c) by specifying five principles that we believe underlie the hypothesis. We turn now to a discussion of how these five principles and four additional ones can be used to illuminate mood effects on memory, judgment, processing, and creativity.

APPLICATIONS TO FOUR PHENOMENA

Mood and Memory

One of the most popular ideas to come out of the mood literature is that moods influence memory (e.g., Bower, Monteiro, & Gilligan, 1978; Isen, Shalker, Clark, & Karp, 1978). In addition to being interesting in its own right, mood-congruent recall offers a powerful explanation for other phenomena. For example, the influence of mood on judgment can be explained by assuming that the accessibility of information for judgment will be biased by mood, creating mood-congruent judgment. However, the effect of mood on memory has not always proved reliable (see Blaney, 1986). Indeed, there are both empirical and theoretical reasons for questioning whether affect should function in this way. Our view of the role of mood in memory is expressed in the following memory principle (Wyer, Clore, & Isbell, 1999).

6. *The memory principle: Affective feelings may activate specific concepts for interpreting them, but such affect is not itself stored in declarative memory and does not automatically influence the accessibility of similarly valenced semantic concepts and declarative knowledge.* Emotional feelings are an experiential representation of emotional significance. The same significance can also be represented as emotion concepts. Emotion concepts can in turn prime related memories and concepts in declarative memory. For example, if one were frightened, conceptualizing one's situation as "being frightened" might make memories of other frightening situations more accessible. But that would be an example of ordinary cognitive priming. Although the experience of affect might make such conceptualization more likely, there is no reason to assume that it would serve as some kind of energy that would automatically activate similarly valenced memories. We propose that when mood-congruent memory does occur, it is a function of affective concepts rather than of affective feelings.

We are not proposing that happy and sad moods cannot influence memory, only that the process does not involve the spontaneous activation by the affect itself of affectively similar concepts and memories. People do pursue consistent lines of thought. Thus, if one person tells of a harrowing traffic accident, it is likely that others will be able to recall similar experiences. That illustrates conceptual, but not affective, priming. It would be odd to respond to the traffic accident story with random negative memories. Affect might play two different roles in such a situation. The affect originally experienced in the traffic accident should increase the general memorability of that event, and the affect displayed by others during their stories might ensure sufficient attention to make conceptualization and conceptual priming likely. Neither of these, however, involves automatic affective priming.

In addition to asserting that affect does not prime similarly valenced material in memory, the memory principle also says that affect cannot be stored in memory. One can, of course, store concepts and propositions about emotional experiences. Thus one may remember the fact of having been angry, anxious, or pleased in some situation, but that remembering simply involves retrieving facts, not experiences.

Although one can retrieve facts about emotions, those conceptualizations of emotion are generally less vivid and compelling than actual emotions. This fact explains Lowenstein's (1996) important observation that people routinely underestimate the impact of emotional and other visceral experiences in decisions. He notes that in judgments about one's own past behavior, forecasts of one's future behavior, and considerations of others' behavior, people often fail to appreciate the role played by subjective experience. For example, when making decisions about alcohol, drugs, and sexual behavior, people find it difficult to take fully into account how they felt the previous time or how they or others will feel later. One result is that people may be unsympathetic and react with blame when viewing at a distance their own or others' failures of will. We propose that people underestimate the impact of emotional experience because they have no way of storing the experience so that it can be retrieved later when needed.

Constructive Memory. When memory theorists say that memory is constructed (e.g., Bartlett, 1932), they mean that memory for experiences is constructed because it cannot be stored. Facts, beliefs, and a variety of complex information can be stored and directly retrieved. These may be helpful in staging mental reenactments of experiences. If one were to reconstruct an important experience with vividness, one might feel emotional again, but that would be using imagination to generate new feelings, not memory to retrieve old feelings. Such reenactments are probably necessary for a past event to be experienced in the present. It is less clear that the same is true of semantic knowledge. One may not have to replay the conditions under which one learned a particular fact in order to use it to solve a problem.

Conditioning. Emotional conditioning might initially seem to provide evidence against the proposal that affect cannot be stored. Imagine a person who feels anxious around people with red hair because of a traumatic experience of having been abused by a person who had red hair. Would the conditioned anxiety be an example of memory for feeling itself? We suggest not. An S-S, as opposed to an S-R, account of conditioning (Hebb, 1949) would suggest that it is not the fear response itself that might be conditioned to red hair but an abstract representation of threat that in turn elicits fear. Emotions occur when the cognitive eliciting conditions of emotions are satisfied (Ortony et al., 1988). Memory is a cognitive process that allows for the storage and retrieval of eliciting conditions but not of feelings.

Emotional Memories. The assertion that subjective experience is not stored does not imply that emotion is not important for memory. Memory is often especially strong when accompanied by emotional experience. It probably makes good evolutionary sense that one should remember well situations involving emotions. Thus many people recall well where they were when they heard of various tragic events (e.g., the Kennedy and King assassinations, the Challenger explosion, the Nicole Brown Simpson murder, or the Oklahoma City bombing). But such recollections are likely to be cued by thinking about relevant content (e.g., assassinations, civil rights, civilians in space, TV in courtrooms, or militia groups). Or they could be cued by emotional concepts ("a time when I was angry, shocked, or sad"). However, we do not believe that feelings of anger, shock, or sadness by themselves make other affect-congruent events come to mind, nor that it would be advantageous for them to do so.

Emotions as Species-Level Memories. We have argued that feelings cannot be stored and retrieved. One might even speculate that the evolution of emotions themselves was occasioned by the inability to retrieve feelings. Behavior is most effectively guided by immediate consequences. What emotions do is to represent long-term positive and negative outcomes in terms of immediate feelings (Frank, 1988; Ketelaar & Clore, 1997). For example, left unpunished, insults to one's honor, theft of one's property, or violation of one's rights would eventually leave one without standing in one's community. Frank (1988) argues that the immediately felt aversiveness of anger motivates one to seek redress now and serves as a cost against not doing so. Similarly, guilt at taking advantage of a friend may represent (as immediate unpleasant feelings) the long-term negative consequences of being known as untrustworthy. Thus the emotion elicitation process may serve as a species-level emotional memory, enforcing lessons that would otherwise be ineffective because individual memories are unable to store as experiences the joy and pain of positive and negative consequences.

Evidence. Wyer and Srull (1989) have also argued that mood and memory effects are based on cognitions about being in a mood rather than on mood itself. In a relevant study, Parrott and Sabini (1990) assessed students' moods on sunny and pleasant or rainy and unpleasant days in the spring and then asked them to write down an event in their recent past. Because the mood states were assumed to be caused by the weather, they presumably had little cognitive content. It is especially instructive then that mood-congruent memory was not found except in a separate condition in which participants were led to label their moods. Rothkopf and Blaney (1991) report similar conclusions. Riskind (1989) also showed that cognitive content, rather than the arousal component of mood, produced the mood-congruity effect. He too noted the general ineffectuality of subjective feelings as a retrieval cue and focused on the importance of cognitive priming as the active process in mood effects. In a related study on attention, Niedenthal and Setterlund (1994) examined lexical decisions about words related to participants' emotional states. They found attentional effects for stimuli congruent with the emotional content but not for stimuli that were only valence-congruent. Thus, if a difference between moods and emotions is that emotions have cognitive content that moods do not, we should expect emotion congruence, but not necessarily mood congruence, in attention and memory.

As a further test of the memory principle, Garvin (1999) not only induced mood by playing both happy and sad music but also exposed participants to a standard priming task (a sentence completion task) in which the concepts "happiness" and "sadness" were primed. Participants then read an adaptation of a story used previously by Bower, Gilligan, and Monteiro (1981) in which a character relates an equal number of happy and sad memories during psychotherapy. Consistent with the memory principle, the results show evidence of prime-congruent but not of mood-congruent recall. This project is ongoing, but the data are consistent with the hypothesis that affect, although it may be produced by material in declarative memory and may be represented by concepts from declarative memory, is not itself part of declarative memory (Wyer et al., 1999).

To summarize, we proposed that the subjective experience of affect cannot be stored in declarative memory, a fact that explains people's inability to anticipate fully the role of affect in their past or future behavior. We also proposed that affect itself does not spontaneously activate similarly valenced material in memory, as is generally believed. Hence, we hypothesized that any relationship between mood and memory actually reflects priming by concepts about affect rather than priming by affect itself. Data from various sources suggest that mood-congruent recall occurs mainly when the induction procedures encourage people to label their moods.

We turn now to the role of mood in evaluative judgment. In contrast to their indirect role in mood-congruent memory, we believe that affective feelings play a direct role in mood-congruent judgment.

Mood and Judgment

The idea that there is a relationship between feelings, beliefs, and judgments is a central one for novelists and playwrights. Modern psychologists too have observed that judgments tend to involve consistency of beliefs and feelings (e.g., Rosenberg & Abelson, 1960). But it was not until psychologists varied affective feelings independently of evaluative beliefs that it became clear that the feelings themselves influence judgment (e.g., Gouaux, 1971; Griffitt & Veitch, 1971; Lott & Lott, 1960; Nunnally, Duchnowski, & Parker, 1965; Staats & Staats, 1958). By showing happy or sad films (Gouaux, 1971) and by having participants write about happy or sad events (Schwarz & Clore, 1983), one can observe that mood can influence a variety of evaluative judgments.

There are two common ways of explaining the effects of mood on judgment. Memory-based approaches assume that the affective feelings prime affect-congruent beliefs about objects, which are then more accessible as a basis for judgments about them (Bower, 1981; Forgas & Bower, 1988; Isen et al, 1978). Like the previously discussed impression formation (Anderson, 1971) and attitude theories (Fishbein & Ajzen, 1975), the memory-based explanation of mood effects on judgment assumes that judgments are based directly on beliefs and only indirectly on affect. However, consistent with the experience principle, we assume that affective feelings accessible at the time of judgment often contribute directly to evaluative judgments.

According to the information principle, emotional feelings are a conscious representation of unconscious appraisal processes. Thus any subjective experiences that arise while we consider a decision alternative, a political candidate, or a possible mate may accurately index our evaluation. There is, therefore, no reason to assume as is so often done in the judgment and decision literature that decisions based on feelings must be biased. By reflecting one's evaluative representation of the object of judgment, feelings may be highly informative.

Of course, using a subjective basis for judgment is often thought to be inappropriate. Examples include judgments by referees, judges, or personnel managers. We contend, however, that the essential process of judgment is similar whether situations require objectivity or not. The only issue is whether referees, judges, and personnel managers focus on task-relevant goals and standards rather than on purely personal goals. To the extent that personnel managers, for example, focus on the requirements for particular positions, it is reasonable for them to rely on their feelings as data about whether to hire someone. Indeed, once relevant standards and goals have been accessed, we would contend that reliance on intuitions and feelings is the essence of the judgment process. There is no necessary problem presented by the fact that a different appraisal might be given when focusing on different standards and goals (e.g., "Would I choose this person as a friend or confidant?"). At the same time, there clearly can be conflicts of interest (e.g., a mixture of personal and job-relevant criteria), as, for example, when an applicant is a friend or relative of the person making the decision.

Evidence. Evidence that judgments are often influenced directly by feelings comes from early experiments contrasting feeling-based explanations with priming or memory-based explanations. The priming hypothesis maintains that mood effects are mediated by participants' interpretations of ambiguous situations and that mood activates mood-congruent material that biases interpretations and, hence, judgments. However, Schwarz, Robbins, and Clore (1985) found strong mood effects even when situations were evaluatively unambiguous so that they did not lend themselves to varied interpretations.

Other research (Clore & Wilkin, 1985) contrasted the effects of introducing mood before or after presentation of the information to be judged. Mood effects were found to occur at the point of judgment, well after the information had already been interpreted. This finding is notable because it does not match what we know from the literature on cognitive priming (e.g., Massad, Hubbard, & Newtson, 1979; Srull & Wyer, 1979). Priming manipulations typically have effects only at the encoding stage of processing, when stimulus materials are first interpreted. When introduced later at the output stage, attempts at priming generally have no effect on judgment at all. Consistent with the information principle, then, mood may exercise its influence not by coloring initial interpretations at encoding but by affecting evaluations at judgment. After reviewing these studies, Clore and Parrott (1991) concluded:

> In several studies, therefore, mood effects occurred in situations that should not produce priming and did not occur in situations that should produce

priming. Such findings suggest that the influences of mood on judgment in these studies may not have been due to cognitive priming. (p. 117)

According to the attribution principle, feelings must be seen as a reaction to (must be attributed to) the object of judgment in order to have a direct influence. These attributions are generally assumed to be automatic and implicit (the experience principle), just as the movement of a soccer ball is attributed automatically to the foot that kicks it. The primary evidence for the hypothesized role of subjective experience comes from misattribution studies in which causes for feelings that render them irrelevant to the judgment are made salient. As a result, when affect is no longer experienced as a reaction to the object of judgment, judgments no longer show their influence. What is important, however, is not whether the affect has a clear cause, but whether at the moment of judgment, that cause is more salient than other plausible causes.

In one of the original Schwarz and Clore (1983) studies, participants were asked as part of a telephone interview about their life satisfaction. Calls were made either on the first warm, sunny days of spring, when people were presumably in good moods, or on subsequent cold and rainy spring days, when they were not. It was found that mood influenced the judgments of respondents about their life satisfaction. However, in some cases the interviewer, pretending to call from another town, asked first about the weather. Answering that question caused respondents to attribute their feelings to the weather, which eliminated the relationship between mood and judgment. The attributional manipulation did not affect the moods themselves but only the information value of the moods for making the judgment.

Unconscious Activation of "Affect." In keeping with the experience principle, we have emphasized the role of conscious affective experience, but much work currently focuses on unconscious activation of what some refer to as "affect" (e.g., Winkielman, Zajonc, & Schwarz, 1997). In the standard experiment, an affective stimulus (word, face) is exposed briefly followed by another stimulus (which serves as a pattern mask that interferes with recognition of having seen the affective stimulus). What is found is that the affective stimulus influences the evaluation of subsequent stimuli even though participants are unaware of having seen it (Bargh, 1997). Do such results contradict the experience principle? We would argue that they do not for either of two reasons: (a) Lack of awareness of having seen the affective stimulus does not guarantee that there is no affective experience and no information, and (b) in studies that show nonconscious priming effects without generating affective feelings (e.g., Winkielman et al., 1997), we assume that the phenomena are not really examples of primed affect but of primed affective meaning. Indeed, the primes are often mildly positive or negative words (e.g., Bargh, 1997), stimuli that would be unlikely to produce affective feelings even if presented in full awareness. Also, because the same kind of priming effects occur when male and female names are used to prime expectations of gender (Greenwald, Draine, & Abrams, 1996), there is no reason to assume that such studies have important implications for hypotheses about affect.

We contend that such studies illustrate the attributional constraint principle—the idea that opportunities for the misattribution of affect are constrained by the salience of the source or object of the affect (see Bornstein, 1992, for a similar argument). Without access to the source of the affective stimulus, attribution of its affective meaning is completely unconstrained. Thus what is interesting about subliminal affect studies is not what they tell us about lack of awareness but what they say about the difficulty of making correct attributions about mental content that has no clear source (Clore & Ketelaar, 1997; Clore & Ortony, 2000; Ketelaar & Clore, 1997). The same effects occur regardless of whether the stimulus is presented outside of awareness, consciously but incidentally as part of another task, or even in full awareness but in situations in which participants are simultaneously engaged in a secondary task that occupies their attention (Martin, Seta, & Crelia, 1990). What appears to be important is not whether the stimulus is conscious or unconscious but whether the experimental techniques make the proper attribution easy or difficult.

Freud. This approach is similar to Freud's theory of displacement. In his essay, "Instincts and Their Vicissitudes," Freud (1915/1959) outlined a remarkably modern cognitive psychology. He insisted that ideas must be activated to become conscious and that this activation spreads throughout a network of associated memories and determines our train of thought. Repression, he suggested, involves splitting activation off from an unacceptable idea. The unattached activation (what he called affect) can then attach itself to any associated idea and drive it into consciousness, perhaps giving it undue importance. Interestingly, for Freud as well as for modern attribution theory, what allows affect to influence belief is lack of awareness of the true source of the affect. By implication, freeing someone from affectively biased beliefs requires getting them to attribute the affect to its true source, which is, as it happens, the object of Freud's insight-oriented psychotherapy.

Mood and Processing

Much of the research on mood has focused on mood-congruent judgment, which appears to be one of the more reliable effects of mood. However, according to the immediacy principle, the information value of affective feelings depends in part on one's focus of attention. If, instead of focusing on an object with the goal of evaluating it, one is focused on a task with goals relevant to learning and performance, then affective cues may be experienced as feedback about currently accessible cognitive content. Such content may include beliefs, expectations, expertise, intuitions, strategies, responses, inclinations, and so on. This idea is summarized in the processing principle.

7. *The processing principle: When one is task-oriented, affective feelings may be experienced as feedback about one's performance and about the value of accessible information.* This principle suggests that positive affective cues serve as an incentive, reward, or "go" signal for using currently accessible information and pursuing currently accessible inclinations, whereas negative affective cues serve as an inhibition, punishment, or "stop" signal. Thus, in addition to indicating whether situations are benign or problematic (Schwarz, 1990; Schwarz & Clore, 1996), affective feelings are often about oneself, one's responses, and one's expectations, inclinations, and desires in relation to the situation.

We assume that all information processing involves an interplay of old and new information, of what is already believed and what is being experienced, or of top-down and bottom-up processing. For example, in visual perception, what one sees depends on both internal, conceptual information and external, sensory information (Palmer, 1975). Positive affect serves as an incentive to use accessible information, privileging the expectation-driven or top-down aspects of this process, whereas negative affect inhibits the use of accessible information, resulting in greater reliance on data-driven or bottom-up aspects. Thus the influence of affect on processing often concerns whether one assimilates sense data to existing knowledge, expectations, and intuitions or accommodates such expectations and conceptions to new data. Whether experienced as self-confidence, as success, or as an indication that one's beliefs and expectations are valid, positive affect should serve as a go signal (or reward) and negative affect as a stop signal (or punishment) for using whatever goal, strategy, information, or response is most accessible. It would be a mistake to assume that accessible response are necessarily shallow or error prone. In a study of young doctors (Isen, Rosenzweig, & Young, 1991), the most accessible response drew on a well-learned body of medical knowledge.

The assertion that success feedback should lead to the use of prior knowledge, whereas failure feedback should lead to learning, is not a new one. Analogous proposals can be found in (or at least easily read into) a variety of writings. The idea that the experience of failure and disconfirmation of expectations is essential for learning is central to McDougall's (1923) theory of learning, Kelly's (1955) philosophy of science, Dewey's

(1916) approach to education, and Piaget's (1954) theory of cognitive development. The idea is also evident in Gray's (1971) discussion of his experiments on rats, in which he proposed that positive affect elicits the use of habit and negative affect elicits new learning. Also, in studies of evoked brain potentials, the P-300 wave is seen as a measure of the cognitive updating of a situation following expectation violation (Donchin, 1981). On the basis of the information and immediacy principles, we predict an association between positive affect and reliance on accessible knowledge, beliefs, and expectations and an association between negative affect and attention to new information.

Stereotype Use.   An example of this process is evident in recent experiments on stereotype use (Isbell, Clore, & Wyer, 2000). Participants heard a story about a day in the life of a woman named Carol. She was initially described either as an introverted librarian or as an extraverted salesperson, but the story included equal numbers of introverted and extraverted actions. Later, when asked about how introverted or extraverted Carol was, ratings by those in happy moods reflected the expectations associated with the stereotype they had received, whereas those in sad moods reflected the equal balance of introverted and extraverted acts in the story. In addition, recall measures showed that happy participants could recall more stereotype-incongruent behaviors from the story, indicating that they had actively used their stereotyped expectations to organize incoming information.

In some versions of the experiment, the affect-as-information interpretation was tested directly by including an attribution condition. In those conditions, participants rated other possible reasons for their feelings, which should have interfered with attributing the feelings to the task and inhibited their use. The results supported the idea that normal processing involves both expectation-driven and data-driven processing. They showed that interfering with one of those processes allowed the other to dominate processing, yielding reversals of the usual mood and processing relationship in the attribution condition. We interpreted the result as evidence of the role of affect-as-information—in this case, information about the appropriate style for processing information about Carol.

Anger.   Before leaving the topic of mood and processing, it is important to note findings by Bodenhausen, Sheppard, and Kramer (1994) that seem at first to challenge this generalization. They showed that happy and angry participants were both more likely than sad participants to use an ethnic stereotype to convict a defendant in a mock trial situation. The fact that both a positive and a negative state triggered stereotype use appears at first problematic, but we assume that the key lies in the information provided by the affective cues of happy and angry states. Anger, like happiness, implies the validity of the person's own beliefs. Indeed, anger appears to be an emotion concerned with reasserting one's own perspective. So individuals who feel aggrieved may, even more than those in positive moods, feel empowered to rely on accessible beliefs, expectations, and inclinations.

Before leaving the topic of mood and processing, we turn briefly to the relationship between this approach and previous affect-as-information treatments of processing.

Relation to Previous Treatments. In previous work, the influence of mood on information processing has been conceptualized as an example of Chaiken's (1987) heuristic–systematic processing distinction. In this view, positive affect has been interpreted as leading to heuristic processing and negative affect as leading to systematic processing (Bless, Bohner, Schwarz, & Strack, 1990; Schwarz & Clore 1996). Schwarz (1990) suggested that positive affect may signal that a current situation is benign, whereas negative affect signals that it is problematic. As a result, negative affect should motivate participants to be systematic, whereas positive affect suggests that further investment of such processing resources is not necessary.

This view is a straightforward application of the general affect-as-information hypothesis (Schwarz & Clore, 1983), but two comments seem important: (a) The use of the term *heuristic* (Schwarz & Clore, 1988) implies that the strategies followed by individuals in positive moods are shortcuts, an idea that has been interpreted as evidence that positive moods motivate individuals to save cognitive effort (for a critique, see Bless, Clore, Golisano, Rabel, & Schwarz, 1996); and (b) this view has also been interpreted as implying that mood should have a main effect on processing in which positive and negative affect always tend to trigger heuristic and systematic processing (for a critique, see Martin, Ward, Achee, & Wyer, 1993). These may or may not be necessary implications of the original formulation, but we agree with the conclusions of Bless and colleagues (1996) that the processing influences of positive affect need not involve reduced processing motivation and with the conclusions of Martin and colleagues (1993) that the informational influences of affect should be thought of as flexible and as dependent on the active goal. This latter point raises an important issue. The processing principle assumes that one is primarily motivated to perform adequately. To cover cases in which this is not the case, we need another principle (see Wyer et al., 1999).

8. *The enjoyment principle: When an enjoyment rather than a performance goal is paramount, positive and negative affect may be experienced as enjoyment and lack of enjoyment, leading to greater and lesser persistence at the activity or*

task. Instead of a task orientation in which one is motivated to perform well, one may engage in some activities just for fun. Then positive affective feelings may be experienced as feedback about enjoyment goals rather than as feedback about performance goals. Given a concern with enjoyment, positive affect may lead to judgments that tasks are more enjoyable (Martin et al., 1993) and hence to more involvement and systematic processing (Wegener, Petty, & Smith, 1994) and to greater creativity (Isen, 1987) on these tasks because they are experienced as enjoyable.

It can be seen that the utterly generic nature of affective feedback and the fact that it can provide positive and negative feedback about whatever is currently on one's mind means that it may often be difficult to make accurate predictions about the impact of mood and emotion in uncontrolled situations. It all depends on what is accessible to the person in the moment, information that is not necessarily publicly available.

In short, the processing principle holds that positive affect often provides a "go" signal and negative affect a "stop" signal, leading to increased and decreased reliance on accessible information. In addition, the enjoyment principle proposes that positive affect may lead to greater persistence on tasks that provide enjoyment. There is, however, still another effect of mood on processing by which positive affect appears to generate an integrative, global, categorical, or relational focus as opposed to negative affect, which generates an analytical, local, item-level focus. This latter tendency is most relevant to the next issue, the role of mood in creativity.

Mood and Creativity

It is easy enough to see how positive affect might lead to novel responses from our perspective. Although positive mood sometimes (Isen, 1987) leads to better performance on creativity tests such as the Remote Associates Test (RAT), Gasper (1999) finds that happy moods also lead sometimes to more responses and more errors. Because positive affect may signal success on a task, it may lead to an early exit from any particular stage of processing. This may result in impulsivity and a tendency to go with whatever responses come to mind, including novel ones. However, creativity also involves relational, holistic, integrative thinking.

Creativity in both art and science involves finding ways in which superficially different things share something in common; that is, finding unity in variety (Bronowski, 1956). For example, the French impressionist painters depicted everything as points of reflected light, the cubist painters saw everything as geometric forms, and the surrealists saw everything as united by fluidity of form and absurdity of content. Similar examples abound in science, as when Darwin proposed that the varied species of plants and animals all emerged through natural selection. Such creativity often appears to have an emotional engine. Jamison (1993) has documented the extraordinary prevalence of mania and depression among great poets, novelists, and composers. Experimentally, too, psychologists have found links between emotion and creativity (Isen, 1987).

The typical effects of positive mood on processing involve greater use of stereotypes, categories, schemas, and scripts. In the previous section we treated these as examples of the use of accessible knowledge and expectations. But these are also examples of adopting a global rather than a local focus, of relying on general, categorical knowledge rather than local and specific facts. In much of the research to date these two factors have been confounded, so that it is unclear whether mood provides information about the validity of accessible knowledge, expectations, and inclinations on the one hand or elicits global versus local processing on the other. Alternatively, a global focus may be associated with positive affect because it is one example of a generally accessible response. Thus a corollary to the processing principle is what might be called the level-of-focus principle.

9. *The level-of-focus principle: Affective feedback about the success or failure of one's efforts and appropriateness of accessible beliefs should also influence the global-versus-local focus of processing.* The kind of top-down, theory-driven processing we have associated with positive mood is inherently integrative, tending to assimilate details into larger wholes. Conversely, the kind of bottom-up, data-driven processing we have associated with negative mood is inherently analytical, tending to focus on distinctions to which concepts must then accommodate. A related idea is evident in Wegner and Vallacher's (1986) work on action identification. They showed that in the context of feedback about success and failure people characterize the meaning of their own behavior differently. With success feedback, they describe their behavior as relevant to higher level, more abstract and encompassing goals, and with failure feedback, to lower level, more concrete and disconnected goals. The same relationship has been observed by Ketelaar and Clore (unpublished). In positive moods, participants characterized their behavior of making ratings in an experiment as relevant to abstract goals such as "earning credit for introductory psychology," whereas in negative moods they were more likely to characterize it as relevant to concrete goals such as "completing forms." Thus positive mood might be expected not only to provide positive feedback about reliance on one's expectations but also to encourage a global and integrative orientation as opposed to a local and analytical one.

To the extent that positive affect is an activation of the reward or "go" system and to the extent that it represents an affirmative answer to implicit processing questions, it should promote giving more and faster answers and paying less regard to the possibility of their being incorrect. But it should also encourage integration as opposed to analysis and affirmative answers to implicit questions about whether two things are related. In other words, positive affect should lead to making connections and negative affect to drawing distinctions. In the language of Piaget's assimilation and accommodation concept, positive affect should lead to assimilation of new data to one's own ideas, whereas negative affect should lead to accommodation of one's ideas to new information (learning).

Evidence. To test the idea that happy moods can lead to global processing, Dienes (1996) performed experiments in which participants attempted to learn words that were either easy or hard to categorize. Optimal learning of such lists requires that global, category-level processing be complemented by local, item-level processing (Einstein & Hunt, 1980). This fact allowed Dienes to make strong inferences about the role of mood in processing. For example, the easy-to-categorize list forces attention to categories, because such items as Spain and France or tennis and soccer automatically elicit the categories of countries and sports. As a result, the category-level processing hypothesized to result from happy mood should be redundant with the category-level processing forced by the task, yielding poor recall of easy words by happy participants. In contrast, the item-level processing of sad individuals should complement what is provided by the task, yielding superior recall. Results confirmed these predictions.

In contrast, the hard-to-categorize list forces attention to individual items. So the complementary category-level processing by happy participants should enhance their learning. Consistent with predictions, results showed that happy participants recalled hard-to-categorize words better than did sad participants, whose item-level processing was now redundant. The results show that happy moods led to a global, category-level focus in which connections were sought among the items, whereas sad moods led to a local focus on items without regard to their interconnections. Most important, the contrasting global-versus-local focus led each group to show superior recall of one list and inferior recall of the other.

Although the Dienes (1996) project was not about creativity per se, we include it here as evidence that positive affect leads to the kind of global, integrative focus that is often required for true creativity. It is worth noting that the hard-to-categorize word list consisted of ad hoc categories, so that extra processing was required to generate the categories. Whereas participants in sad moods were content to memorize individual items, those in happy moods appeared to actively seek connections among the items. Although this behavior is consistent with an affect-as-information approach, it is possible that other accounts could arrive at the same predictions. Therefore, an attribution manipulation was added.

In one version of the study, the true source of participants' affective experiences was made salient. When the affective feedback no longer appeared to reflect feedback about the learning task, everything changed. Happy participants inhibited their exclusive reliance on categories and did better at learning easy-to-categorize words; sad participants inhibited their focus on individual items and did worse. Conversely, happy participants did worse and sad ones did better on the hard words, as predicted.

It is noteworthy that we have now shown that attribution manipulations affect the relation between mood and processing in paradigms involving persuasion (Sinclair, Mark, & Clore, 1994), stereotypes (Isbell et al., 2000), and category versus item-level processing (Dienes, 1996). Consistent with the attribution principle, these results imply that the system is keenly sensitive to how one parses one's experience and that the influence of affect depends on what it is experienced as a reaction to.

To summarize, the level-of-focus principle, in which affective feedback about the success or failure of one's efforts should lead to a relatively more global or local focus of processing, is consistent with Wegner and Vallacher's (1986) work on action identification. Positive moods may be associated not only with reliance on accessible knowledge but also with adoption of a global focus involving integrative processing, and negative moods may be associated with a reluctance to rely on accessible information, adoption of a local focus, and pursuit of analytic processing. We hypothesize that all of these effects depend on the experienced meaning of affective feedback.

ADDRESSING THE CONTRIBUTORS' QUESTIONS

1. The reason behind the evolution of your model from a reinforcement one to a cognitive one is not clear. How and why did you move away from a "passive" conditioning model to a more "conscious" cognitive framework?

The reinforcement-affect model of attraction (Clore, 1977; Clore & Byrne, 1974) asserted that the development of liking or disliking for others involved associating them with one's own affective reactions. That account was couched in the language of classical conditioning, which was intended to capture the fact that liking and disliking involve visceral reactions that seem visited on one. Alternative conceptions that were prevalent at the time (e.g., Anderson, 1971; Fishbein & Ajzen, 1975) had no real role for affect except as an attribute of belief. Thus liking for another person was assumed to depend solely on the degree to which they were believed to have likable traits or other positive characteristics. But, of course, listing others' positive traits can only generate beliefs that they might be likable, which is not at all the same thing as finding that one likes them.

By the mid-1970s, the cognitive revolution was well under way, and even former behaviorists such as Albert Bandura had joined it (e.g., Bandura, 1973). In that context, the classical-conditioning language of the reinforcement-affect model of attraction was potentially problematic. On the one hand, research did show that liking could be produced merely by associating a stimulus object with the experience of positive affect, even when the affect came from an irrelevant source (e.g., Griffitt & Veitch, 1971). On the other hand, mere temporal contiguity of affect and object did not seem sufficient. After all, people do not generally develop attraction to the person who delivers their paycheck or to the waiter who brings their food, despite the temporal association of such persons with reward. Moreover, we found that even when associations between affect and objects would otherwise create liking, the process could easily be disrupted by making salient an extraneous plausible cause for the affect (e.g., Schwarz & Clore, 1983). Whether affect becomes linked to an object depends on whether a mental association is formed or not, which in turn depends on how individuals parse their own experience. Liking requires felt affect, but what is made likable by that affect depends on the cognitive connections and perceptual groupings that are made. Thus it became clear that the passive, mechanical processes of classical conditioning, however relevant, were not enough. Therefore, the affect-as-information approach does concern associations between objects and the experience of affect, which can be treated as conditioned affect, but it also assumes that the associations are governed by accessible knowledge structures and implicit attributional processes. So one might assume that both conditioning and cognition play a role. However, such an account implies that these two aspects fit neatly into a single, unitary process, which may represent the system as more orderly than it is.

An alternative possibility is suggested by dual-process models. For example, Clore and Ortony (2000) suggest that understanding alternative routes to emotions may require studying the interplay of two different kinds of processing—associative processing and rule-based processing (Sloman, 1996). In associative processing, objects are organized according to subjective similarity and temporal contiguity in experience. In rule-based processing, reasoning operates on symbolic structures. Presumably, associative and rule-based processing proceed in parallel, and, as a consequence, they can lead to different, even conflicting, outcomes. For example, in a vivid account of his struggle with anxiety and depression, Solomon (1998) recalls lying frozen in bed, crying, because he was too frightened to take a shower, even though he was fully aware at the same time that showers are not scary. His feelings and beliefs were at odds. Similarly, in unpublished research by Weber and Clore (1987), individuals induced to feel anxious through hypnosis avoided bets involving small risks, even though they believed they would win them. Despite the fact that they knew rationally that the bets were advantageous, from an experiential standpoint they felt the bets were too risky. Such felt information is sometimes more compelling than information from knowing. Clore and Ortony (2000) suggest how this process might work:

A situation may be categorized as a threat either because it reminds one of a prior situation that was threatening or because a rule-based analysis shows it to involve risk. In the former instance, one need not rationally believe that the event will actually bring harm. But if one is reminded of a past bad outcome, then a mental representation of that bad outcome comes to mind. Because the triggers for emotions are mental representations of outcomes (rather than actual outcomes), being reminded may be sufficient to elicit an emotion, so that entertaining the possibility can make one feel afraid even when one knows better.

The idea, then, is that associations arising from one's experience and inferences arising from one's beliefs may or may not be one and the same. For example, in a study by Lewicki (1985), participants had a negative affective experience when they were criticized by a person who happened to have curly hair. Much later they had a chance to turn in their materials to one of two individuals seated at a table, one of whom was curly-haired and the other of whom was straight-haired. Although they were apparently not aware of why they did so, these individuals avoided interacting with the curly-haired person. Emotions are generally responses to whatever content is currently in mind. As a result, our thoughts and feelings are usually tightly linked. But Lewicki's results suggest that, even as we use rule-based reasoning to make a sensible plan, aspects of a situation can trigger affective associations that move us in a different direction. If so, it may be inadequate for social cognitive analyses to rely on either cognition or conditioning, as both may always be active at the same time.

2. You frequently mention emotion as the larger context of your work, but there seems to be a conflict between your attribution results and what research has shown about emotion. The studies in which you claim attribution effects seem to suggest that the influence of affect on judgment and processing can be controlled simply through awareness of the source of the affect. Emotions, however, are notorious for being difficult to control. How would you address the criticism that yours is a theory about "pseudoemotions" in sophomores in social psychology experiments rather than about real emotional feelings?

The answer to this question has two parts. The first part argues that the same appraisal processes that are responsible for intense states of passion and terror are also responsible for barely noticeable cues of interest and concern. Although intense emotion may command attention and dictate responses, milder affective feelings do not. A second part of the answer argues that the currently popular idea that affective influences are controlled through intentional corrections may not be the best way to think about the process.

Attention to Affective Cues is Optional. It is surely true that emotions are often powerful states with consequences that are difficult to control. We assume, however, that much of that power is mediated by the intensity of emotional feelings, which are triggered automatically by the appraisal of something as emotionally significant (Lazarus, 1994). The intensity of feeling is presumably an index of the perceived urgency of the situation (Frijda, Ortony, Sonnemans, & Clore, 1992). When they are intense, feelings of arousal and emotion command attention, which in turn influences what cognitions, motivations, and actions are most accessible. In addition, because intense feelings command attention, urgent events are well remembered (Christianson, 1992). This attention-grabbing nature of intense feeling presumably has great survival value, and we might therefore expect that aspect of intense emotion to show little individual variation. However, the same appraisal system that gives rise to strong emotion is also responsible for milder affective feelings typical of those produced in most mood experiments.

We assume that most of our affective experience consists of being pleased rather than overjoyed or concerned rather than terrified. As a model for everyday affect, therefore, intense emotion may have limitations. Whereas both mild and strong feelings convey information, less intense feelings do not compel one to attend to them the way strong feelings do. In fact, for mild affect to influence judgment often requires one to ask implicitly, "How do I feel about this?" (Schwarz & Clore, 1988).

Evidence in support of the idea that individuals do differ in the attention they pay to mild affect and that such differences influence mood effects comes from research (Gasper & Clore, 2000) that found that negative mood states elevated risk estimation only among individuals scoring high on an attention to emotion scale (Salovey, Mayer, Goldman, Turvey, & Palfai, 1995). Low scorers were equally responsive to the mood induction procedure, but without a tendency to focus on feelings, their risk estimates were not influenced by mood.

To examine the attention hypothesis further, some participants in a second experiment were instructed to attend to their feelings and some to attend to the relevant facts. As expected, participants scoring low on the

attention to emotion scale based their risk estimates on feelings of negative affect only after instructions drew attention to them. Those data suggest that low-intensity feelings, despite their accessibility, may remain un-
attended to until brought to one's attention. The same results presumably
would not be found for strong affective reactions, especially if they arose
sharply in response to the appearance of a threat. Under those conditions,
the feelings might be inescapable.

Studies of attributions for affective feelings also show, in contrast to the
dictates of strong emotion, that everyday affective information is only ad-
visory. Mood effects on judgment (e.g., Keltner, Locke, & Audrain, 1993)
and processing (e.g., Sinclair, Mark, & Clore, 1994) are often eliminated
when alternative plausible causes for affective feelings are made salient. In
most real-world situations, similar effects would not be expected, because
emotional reactions usually are relevant to whatever is salient in consciousness at the time. Thus attributional manipulations designed to make
salient the true cause of emotions would generally be redundant. Moreover, misattributions of emotions are presumably less common than
misattributions of moods. Indeed, in emotions, experiences of events and
of feelings are often seamlessly joined, so that attempts to create in everyday life the kinds of misattributions we see in mood experiments should
be unsuccessful. The point of creating misattributions in mood experiments is to separate the Siamese twins of feeling and knowing to see if feeling is a viable cause of behavior on its own. The fact that specialized conditions have to be created to observe these processes at work should not
make less credible the hypothesis that (implicit) attributional connections
mediate the influences of affect on belief.

We have argued that everyday affect and strong emotion are both governed by the same principles but that everyday feelings are more easily
controlled. The topic of how automatic inferences are controlled has become a focus in the social cognition literature more generally (e.g.,
Devine, 1989; Gilbert, 1989). The prevailing model is one in which individuals are believed to exercise control over some automatic inferences by
judging their irrelevance and then correcting for them. Supporting evidence comes from studies employing distracting tasks. When distraction
occupies attentional resources, mood, priming, or other "heuristic" effects
are more likely to occur. Without distraction, irrelevant factors may be
more apparent, so that corrections of judgment can occur. This is a powerful frame for viewing attribution effects. However, to the extent that the
"correction" language suggests that attributional discounting involves
conscious, willful efforts to make corrections, it may be misleading.

A Race Model Interpretation of "Correction" Effects.   Devine (1989)
and Gilbert (1989) have described a process whereby deliberate "corrections" are made when individuals become aware of the possible inappro-

priateness of their initial inclination to respond in a stereotyped, heuristic, or mood-influenced manner. However, such models may be overly dependent on conscious thought and intentional action. In this regard, Read, Vanman, and Miller (1997) have described how connectionist models might be applied to such problems. They propose that some processes that have been treated as conscious, serial, and deliberative can also be thought of as occurring in parallel and as requiring little conscious control.

Until recently, psychologists have implicitly assumed that information is processed serially rather than in parallel, and centrally rather than in a distributed fashion. In social psychology, even dual-process models sometimes imply that people decide whether to respond automatically or to correct for automatic processing. They often assume that automatic processing is motivated by a desire to save cognitive resources. Too often we social psychologists write as though information processing depends on planned, intentional, willful decisions, that alternative processes unfold serially, and that whether systematic or heuristic processing prevails is motivated.

In contrast, we suggest that once one engages a problem with the intention of solving it, learned processing strategies unfold more or less automatically, that multiple processes unfold in parallel, and that the eventual response is simply whichever one first satisfies the multiple accessible constraints imposed by the psychological situation. A central decision maker is not needed in such instances any more than a river decides to follow the path of least resistance. Similarly, heuristic processing is not motivated by a desire to save cognitive resources any more than water avoids going uphill because it wants to conserve resources. The "cognitive miser" metaphor may be no more apt for cognition than an analogous metaphor would be for rivers.

For example, Gilbert (1989) argues that people automatically make dispositional inferences (often termed the "fundamental attribution error") and that doing otherwise requires making a conscious correction. He argues that even if people know better, dispositional inferences will automatically be accessible, so that to incorporate situational factors requires a deliberate correction. Evidence that this requires conscious effort comes from studies that eliminate such "corrections" by introducing a cognitive load (e.g., remembering a nine-digit number). Thus the model assumes that people decide whether to allow themselves to rely on trait attributions (or on affect) or to correct those impulses.

Conscious processing does require attention and is presumably serial in nature. As a result, secondary tasks generally do occupy attention, which should place responses requiring sustained attention to new information at a disadvantage. For example, such tasks should disadvantage interpretations of one's feelings that require attention to the fact that one has just seen an emotional film. As a result, feelings might be experienced as liking for whatever decision alternative is focal at the time of judgment. To make a "correction," one does have to be engaged in the task (i.e., be motivated) and must attend to the true source of affect (i.e., have attentional resources), but with the confluence of these factors, the "correction" itself is automatic and hence does not require effort, intention, or resources. Consider how such a model might apply to attribution effects in studies of mood and processing.

We have examined attribution effects in several mood and processing studies (e.g., Dienes, 1996; Isbell et al., 2000). Often attribution manipulations not only eliminate mood effects but also produce "corrections" or reversals of mood effects. Moreover, such reversals are sometimes more extreme than the initial mood effects. This overshoot might be accounted for by assuming that all informational processing necessarily involves both top-down processing (using accessible knowledge) and bottom-up processing (collecting new data). Although both are necessary (Neisser, 1976), shifting between top-down and bottom-up processing may be subject to something like Miller, Galanter, and Pribram's (1960) TOTE mechanism, in which top-down processing requires an implicit "go" signal (e.g., experiencing a model-to-data match) and bottom-up processing is triggered by an implicit "stop" signal (e.g., a model-to-data mismatch). In a situation in which positive affective feelings would be experienced as a "go" signal, an attribution that interfered with the "go" signal of mood might be expected to inhibit reliance on naturally occuring "go" signals as well. Similarly, discounting attributions for sad affect should interfere with currently accessible "stop" signals. As a result, the individuals in the attribution condition should be in the unaccustomed position of having their top-down processing unconstrained by the discredited stop signal or their bottom-up processing unconstrained by the now-discredited "go" signal. As a result, happy participants would focus exclusively on collecting new data and sad participants on accessible prior information. The idea is that if positive mood, for example, privileges accessible information, then situational attributions for positive mood interfere with the use of accessible information. To successfully interfere with mood effects would require enough free attention to keep the competing attributional information in mind, but the "corrections" themselves should be automatic, requiring neither motivation nor intention.

3. The model assumes that feelings influence judgments directly but that they influence memory only through the specific concepts activated by the experience that induced the feelings. Why does affect "trump" activated concepts with judgment but not with recall? Similarly, given that an affect-inducing experience can activate concepts that in turn can influence

memory, does your model become difficult to distinguish from spreading-activation models? Specifically, doesn't your model allow for an affective experience to activate concepts that could then become the basis for a judgment? If so, then how can you justify the strong claim that affect influences judgments at the time of output?

There are two kinds of situations in which feelings trump concepts in judgment. The first is when the judgment is essentially about one's feelings, including many judgments of liking, preference, and choice. To the extent that a judgment item can be rephrased as, "How do you feel about X?" then we might expect feelings about X to trump concepts about X simply because they are more directly relevant. In the domain of love and romance, for example, we expect feelings to play a large role, although in most real-world situations we also expect feelings and concepts to coincide.

The second instance is when affect is used as a heuristic. A number of studies show that generalized mood is less likely to have an effect when individuals have detailed knowledge about a domain of judgment. This has been shown for political judgments by individuals knowledgeable about politics (Ottati & Isbell, 1996) and for decisions about car buying among individuals knowledgeable about cars (Srull, 1989). It seems likely that affective and factual considerations are generally active simultaneously and that the basis of the final decision depends on which one satisfies the minimal criteria for judgment first. That is, one might assume a race model (Logan, 1997) in which the first process to provide an answer wins. Having expertise involves having relevant and highly specific conceptual information that is readily accessible. When such information is salient and accessible, it should beat out generic feelings of mood as a basis for judgment. But when relevant knowledge is not accessible, general affective inclinations due to mood may be more accessible, so that they win the race and determine the judgment.

We assume that emotional feelings are experiential representations of the appraisals of situations. As such, they are the results of implicit computations of the goodness or badness of situations, results that are accessible as positive or negative experiences. The influence of affective feelings on overt evaluative judgments is not at all surprising. Indeed, it is difficult to imagine an organism in which explicit evaluations would not reflect felt implicit evaluative reactions.

Declarative memory, on the other hand, involves the symbolic representation of general semantic and specific episodic knowledge. The goodness or badness of general concepts and specific episodes is also represented in declarative memory, but such evaluations are presumably represented symbolically rather than experientially. Sad moods, for example, generally involve both sad feelings and sad thoughts, and as a result sad memories are likely to be activated as well. In that sense, moods do influence memory, and they presumably do so by virtue of the kinds of processes outlined in spreading-activation theories. But there is no way for feelings to trump concepts in memory because that is what declarative memory is—a system of interconnected concepts and symbolized episodes. We presume that feelings do not speak the same language as concepts. But once affect is conceptualized, then concepts about affect can and do influence memory. In this sense, affect can influence judgment at encoding as well as at retrieval. However, that role is no different from the role played by any other entity that is referred to by concepts in memory.

It should be clear that the affect-as-information hypothesis is not incompatible with a spreading-activation theory of memory or with an account of affective phenomena based on the influence of concepts about mood in memory. A reading of early papers by Bower (1981) and by Isen (Isen et al., 1978), for example, suggest that they did not make strong distinctions between affective feelings and affective concepts. As a result, our view may not conflict directly with earlier work on mood and memory. Instead, it is a refinement, attempting to differentiate effects that are due to affective concepts and affective experience.

ACKNOWLEDGMENTS

The writing of this chapter was supported by NSF Grant SBR 96-01298, NIMH Grant MH 50074, and John D. & Catherine T. MacArthur Foundation Grant 32005-0 to the Center for Advanced Study in the Behavioral Sciences. After the first two authors, authorship was determined alphabetically.

REFERENCES

Anderson, N. H. (1971). Integration theory and attitude change. *Psychological Review, 78*, 171–206.
Bandura, A. (1973). *Aggression*. New York: McGraw-Hill.
Bargh, J. A. (1997). The automaticity of everyday life. In R. S. Wyer, Jr. (Ed.), *The automaticity of everyday life* (pp. 1–62). Mahwah, NJ: Lawrence Erlbaum Associates.
Bartlett, F. C. (1932). *Remembering*. Cambridge, England: Cambridge University Press.
Blaney, P. H. (1986). Affect and memory: A review. *Psychological Bulletin, 99*, 229–246.
Bless, H., Bohner, G., Schwarz, N., & Strack, F. (1990). Mood and persuasion: A cognitive response analysis. *Personality and Social Psychology Bulletin, 16*, 331–345.
Bless, H., Clore, G. L., Golisano, V., Rabel, C., & Schwarz, N. (1996). Mood and the use of scripts: Do happy moods really make people mindless? *Journal of Personality and Social Psychology, 71*, 665–678.

Bodenhausen, G., Sheppard, L. A., & Kramer, G. P. (1994). Negative affect and social judgment: The differential impact of anger and sadness. *European Journal of Social Psychology, 24*, 45–62.

Bornstein, R. F. (1992). Inhibitory effects of awareness on affective responding: Implications for the affect-cognition relationship. In M. S. Clark (Ed.), *Review of personality and social psychology: Vol. 23. Emotion* (pp. 235–255). Newbury Park, CA: Sage.

Bower, G. H. (1981). Mood and memory. *American Psychologist, 36*, 129–148.

Bower, G. H., Gilligan, S. G., & Monteiro, K. P. (1981). Selectivity of learning caused by affective states. *Journal of Experimental Psychology: General, 110*, 451–473.

Bower, G. H., Monteiro, K. P., & Gilligan, S. G. (1978). Emotional mood as a context of learning and recall. *Journal of Verbal Learning and Verbal Behavior, 17*, 573–585.

Bronowski, J. (1956). *Science and human values.* New York: Messner.

Byrne, D., & Clore, G. L. (1966). Predicting interpersonal attraction toward strangers presented in three different stimulus modes. *Psychonomic Science, 4*, 239–240.

Byrne, D., & Clore, G. L. (1970). A reinforcement model of evaluative responses. *Personality: An International Journal, 1*, 103–128.

Chaiken, S. (1987). The heuristic model of persuasion. In M. P. Zanna, J. M. Olson, & C. P. Herman (Eds.), *Social influence: The Ontario symposium* (Vol. 5, pp. 3–39). Hillsdale, NJ: Lawrence Erlbaum Associates.

Christanson, S. (1992). Remembering emotional events: Potential mechanisms. In S. Christianson (Ed.), *The handbook of emotion and memory: Research and theory* (pp. 307–340). Hillsdale, NJ: Lawrence Erlbaum Associates.

Clore, G. L. (1966). *Discrimination learning as a function of awareness and magnitude of attitudinal reinforcement.* Unpublished doctoral dissertation. University of Texas.

Clore, G. L. (1977). Reinforcement and affect in attraction. In S. Duck (Ed.), *Theory and practice in interpersonal attraction* (pp. 23–49). London: Academic Press.

Clore, G. L. (1992). Cognitive phenomenology: Feelings and the construction of judgment. In L. L. Martin & A. Tesser (Eds.), *The construction of social judgments* (pp. 133–163). Hillsdale, NJ: Lawrence Erlbaum Associates.

Clore, G. L. (1994). Why emotions are felt. In P. Ekman & R. J. Davidson (Eds.), *The nature of emotion: Fundamental questions* (pp. 103–111). New York: Oxford University Press.

Clore, G. L., & Byrne, D. (1974). A reinforcement-affect model of attraction. In T. L. Huston (Ed.), *Foundations of interpersonal attraction* (pp. 143–170). New York: Academic Press.

Clore, G. L., & Gormly, J. B. (1974). Knowing, feeling, and liking: A psychophysiological study of attraction. *Journal of Research in Personality, 8*, 218–230.

Clore, G. L., & Itkin, S. M. (1982). Attraction and conversational style: A three-mode factor analytic study. In N. Hirschberg & L. Humphreys (Eds.), *Multivariate applications in psychology* (pp. 143–162). Hillsdale, NJ: Lawrence Erlbaum Associates.

Clore, G. L., & Ketelaar, T. (1997). Minding our emotions: On the role of automatic, unconscious affect. In R. S. Wyer (Ed.), *Advances in social cognition* (Vol. 10, pp. 105–120). Mahwah, NJ: Lawrence Erlbaum Associates.

Clore, G. L., & Ortony, A. (2000). Cognitive in emotion: Never, sometimes, or always? In L. Nadel & R. Lane (Eds.), *The cognitive neuroscience of emotion* (pp. 24–61). New York: Oxford University Press.

Clore, G. L., & Parrott, W. G. (1991). Moods and their vicissitudes: Thoughts and feelings as information. In J. Forgas (Ed.), *Emotion and social judgment* (pp. 107–123). Oxford, England: Pergamon Press.

Clore, G. L., Schwarz, N., & Conway, M. (1994). Affective causes and consequences of social information processing. In R. S. Wyer & T. Srull (Eds.), *Handbook of social cognition* (2nd ed., pp. 323–417). Mahwah, NJ: Lawrence Erlbaum Associates.

Clore, G. L., & Wilkin, N. (1985, May). *Does emotional bias occur during encoding or judgment?* Paper presented at the meeting of the Midwestern Psychological Association, Chicago.

Clore, G. L., Wong, G., Isbell, L., & Gasper, K. (1994, July). *Odor, experiential orientation, and affect.* Paper presented at the Meeting of the International Society for Research on Emotion, Cambridge, England.

Damasio, A. R. (1994). *Descartes' error: Emotion, reason and the human brain.* New York: Grosset/Putnam.

Devine, P. G. (1989). Stereotype and prejudice: Their automatic and controlled components. *Journal of Personality and Social Psychology, 56,* 5–18.

Dewey, J. (1916). *Democracy and education.* New York: Macmillan.

Dienes, B. P. A. (1996). *Mood as information: Affective cues for cognitive processing styles.* Unpublished doctoral dissertation, University of Illinois.

Donchin, E. (1981). Surprise! . . . surprise? *Psychophysiology, 18,* 493–513.

Einstein, G. O., & Hunt, R. R. (1980). Level of processing and organization: Additive effects of individual-item and relational processing. *Journal of Experimental Psychology: Human Learning & Memory, 6,* 588–598.

Ekman, P. (1984). Expression and the nature of emotion. In K. R. Scherer & P. Ekman (Eds.), *Approaches to emotion* (pp. 319–343). Hillsdale, NJ: Lawrence Erlbaum Associates.

Fishbein, M., & Ajzen, I. (1975). *Belief, attitude, intention, and behavior.* Reading, MA: Addison-Wesley.

Forgas, J. P., & Bower, G. H. (1988). Affect in social and personal judgments. In K. Fiedler & J. P. Forgas (Eds.), *Affect, cognition and social behavior* (pp. 183–208). Toronto, Ontario, Canada: Hogrefe.

Frank, R. H. (1988). *Passions within reason: The strategic role of the emotions.* New York: Norton.

Freud, S. (1959). Instincts and their vicissitudes. In E. Jones (Ed.), *Sigmund Freud: Collected papers* (Vol. 4). New York: Basic Books. (original work published 1915)

Frijda, N., Ortony, A., Sonnemans, J., & Clore, G. (1992). The complexity of intensity: issues concerning the structure of emotion intensity. In M. S. Clark (Ed.), *Review of personality and social psychology* (Vol. 11, pp. 60–89). Beverly Hills, CA: Sage.

Garvin, E. (1999). *Mood and memory? Forget about it.* Unpublished Master's thesis, University of Illinois.

Gasper, K. (1999). *How thought and emotional awareness influence the role of affect in processing: When attempts to be reasonable fail.* Doctoral dissertation, University of Illinois at Urbana-Champaign.

Gasper, K., & Clore, G. L. (2000). Do you have to pay attention to your feelings to be influenced by them? *Personality and Social Psychology Bulletin, 26,* 698–711.

Gasper, K., & Clore, G. L. (1998b). The persistent use of negative affect by anxious individuals to estimate risk. *Journal of Personality and Social Psychology, 74,* 1350–1363.

Gilbert, D. T. (1989). Thinking lightly about others: Automatic components of the social inference process. In J. Uleman & J. A. Bargh (Eds.), *Unintended thought* (pp. 189–211). New York: Guilford.

Gohm, C., & Clore, G. L. (2000). Individual differences in emotional experience: A review of scales. *Personality and Social Psychology Bulletin, 26,* 679–697.

Gouaux, C. (1971). Induced affective states and interpersonal attraction. *Journal of Personality and Social Psychology, 20,* 37–43.

Gray, J. A. (1971). *The psychology of fear and stress.* London: Weidenfeld & Nicholson.

Greenwald, A. G., Draine, S. C., & Abrams, R. L. (1996). Three cognitive markers of unconscious semantic activation. *Science, 273,* 1699–1702.

Griffitt, W., & Veitch, R. (1971). Hot and crowded: Influences of population density and temperature on interpersonal behavior. *Journal of Personality and Social Psychology, 17,* 92–98.

Hebb, D. O. (1949). *The organization of behavior.* New York: Wiley.

Heider, F. (1958). *The psychology of interpersonal relations.* New York: Wiley.

Higgins, E. T., Rholes, W. S., & Jones, C. R. (1977). Category accessibility and impression formation. *Journal of Experimental Social Psychology, 13,* 141–154.

60 CLORE ET AL.

Isbell, L., Clore, G. L., & Wyer, R. S. (2000). *Mood, stereotype use and memory for stereotype-inconsistent information.* Unpublished manuscript, University of Illinois.

Isen, A. M. (1987). Positive affect, cognitive processes, and social behavior. In L. Berkowitz (Ed.), *Advances in experimental social psychology* (Vol. 20, pp. 203–253). New York: Academic Press.

Isen, A. M., Rosenzweig, A. S., & Young, M. J. (1991). The influence of positive affect on clinical problem solving. *Medical Decision Making, 11,* 221–227.

Isen, A. M., Shalker, T. E., Clark, M., & Karp, L. (1978). Affect, accessibility of material in memory, and behavior: A cognitive loop? *Journal of Personality and Social Psychology, 36,* 1–11.

Jamison, K. R. (1993). *Touched with fire: Manic-depressive illness and the artistic temperament.* New York: Free Press.

Kelly, G. A. (1955). *The psychology of personal constructs.* New York: Norton.

Keltner, D., Locke, K. D., & Audrain, P. C. (1993). The influence of attribution on the relevance of negative feelings to personal satisfaction. *Personality and Social Psychology Bulletin, 19,* 21–29.

Ketelaar, T., & Clore, G. L. (1997). Emotions and reason: Proximate effects and ultimate functions. In G. Matthews (Ed.), *Personality, emotion, and cognitive science* (pp. 355–396). Amsterdam: Elsevier Science.

Ketelaar, T., & Clore, G. L. (unpublished). *Action identification and mood.* University of Illinois at Urbana-Champaign.

Lazarus, R. S. (1994). Universal antecedents of the emotions. In P. Ekman & R. J. Davidson (Eds.), *The nature of emotion: Fundamental questions* (pp. 163–171). New York: Oxford University Press.

LeDoux, J. E. (1996). *The emotional brain.* New York: Simon and Schuster.

Lewicki, P. (1985). Nonconscious biasing effects of single instances of subsequent judgments. *Journal of Personality and Social Psychology, 48,* 563–574.

Logan, G. D. (1997). The automaticity of academic life: Unconscious applications of an implicit theory. In R. S. Wyer (Ed.), *Advances in social cognition: Vol. 10. Automaticity in everyday life* (pp. 157–179). Mahwah, NJ: Lawrence Erlbaum Associates.

Lott, B. E., & Lott, A. J. (1960). The formation of positive attitudes toward group members. *Journal of Abnormal and Social Psychology, 61,* 297–300.

Lowenstein, G. (1996). Out of control: Visceral influences on behavior. *Organizational Behavior and Human Decision Processes, 65,* 272–292.

Martin, L. L., Seta, J. J., & Crelia, R. A. (1990). Assimilation and contrast as a function of people's willingness and ability to expend effort in forming an impression. *Journal of Personality and Social Psychology, 59,* 27–37.

Martin, L. L., Ward, D. W., Achee, J. W., & Wyer, R. S. (1993). Mood as input: People have to interpret the motivational implications of their moods. *Journal of Personality and Social Psychology, 64,* 317–326.

Massad, C. N., Hubbard, M., & Newtson, D. (1979). Perceptual selectivity: Contributing process and possible cure for impression perseverance. *Journal of Experimental Social Psychology, 15,* 513–532.

McDougall, W. (1923). *Outline of psychology.* New York: Charles Scribner & Sons.

Miller, G. A., Galanter, E., & Pribram, K. H. (1960). *Plans and the structure of behavior.* New York: Holt, Rinehart, & Winston.

Neisser, U. (1976). *Cognition and reality.* San Francisco: Freeman.

Niedenthal, P. M., & Setterlund, M. (1994). Emotion congruence in perception. *Personality and Social Psychology Bulletin, 20,* 401–411.

Nunnally, J. C., Duchnowski, A. C., & Parker, R. K. (1965). Association of neutral objects with rewards: Effect on verbal evaluation, reward expectancy, and selective attention. *Journal of Personality and Social Psychology, 1,* 270–274.

Ottati, V. C., & Isbell, L. M. (1996). Effects of mood during exposure to target information on subsequently reported judgments: An on-line model of assimilation and contrast. *Journal of Personality and Social Psychology, 71,* 39–53.

Ortony, A., Clore, G. L., & Collins, A. (1988). *The cognitive structure of emotions.* New York: Cambridge University Press.

Palmer, S. E. (1975). Visual perception and world knowledge: Notes on a model of sensory-cognitive interaction. In D. A. Norman, D. E. Rumelhart, and the LNR research Group (Eds.), *Explorations in cognition* (pp. 279–307). San Francisco: Freeman.

Parrott, W. G., & Sabini, J. (1990). Mood and memory under natural conditions: Evidence for mood incongruent recall. *Journal of Personality and Social Psychology, 59,* 321–336.

Piaget, J. (1954). *The construction of reality in the child.* New York: Free Press.

Read, S. J., Vanman, E. J., & Miller, L. C. (1997). Connectionism, parallel constraint satisfaction processes, and gestalt principles: (Re)Introducing cognitive dynamics to social psychology. *Personality and Social Psychology Review, 1,* 26–53.

Riskind, J. H. (1989). Will the field ultimately need a more detailed analysis of mood-memory? Comments on Ellis and Ashbrook. *Journal of Social Behavior & Personality, 4,* 39–43.

Rosenberg, M., & Abelson, R. (1960). An analysis of cognitive balancing. In C. Hovland & M. Rosenberg (Eds.), *Attitude organization and change* (pp. 112–163). New Haven, CT: Yale University Press.

Russell, J. A. (1980). A circumplex model of affect. *Journal of Personality and Social Psychology, 39,* 1161–1178.

Salovey, P., & Mayer, J. D. (1990). Emotional intelligence. *Imagination, Cognition, and Personality, 9,* 185–211.

Salovey, P., Mayer, J. D., Goldman, S. L., Turvey, C., & Palfai, T. P. (1995). Emotional attention, clarity, and repair: Exploring emotional intelligence using the Trait Meta-Mood Scale. In J. Pennebaker (Ed.), *Emotion, disclosure, & health* (pp. 125–154). Washington, DC: American Psychological Association.

Schwarz, N. (1990). Happy but mindless? Mood effects on problem-solving and persuasion. In R. M. Sorrentino & E. T. Higgins (Eds.), *Handbook of motivation and cognition* (Vol. 2, pp. 527–561). New York: Guilford Press.

Schwarz, N., & Clore, G. L. (1983). Mood, misattribution, and judgments of well-being: Informative and directive functions of affective states. *Journal of Personality and Social Psychology, 45,* 513–523.

Schwarz, N., & Clore, G. L. (1988). How do I feel about it? Informative functions of affective states. In K. Fiedler & J. Forgas (Eds.), *Affect, cognition, and social behavior* (pp. 44–62). Toronto, Ontario, Canada: Hogrefe International.

Schwarz, N., & Clore, G. L. (1996). Feelings and phenomenal experiences. In E. T. Higgins & A. Kruglanski (Eds.), *Social psychology: A handbook of basic principles* (pp. 433–465). New York: Guilford.

Schwarz, N., Robbins, M., & Clore, G. L. (1985, May). *Explaining the effects of mood on social judgment.* Paper presented at Midwestern Psychological Association, Chicago.

Sinclair, R. C., Mark, M. M., & Clore, G. L. (1994). Mood-related persuasion depends on (mis)attributions. *Social Cognition, 12,* 309–326.

Sloman, S. A. (1996). The empirical case for two systems of reasoning. *Psychological Bulletin, 199,* 3–22.

Solomon, A. (1998, January 12). Anatomy of melancholy. *The New Yorker, 73*(42), 46–61.

Srull, T. K. (1989). Advertising and product evaluation: The relation between consumer memory and judgment. In C. Patricia & A. M. Tybout (Eds.), *Cognitive and affective responses to advertising* (pp. 121–134). Lexington, MA: Heath/Lexington Books.

Srull, T. K., & Wyer, R. S., Jr. (1979). The role of category accessibility in the interpretation of information about persons: Some determinants and implications. *Journal of Personality and Social Psychology, 37,* 1660–1672.

Staats, A. W., & Staats, C. K. (1958). Attitudes established by classical conditioning. *Journal of Abnormal and Social Psychology, 57,* 37–40.

Weber, E., & Clore, G. L. (1987). *Anxiety and risk-taking.* Unpublished data, University of Illinois at Urbana-Champaign.

Wegener, D. T., Petty, R. E., & Smith, S. M. (1995). Positive mood can increase or decrease message scrutiny: The hedonic contingency view of mood and message processing. *Journal of Personality and Social Psychology, 69,* 5–15.

Wegner, D. M., & Vallacher, R. R. (1986). Action identification. In R. M. Sorrentino & E. T. Higgins (Eds.), *Handbook of motivation and cognition: Foundations of social behavior* (pp. 550–582). New York: Guilford.

Winkielman, P., Zajonc, R. B., & Schwarz, N. (1997). Subliminal affective priming resists attributional interventions. *Cognition and Emotion, 11,* 433–465.

Wyer, R. S. (1974). *Cognitive organization and change: An information processing approach.* Potomac, MD: Lawrence Erlbaum Associates.

Wyer, R. S., Jr., & Carlston, D. E. (1979). *Social cognition, inference, and attribution.* Hillsdale, NJ: Lawrence Erlbaum Associates.

Wyer, R. S., Clore, G. L., & Isbell, L. (1999). Affect and information processing. In M. P. Zanna (Ed.), *Advances in experimental social psychology* (Vol. 31, pp. 3–78). Mahwah, NJ: Lawrence Erlbaum Associates.

Wyer, R. S., & Srull, T. K. (1989). *Memory and cognition in its social context.* Hillsdale, NJ: Lawrence Erlbaum Associates.

Chapter 3

Mood and Processing: A View From a Self-Regulation Perspective

Ralph Erber
DePaul University

Maureen Wang Erber
Northeastern Illinois University

The idea that our transient moods can have a profound impact on our judgments, our behavior, and a variety of cognitive processes is neither new nor very controversial. It seems that when Alice Isen surprised mall shoppers with an unexpected dime in the return slot of a public phone and found that they were subsequently more willing to assist a hapless passerby who had dropped a stack of papers (Isen & Levin, 1972), social cognition researchers were on the verge of discovering the missing link between "hot" affect and "cold" cognition. What has been controversial, however, are the precise reasons why these and other effects of mood come about in the first place. Over the years, a number of models have been advanced to account for the many effects moods have been shown to have. Some of them, especially early ones, have emphasized the importance of mood priming mood-congruent thoughts (e.g., Bower, 1981; Bower, Gilligan, & Monteiro, 1981; Clark & Isen, 1982). According to this view, good (i.e., happy) moods make positive thoughts about helping more accessible, resulting in increased willingness to help. Unfortunately, it soon became evident that negative (i.e., sad) moods carried a similar proclivity to respond with help to an emergency, at least under some conditions (Carlson & Miller, 1987). Research concerned with the effects of moods on social judgments and recall soon ran into rough waters as well. Although many experimental investigations confirmed speculations consistent with the idea that happy moods increased the accessibility of congruent thoughts, the idea that sad moods would yield mirror-image results frequently remained unsupported (cf. Blaney, 1986; Isen, 1984, for reviews).

Over the years, researchers interested in the study of moods have responded to these types of difficulties in several ways. Some have deemphasized the idea that moods prime mood-related thoughts and instead focused on the informational and motivational aspects of mood (Bless, Bohner, Schwarz, & Strack, 1990; Schwarz & Clore, 1983, 1988). Others have suggested that mood effects are less the result of automatic priming than of the context (Martin, chapter 6, this volume; see also Martin, Abend, Sedikides, & Greene, 1997; Martin & Stoner, 1996; Martin, Ward, Achee, & Wyer, 1993). Yet others (e.g., Forgas, 1995; Mayer, Gaschke, & Braverman, 1992) have more or less explicitly stuck with the idea that mood effects can ultimately be considered priming effects. And although all these approaches have furthered our understanding of how moods affect processing, in this chapter we contend that a full understanding of this relationship can only be achieved when we take into account how people manage or regulate their moods.

MOOD REGULATION

The Mood Repair Hypothesis

To be sure, the idea that people do not automatically and invariably succumb to their moods but instead manage, control, or regulate them has been proposed before, albeit not in a terribly sophisticated way. Faced with mounting experimental evidence showing that happy but not sad moods usually lead to mood-congruent judgments, recall, and behavior, Isen (1984; Clark & Isen, 1982) introduced the notion of "mood repair." In essence it is an elaboration on what had been known as the "goody-goody" hypothesis (Bower et al., 1981). In a nutshell, it predicts that all else being equal, people would prefer pleasure over pain, ergo good moods over bad ones. As a result, different kinds of moods lead to vastly different motivational and processing tendencies. Good moods are entertained, and bad moods are banished. Thus, when we ask our participants to watch a cheerful video, listen to upbeat music, or recall the happiest moment in their lives with great detail and vividness, they will be more than willing to comply, experiencing the happy mood that usually follows such experimental manipulations. On the other hand, when we ask them to watch a depressing video, listen to plaintive music, or recall the saddest moment in their lives, they will fend off the resulting mood by any means necessary (Isen, 1984; Taylor, 1991). Of course if such efforts at mood repair among our participants are successful, there is no reason to expect that the mood we tried so hard to induce would indeed be reflected on some relevant dependent measure.

The mood-repair hypothesis is enjoying immense popularity to this very day, perhaps in part because it has been a convenient way to account for the many asymmetrical findings for positive and negative moods. Moreover, it has been incorporated into many theoretical models of how mood affects processing in general. Figure 3.1 is an attempt to depict the modal features of this type of model. It is not a model for which a single researcher in the area of mood and processing would claim ownership but rather one that reflects the most commonly held assumptions of these approaches.

According to this type of model, positive and negative moods have somewhat different implications for both processing and motivation. Looking at positive mood first, an event that makes us happy (e.g., being greeted by a sunny day when we open the curtains in the morning) is hypothesized to increase the accessibility of happy and perhaps more generally positive thoughts (initial mood priming). Some (Clark & Isen, 1982) have characterized this state as one in which we see the world through rose-colored glasses. These positive thoughts subsequently bias our judgments in a mood-congruent fashion, and they further allow us to rely on

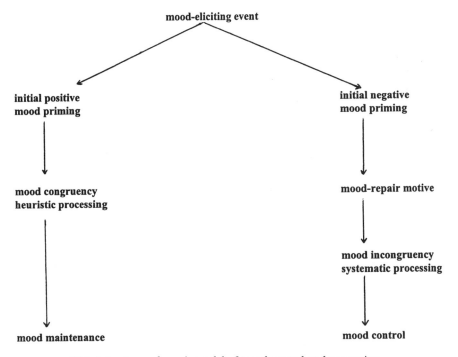

FIG. 3.1. A mood-repair model of mood control and processing.

heuristic processing (e.g., Bless, chapter 1, this volume). This, in turn, leads to positive moods being maintained even in the absence of any explicit motive to do so. An event that makes us sad (e.g., being greeted by a rainy and dreary day in the morning) may similarly prompt an initial increase in sad or generally negative thoughts. But this is where the similarity ends. A strong version of the mood-repair hypothesis (the one depicted in Fig. 3.1) suggests that people would immediately engage in counteracting processes on realizing the aversive nature of their affective state (Isen, 1984; Taylor, 1991). A weaker version (Forgas, 1995) would suggest that the initial mood priming might persist until some threshold of aversiveness is reached (e.g., when we additionally learn that the bad weather has led to unbearable traffic tie-ups). Thus, although mood-congruent thinking and perhaps heuristic processing may be observed at low levels of negative mood, once a threshold is reached, a motivation to repair one's mood would compel one to engage in systematic processing in the ultimate service of mood control. These differences aside, both the strong and the weak version predict processing shifts once a mood-repair motive has been aroused.

Debunking Mood Repair

We believe that there are several problems with this type of model. First, as Martin (chapter 6, this volume) points out, what effects moods have depends on the context in which they are encountered or experienced. Whether or not a sunny day will, in fact, bring on a happy mood depends on a number of things. If we can take advantage of it by reserving a tee time or by catching up on much-needed yard work, it may indeed make us happy (assuming that yard work is a positively valenced activity). On the other hand, if it happens on a day that is filled with meetings and appointments, it may not make us feel better and may even make us feel worse when we realize that we cannot take advantage of it. By the same token, a rainy day may primarily make us feel bad when it prevents us from playing golf or doing yard work, but it may not affect us much when it provides the context for a busy day at the office, and it may even make us feel good when our goal is to curl up in front of the fireplace. Thus, if mood-congruent thinking and heuristic processing depend on some initial mood priming, whether or not these processes are set in motion ultimately depends on the context as well.

The very simple assumption that people prefer to avoid sad moods and instead prefer happy moods, which lies at the heart of the mood-repair hypotheses, is problematic as well. For one thing, it implies that pleasure and pain are indeed our "sovereign masters," as Bentham (1789, p. 1) suggested. Proponents of the view that human motivation can be captured entirely in terms of seeking pleasure and avoiding pain have been on the retreat at least since McDougall (1923) pointed out that pleasure and pain, rather than being motivational forces, may be mere signposts for other things (e.g., that tasks have been accomplished or remain undone). However, given the present state of theorizing, it appears that "goody-goody" theories have found a refuge in the study of how we regulate our moods (Erber, 1996). But if we, like Allport (1954, p. 7), "appeal to common observation," we can readily generate countless examples of behavior that seems to violate hedonistic principles. People often choose to read stories with tragic rather than sugarcoated happy endings. They listen to plaintive music instead of silly love songs, and they often spend a great deal of money to watch really sad movies. A case in point is the success of the movie *Titanic*, which as of this writing had just become the highest grossing motion picture of all time. But unlike *Star Wars*, the previous record holder, *Titanic* does not afford us the pleasure of watching the forces of good conquer the forces of evil. Instead, as everybody knows beforehand, the ship sinks, and the lovers are sadly torn apart when Jack drowns in the icy waters of the North Atlantic. From a hedonistic point of view, it is interesting that people would go to see this movie in the first place. And it seems that even the most hardened hedonist would have a difficult time explaining why many people would see this movie repeatedly (as seems to be the case), knowing full well that Lloyd Bridges never comes to a daring, last-minute rescue.

If we agree that pleasure seeking and pain avoidance may insufficiently characterize how we regulate our emotional life, the power of the motive to repair negative moods that are encountered because of misfortune or random assignment is similarly called into question. This is not to say that mood repair never occurs. In fact, there is evidence that people find ways to combat the affective consequences of highly threatening life events such as the loss of a job or a loved one or experiencing strong rejection (Gilbert, Pinel, Wilson, Blumberg, & Wheatley, 1998). But when it comes to the kinds of negative mood manipulations employed in a typical mood experiment (e.g., watching a video or reading a story about someone else's misfortune; recalling a sad event from years past), it is at least doubtful whether participants would be equally compelled to rid themselves of the corresponding affect. In fact, most studies that refer to mood repair as the mechanism responsible for the lack of findings for negative moods provide no evidence that it occurred, instead inferring it from the lack of findings. This alone could give rise to the suspicion that mood repair is perhaps more a myth than a reality. To turn this suspicion into conviction, consider the experimental strategy of a series of studies on the effects of mood on creative problem solving that is frequently cited as showing evidence for mood repair (Isen & Daubman, 1984). The first study induces

68   ERBER AND ERBER

happy, neutral, and sad moods via video manipulations and then measures the unusualness of word associations. A significant effect on this measure is reported when those in happy moods are compared with those in neutral moods. The corresponding effect for those in sad moods, a manipulation that involved a much smaller number of participants, is marginally significant. But rather than acknowledging that the failure to reach a conventionally accepted level of significance might be due to the relatively lower number of participants in the sad-mood condition, the researchers instead concluded that mood repair was responsible for the lack of effect. Furthermore, sad mood is subsequently dropped from additional studies, thus providing overwhelming evidence for the effects of happy moods with really no evidence for the effects of sad moods.

But even if one granted that a mood-repair motive might operate on some level, even in response to relatively benign inductions of sadness, the conditions under which it would occur and the means by which participants would achieve a successful attenuation of their sad moods are far from clear. In a series of studies, we (Erber & Erber, 1994; Erber & Tesser, 1992) found that only tasks that are mentally taxing bring about an attenuation of previously induced mood, primarily because they prevent mood-congruent thinking. Specifically, these and other studies showed that completing a series of difficult math problems (Erber & Tesser, 1992) or difficult anagrams (Erber et al., 1999), and even exercise (Erber & Therriault, 1994) brought about an attenuation of both happy and sad moods. Doing simple math problems, solving simple anagrams, watching an exercise movie, or simply sitting around for a comparable amount of time had no attenuating effect on either type of mood.

Thus it appears that whether or not mood repair, and to some extent mood maintenance, occur (in the psychological laboratory as well as real life) and influence processing accordingly depends on a combination of motivation and ability. In light of the problems that the mood-repair hypothesis has in accounting for the entire range of mood regulation, we (Erber, 1996; Erber, Wegner, & Therriault, 1996) have proposed a model delineating the conditions that would lead to two types of mood regulation: mood maintenance and mood control. Because we have elaborated on this model elsewhere, we will briefly summarize its major assumptions and propositions before outlining its implications for processing.

The Social-Constraints Model of Mood Regulation and Processing

The social-constraints model of mood regulation starts with an assumption that is very similar to the one espoused by Martin (chapter 6, this volume), namely that the effects of moods are context-dependent. However, we carry this a step further by suggesting that the experience of moods as a result of a mood-eliciting event may itself may be context-dependent. Context variables of any sort can often act as powerful constraints on our emotional experience and expression. In some cases they compel us to rid ourselves of inappropriate affect. We sometimes work hard not to appear as though we are happy when we have to deliver bad news to someone (Tesser & Rosen, 1975). And we often work just as hard not to look depressed as we join a birthday party, even though we may have been at the receiving end of bad news. In other cases, situational constraints may suggest that we at least try to get into a certain type of mood (e.g., to be happy at someone's wedding or to be sad at someone's funeral), even though our present emotional state may not resemble the desired state. On the other hand, situations characterized by relative solitude may create a context to indulge in whatever mood we might be in at the time.

These considerations, then, suggest a very different model of how mood might affect processing. It is depicted in Fig. 3.2. This model proposes that whether a mood-eliciting event leads to the experience of a corresponding mood does not primarily depend on the valence implications

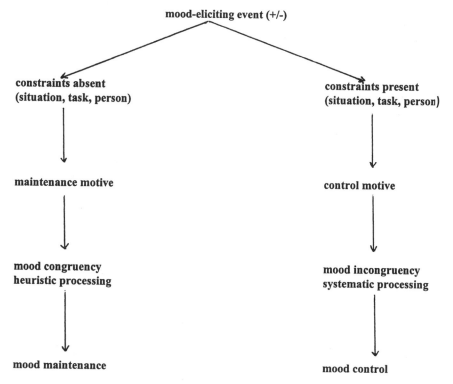

FIG. 3.2. The social-constraints model of mood control and processing.

of the event. Instead, both positive and negative events will likely result in positive and sad moods in the absence of any situational constraints. Under such circumstances people may maintain even a negative mood for a number of reasons. It may be because the absence of a control motive leads to a passive priming of mood-congruent material. It may be because appropriate ways to get rid of the mood may not be readily available (Erber & Tesser, 1992) or because the negative mood provides an opportunity to focus attention inward toward the self (Salovey, 1992; Wood, Saltzberg, & Goldsamt, 1990). As a consequence, processing may proceed in a mood-congruent and heuristic fashion, which ultimately results in mood maintenance.

A very different picture emerges, however, when a mood-eliciting event is encountered in the presence of situational constraints. In such cases, people may be compelled to control the implications of the event by accessing mood-incongruent information or by engaging in cognitively taxing tasks in the ultimate service of mood control. Just why this would be the case becomes clearer when one takes a closer look at the kinds of constraints that may be present in a given situation. First off, it is probably a basic fact of life that we frequently find ourselves in the presence of others (e.g., at work with colleagues, at home with family, at a ball game with strangers of varying levels of intoxication). Because the real, imagined, and implied presence of others has a profound impact on our thoughts, feelings, and behavior (Allport, 1954), it stands to reason that the presence of others on any level should influence our moods and our motivation to indulge in them as well.

Evidence for the model comes from a series of studies in which we (Erber et al., 1996) led happy or sad participants to believe that they would be doing an unspecified task either with a stranger (i.e., another participant ostensibly doing the same experiment in the next room) or by themselves. As expected, when participants were asked to indicate their preference for cheerful or depressing newspaper stories, those who expected to complete the upcoming task by themselves preferred mood-congruent stories. In other words, happy participants preferred cheerful stories, whereas those who were sad preferred depressing stories. However, this preference for mood-congruent information shifted to a preference toward mood-incongruent information among those who expected to complete the task with a stranger. Happy individuals preferred depressing stories, whereas sad ones preferred cheerful stories, ostensibly in order to regulate their moods for the anticipated interaction. Preliminary evidence indicates that this preference for mood-incongruent material may in part be caused by concerns regarding the appropriateness of a happy or sad mood in social interactions. It appears to be most pronounced when it comes to real or imagined interactions with critical others, but when the target of the anticipated interaction is a close other, mood congruency prevails (Commons & Erber, 1997).

Whether or not a mood-eliciting event results in the experience of a corresponding affective state may similarly be constrained by task-related variables to the extent that moods may have detrimental effects. Specifically, it appears that tasks that are perceived to be cognitively taxing (Erber & Erber, 1994) or that require accuracy (Therriault, Erber, & Oktela, 1996) prompt attempts toward mood control. Finally, a number of individual differences may help to determine the extent to which mood control motives may come into play. People with chronic proclivities to regulate negative moods are likely to respond to sadness with attempts toward control even in the absence of situational or task variables (Catanzaro & Mearns, 1990; Smith & Petty, 1995). Deliberative mind-sets should promote a general tendency toward mood congruency and mood maintenance, whereas implemental mind-sets may trigger a desire to rid oneself of one's mood (Gollwitzer, Heckhausen, & Steller, 1990). Similarly, ruminative self-focus may compel people to indulge in their moods, whereas reflective self-focus may lead to self-regulation efforts (Campbell et al., 1996).

In light of these considerations, it is important to note that the model we are proposing here is not an override model of mood regulation. Unlike mood-repair theories that suggest that moods are repaired once they have been encountered, the present model proposes that individuals would evaluate the implications of a mood-eliciting event in light of situational or task-related constraints, as well as of constraints imposed by a disposition. The general principle suggested by these constraints is that people strive to attain moods that promote goal attainment. Neutral moods may be particularly appropriate when we expect to meet a stranger or have to think clearly, and thus we work to attenuate the impact of a mood-eliciting event in light of these constraints. By the same token, we may try to enhance the impact of a positive event when we expect to go to a party and enhance the impact of a negative event when we are about to go to a funeral.

ADDRESSING THE FOUR MAJOR ISSUES

The social-constraints model is first and foremost a framework within which one can examine people's propensity to regulate their moods. That is, its primary focus is on the kinds of conditions that may bring about spontaneous attempts at attenuating or enhancing the consequences of a mood-eliciting event. However, it has some straightforward implications for the four major issues involved in mood and processing: (a) mood-congruent and -incongruent recall, (b) mood-congruent and -incongruent judgment, (c) the fostering of more heuristic processing and creativity by positive moods, and (d) the promoting of more systematic processing by negative moods.

Mood Congruent Recall

Mood-repair models essentially predict that people in both positive and negative moods will always recall positive material from memory, albeit for different reasons. In the case of positive mood, it is automatic priming that leads to the superior recall of positive material, whereas in the case of negative moods, it is caused by a motive to repair one's mood. Our model, on the other hand, suggests that whether recall proceeds in a positive or negative direction depends both on the mood and the nature of the particular constraints of the situation. Mood-congruent recall should be observed when the absence of constraints allows an engaging personal reverie (either as a result of passive priming or an explicit motive), regardless of whether the mood is positive or negative to begin with. On the other hand, mood-incongruent recall should be obtained when the nature of the situation, the task, a personal disposition, or a combination of these imply a motive to either quelch or enhance one's mood.

This general prediction is well supported by several studies showing evidence of spontaneous mood-incongruent recall. Parrott and Sabini (1990) asked students in a large psychology class who had just received their grades on an exam to recall three events from their high school days. Those who had done worse than expected on the exam tended to recall more positive events when their first memory was examined than those who had done better than expected. And although this finding can just as easily be taken as an indication of mood repair, the results of additional studies show that this kind of mood-congruent recall cuts both ways. Students who were given the same recall task as they were entering the library on a sunny day (which supposedly made them happy) tended to recall less pleasant memories than those queried on a cloudy day. Our model suggests that the public nature of these contexts or the fact that these students were getting ready to do some thinking may have triggered a motive to either attenuate the moods brought on by the exam feedback or the nice whether or even to prevent their onset altogether. Note that Parrott and Sabini (1990) replicated these findings under more controlled laboratory conditions. For example, one study asked participants simply to listen to cheerful or depressing music and then gave them the same recall task. Again, a look at the first memory recalled showed evidence of mood-incongruent recall, with supposedly happy participants recalling more unpleasant memories than sad participants. Given the nature of the instructions, it may well have been that participants expected some future interaction with the experimenter. Perhaps realizing that listening to music could not be the whole story, they may have expected to receive further instructions about the "real" experiment yet to come. Alternatively, they may have wondered whether there would be a zillion-item questionnaire, requiring cognitive resources and accuracy, to fill out at the conclusion of the study.

Evidence that expectations about upcoming tasks even in the absence of anticipation of interaction may prompt attempts at mood regulation via mood-incongruent recall was obtained in a study in which participants in happy and sad moods were asked to recall an event from high school either at the beginning or the end of a class period (Erber & Erber, 1994, Study 2). Reasoning that there were more constraints present at the beginning of the class period (i.e., resources need to be allocated to comprehend the lecture) than at the end, we predicted that participants should be more motivated to regulate both their happy and sad moods at the beginning of class. Consistent with this speculation, we found that participants recalled mood-incongruent memories when the experiment was conducted at the beginning of the class period, whereas they recalled mood-congruent memories when it was done at the end of class.

Finally, the idea that individual dispositions may similarly influence the extent to which people are motivated to regulate their moods was borne out in a series of studies that compared recall following a negative mood induction between participants high and low in self-esteem (Smith & Petty, 1995). By and large, low-self-esteem participants recalled mood-congruent memories, whereas high-self-esteem participants recalled mood-incongruent memories. It appears that high self-esteem and its resulting tendency to protect it against threats acted as an important constraint preventing participants from indulging in their negative moods.

Mood-Congruent and Mood-Incongruent Judgments

Much of what we said about the relationship between mood and recall also holds for the relationship between mood and judgment. Judgments should be mood congruent in the absence of any constraints. Under such circumstances there is really nothing that should prevent happy people from believing that others are basically good (Forgas & Bower, 1987; Forgas, Bower, & Krantz, 1984), that our relationships with close others are free of conflict (Forgas, Levinger, & Moylan, 1994), or that our coffeemakers will never fail to deliver that much-needed caffeine (Isen, Shalker, Clark, & Karp, 1978). Analogously, sad people should be more prone to find flaws in others, to dwell on the downside of their relationships, or to take into account the repair history of a household appliance.

On the other hand, when social constraints suggest that mood control may be in order, the effects of moods on judgments may well be reversed. Happy people who feel as though they are sitting on top of the world may remind themselves that it turns over once every day, and sad people likewise may do the same with opposite results.

Having said this, it is important to point out an important difference in the respective relationships between mood and recall and mood and judgment. As Eich and Metcalfe (1989) have pointed out, recall is primarily driven by internal input (e.g., life during our last year in graduate school). Judgments, on the other hand, are primarily driven by external input (e.g., the features and performance of our coffeemakers). And whereas our recollections of graduate school are likely a mix of dread (too many late nights spent analyzing data) and exuberance (too many late nights out drinking with fellow students), our coffeemakers generally do not provide us with such a mixed bag of ups and downs (they just make coffee predictably and reliably). Thus it is not surprising that Strack, Martin, and Stepper (1988) found that happy and sad moods affected how amused participants were by a cartoon (presumably an internally based judgment) but not how funny they thought the cartoon was compared with some objective standard (presumably an externally based judgment).

From this perspective, the nature of the judgment task can act as an important constraint, not so much on our ability to experience a happy or sad mood as on our ability to let our mood influence our judgment. Clearly, when someone's mood has no implication for a judgment domain (e.g., one's sadness and the stellar performance of one's coffeemaker), there is little reason to expect it to be influenced by mood. On the other hand, judgments that carry at least some ambiguity in terms of their evaluative implications are likely to be affected by one's mood (Erber, 1991).

Positive Moods Foster Heuristic Processing and Creativity

The notion that moods might enhance creativity is intriguing not only because of the allure of understanding an elusive topic but also because of the many tantalizing intuitive, logical, and theoretical contradictions found in its exposition. One does not need to be a scientist to postulate a connection between mood and creativity. Many have remarked on the ostensible links among poverty, depression, sadness, and creativity in art and music. Indeed, clinical research on depression finds a great deal of correlational evidence demonstrating the greater artistic and creative genius of sad and depressed individuals (Ludwig, 1994; Schildkraut & Otero, 1996). At the same time, most of the social psychological research to date has found that it is positive and not negative mood that leads to increased creativity (cf. Hirt, Melton, McDonald, & Harackiewicz, 1996; Isen & Daubman, 1984; Sinclair & Mark, 1992).

Attempts directed at explaining this link between positive mood and creativity have included the following suggestions: positive mood leads to increased cognitive flexibility (Murray, Sujan, Hirt, & Sujan, 1990), more inclusive categorization in organization tasks (Isen & Daubman, 1984), increased efficiency (Isen, 1993), use of truncated processing strategies (Forgas, Burnham, & Trimboli, 1988), and, similarly, increases in heuristic processing (Isen, 1984). Whereas some of these sound like good candidates for the role of mediators (e.g., cognitive flexibility), others appear to be less so. Heuristic processing can, of course, lead to increased efficiency and the use of truncated processing strategies. However, given the nature of heuristics as rule-of-thumb type mental shortcuts, it is much less clear how the use of heuristic processing can lead to greater flexibility, more thorough categorization, or increased creativity in general. In other words, if Monet had used a purely heuristic approach, his paintings of haystacks in the South of France would likely not show evidence of creative use of color and brushstrokes.

The suggestion that increased cognitive flexibility and broader categorization resulting from positive moods can enhance problem solving and aid in the generation of creative solutions is further complicated by evidence that negative mood influences creativity as well. Martin and Stoner (1996) found results similar to those of Isen and colleagues in terms of positive moods leading to more creativity than negative ones. However, they also created situations in which positive and negative moods led to similarly creative outcomes, as well as cases in which negative moods lead to greater creativity than positive moods. Further, Kaufmann and Vosberg (1997) showed that participants in positive moods performed more poorly on an insight task than participants in neutral or sad moods (who came up with the most creative solutions).

Of course, mood-repair models might try to explain the finding that both positive and negative moods can lead to enhanced creativity by proposing separate mechanisms. However, given the finite number of possible mediators (e.g., cognitive flexibility, heuristic processing) that have been proposed, it may be more useful to predict that they can come into play for both positive and negative moods. From our perspective, what really matters is the absence or presence of social and other constraints. When they are absent, both types of moods may lead to more cognitive flexibility and perhaps heuristic processing resulting in greater creative solutions. However, when their use is constrained by a motive to control one's mood, creativity should be unaffected by either type of mood.

Unique characteristics of the task at hand may also impose constraints on the use of flexible or heuristic processing much in the same way in which they impose constraints on mood-congruent judgment. In the case of creativity this relates to the distinction between creative inspiration and creative production or output. With regard to the issue of inspiration or the generation of the unique, we have already seen that it can be the result of both positive and negative mood states (cf., Kaufmann & Vosberg, 1997). That is, the generation of creative solutions might be aided to a greater degree by the absence of social constraints (i.e., in which heuristic processing occurs) rather than by a particular mood state per se. On the other hand, creative production may be facilitated by the presence of constraints that may lead to motivated processing. Support for this idea comes from research that looked at how informational or social constraints interact with mood to predict performance on a task (Hirt et al., 1996; Martin et al., 1993). For example, Hirt and colleagues found that task interest affected the number of responses (i.e., production) participants generated but did not influence the quality (i.e., creativity) of their responses.

Furthermore, elements of evaluation inherent in some types of tasks or the instructions given to participants may be another type of task-related social constraint. Both Hirt et al. (1996) and Martin et al. (1993) examined how instructions can influence processing goals. From our perspective, their "stop rules" can be viewed as task-related social constraints. For example, participants in the "time to stop" condition who ask themselves, "Do I think it is a good time to stop?" are being directed explicitly to evaluate or judge their responses before continuing. Similarly, participants under the "enjoy" instructions ask themselves, "Do I feel like continuing with this task?," once again directing participants to engage in a self-evaluation. Because asking these questions influenced the number of responses generated but not the quality of those responses, it appears that they may have acted as constraints to the effects of mood on creativity.

Negative Mood Promotes Systematic Processing

In addressing the relationship between positive mood and creativity, we have been dancing all around the issue of exactly what happens when we are in bad moods. It is commonly held that individuals in positive moods tend to engage in heuristic processing, whereas those in negative moods engage in the systematic processing of information (e.g., Bless et al., 1990). Consequently, "smiling happy people" tend to perform better on creative tasks, whereas sad people tend to outperform happy individuals on analytic tasks (Sinclair & Mark, 1995).

Thus many researchers have advocated that positive and negative moods operate under entirely different sets of guidelines and rules and mediate cognitive processing in very different ways. With regard to the effects of mood on persuasion, early research suggested that participants in positive moods were more easily swayed by persuasive messages (i.e., engaging in heuristic processing and concentrating on peripheral cues), whereas sad participants engaged in the systematic processing of persuasive messages and were thus not influenced by peripheral cues.

By now it will come as no surprise to hear that we do not believe that moods and processing are as neatly and exclusively tied to one another (i.e., happy belongs to heuristics, sad is wed to systematic) as is commonly proposed. Instead, from our perspective, processing style results from an interaction between mood and the presence or absence of constraints. We can say this with some audacity for several reasons. The tendency of happy people to arrive at social judgments in a heuristic fashion by relying on their stereotypes is greatly attenuated when they are accountable for their judgment (Bodenhausen, Kramer, & Suesser, 1994, Study 4). Similarly, the frequently observed tendency of sad participants to forgo the use of stereotypes in favor of more substantive processing is primarily observed when the stereotype is somewhat inappropriate for the judgment (Lambert, Khan, Lickel, & Fricke, 1997). In other words, whether happy moods engender heuristic processing and whether sad moods engender substantive processing depends to some extent on the constraints that are placed on one's judgment. Research on mood and persuasion has similarly demonstrated important exceptions to earlier conclusions and supports our position at least indirectly. Mackie and Worth (1989) suggested that mood effects on persuasion are mediated primarily by capacity limitations rather than mood-induced differences in processing. When given only a limited amount of time, happy participants were influenced by peripheral cues (i.e., use of heuristic processing), whereas participants in negative moods were influenced by strong messages, thus showing evidence of systematic processing. However, when participants were given an unlimited amount of time to read the messages, the results were reversed. Participants in positive moods now spent more time on the arguments and demonstrated that they had processed central issues and used systematic processing. Thus, when given additional time, individuals in positive moods were able to overcome capacity deficits and process information just as systematically as did those in negative moods.

Wegener, Petty, and Smith (1995) propose that, instead of capacity limitations, mood effects in persuasion messages are reflections of motivational differences grounded in hedonistic principles. That is, moods mediate our choice of activities insofar as they direct us toward pleasurable, enjoyable (rewarding) activities and away from unpleasant, noxious (punishing) activities. For individuals in bad moods, almost any activity (e.g., mildly negative, neutral, positive) is rewarding because it is more positively valenced than their current mood state. Unfortunately, happy individuals face a more limited choice in potential activities: Fewer activities are rewarding. Thus, because engagement in most activities will be less pleasant than their current mood state (punishing), happy individuals should be less motivated and therefore less willing to allocate cognitive resources to engage in systematic processing of these activities.

In sum, according to this hedonic contingency approach, processing depends on the comparison between perceiver mood and task valence. Thus, processing, whether heuristic or systematic, is not tied as much to mood state as it is to the relative hedonic value of the task. In other words, people should choose to engage in activities that are as positive as if not more positive than their current mood states. In persuasion, then, happy individuals will be more likely to process positive messages systematically. Sad people, for whom a broader range of messages are hedonically rewarding, should likewise process a larger variety of messages in a systematic fashion.

We agree with one general message from both lines of work, namely, that happy people can also engage in systematic processing as well. However, we also think that the results of both sets of studies are far from unequivocal. Bless (chapter 1, this volume), for example, questions whether the use of heuristic cues or attention to message content does in fact imply limited capacity or motivated processing. In fact, Bless et al. (1990) found no mood effects for the number of cognitive responses produced by participants. Further, although happy participants responded to peripheral cues, they were just as likely as sad participants to notice message quality differences and recall similar details from messages.

Additionally, Wegener and colleagues' (1995) model, at one level, is consistent with our social-constraints approach. Task constraints (valence of task and match to mood) mediate type of processing. However, our approaches differ fundamentally in that the hedonic contingency model is based on the "goody-goody" hypothesis proposing that people are motivated to seek out pleasurable experiences and avoid unpleasant ones. Our research suggests that this is not universally true, nor is it the default. Indeed, happy participants in our study (Erber, Wegener, & Therriault, 1996) sought out mood-incongruent activities, preferring to read sad rather than happy news stories when a social constraint was present.

In closing, we recognize the fact that it is difficult to apply a single model to such a variety of research areas and topics. Thus some of our speculations might be a bit of a stretch. However, although it may not be possible to apply our model directly to every topic, we believe that it is entirely feasible to generalize some of its more basic principles. Thus, from our perspective, the work on mood and persuasion is interesting and significant because it demonstrates that systematic processing is not strictly tied to negative moods and that other mediators might be influencing processing. We have reason to believe that those mediators can be found when one looks at the range of social constraints that may be present.

ADDRESSING CONTRIBUTORS' THREE IMPORTANT QUESTIONS

1. The model assumes that individuals attempt to experience whatever feeling is appropriate for the situation. The model further assumes that individuals are able to do this because they have social knowledge that tells them which feelings are appropriate for various social contexts. What is not clear, though, is how individuals determine which moods are appropriate for which performance tasks. For example, how do individuals know what mood to be in to perform optimally on a math or spelling test? Does the model assume that individuals have insight into the consequences of different moods for different tasks? Do individuals possess naive theories of mood effects on different tasks?

There is reason to believe that people attempt to match their moods to the demands of a task in much the same way they attempt to match their moods to a social situation. More specifically, it is not unreasonable to suggest that most people have at least a rudimentary understanding of the Yerkes–Dodson law: Moods and emotions carrying too little or too much arousal can be detrimental to task performance. Because many performance tasks carry a predilection for levelheadedness (e.g., a math test, buying a car), relatively neutral moods might be considered appropriate in many cases. Then again, the wide world of sports provides plenty of examples of specific moods and levels of arousal being beneficial in the service of task completion. Sports commentators often caution against letdowns resulting from a big game the previous night, and they occasionally observe that teams are "flat" or are "looking ahead." In such instances, athletes often use "trash talk," pumping their fists and celebrating after a score not so much to denigrate their opponents as to get themselves up to the task. On the other hand, the pitcher who comes in in the bottom of the ninth inning with the game on the line, three on base and no outs, often puts on his game face, marked by a seemingly complete detachment from the proceedings. Naturally, to some extent he does this to intimidate his opponents, but a large part of it may be in the service of conquering the utter terror he might be experiencing.

Of course, if everybody had perfect social knowledge about which moods match which situations and performance-related tasks, Emily Post would be out of business and the New York Knicks would be the NBA champions. Everyone who ever paid a visit to the Department of Motor Vehicles has experienced firsthand that a fair number of individuals lack this type of acuity in rather profound ways. To some extent, individual differences in achieving congruency between one's mood and the task at hand may be a matter of emotional intelligence (e.g., Salovey, Hsee, &

Mayer, 1993). Some failures to adjust one's mood to the situation may stem from a lack of knowledge of what is appropriate. In other cases they may be caused by an inability to make the connection between internal states and external demands, a lack of motivation either to perform well or to abandon a particular mood, or more generally because of a low emotional IQ.

2. The model suggests that relatively neutral moods are beneficial because of the flexibility they afford. On the other hand, there is plenty of evidence that people are often motivated to maintain their mood. More generally, in the absence of constraints, is neutral mood the default or is mood maintenance the default?

According to Newton's first law, in the physical world every body will continue in its state of rest or uniform motion in a straight line except insofar as it is compelled to change that state by impressed force. Perhaps in the affective world, moods remain at rest or in motion unless there is a reason to act on them. In other words, individuals are likely to remain in whatever mood they are in (positive, neutral, sad) unless they are compelled to change their moods in light of perceived constraints. Skeptics about our model often ask why, if neutral moods give us the most flexibility in confronting unknown people and situations, our participants who did not anticipate future interaction with others maintained their positive or negative moods. One answer is that they had no reason to adjust their moods because of the very fact that there were no situational constraints evident to them and thus there was no impressed force to change their state. From this perspective, the model appears to suggest that maintaining a given mood regardless of its valence (positive, neutral, negative) might indeed be the default as long as there are no constraints present. On the other hand, we are hesitant to embrace this position completely. Given the social nature of our existence, there may be few cases in which our emotional experience is completely unconstrained. Thus proposing defaults in the absence of constraints would come at the considerable and unnecessary epistemic expense of deemphasizing the importance of context.

3. The model suggests that the presence of situational constraints might engender a self-regulation motive, which in turn is associated with systematic processing. The model further predicts that the effect of this systematic processing will be mood control and mood-incongruent effects (e.g., judgment, recall). It is unclear, though, why this should be the case. Couldn't systematic processing also lead to mood maintenance and greater affect infusion (e.g., Forgas)? More generally, does your model need to distinguish between systematic, substantive processing on the one

hand and motivated processing in the service of mood control on the other?

There may indeed be good reason to distinguish between motivated processing on the one hand and heuristic versus systematic processing on the other as some of our theoretical competitors have done. However, we would like to slice up the pie in a somewhat different way. If Newton's law has any bearing on the issue, then much less effort needs to be applied to maintaining our moods than to changing them. In fact, our studies on the mood-absorbing qualities of cognitively demanding tasks (Erber & Erber, 1994; Erber & Tesser, 1992) suggest just that. From this perspective, it appears that heuristic processing will likely aid in maintaining moods, whereas systematic or substantive processing may eradicate them. Either processing strategy can be an instance of motivated processing to the extent that they follow from a motive to either maintain one's mood in the absence of constraints or to control one's mood when constraints are present. However, it is entirely possible that systematic processing may lead to mood maintenance under some circumstances as well. Whether or not it does depends to some extent on the nature of what is being processed. If individuals were to engage in the systematic processing of information relevant to their current moods, as is the case for rumination, this kind of processing should lead to mood maintenance. If, on the other hand, individuals were to engage in the systematic processing of information irrelevant to their current moods, as is the case when we solve difficult math problems or process persuasive messages, this same type of processing should lead to mood control.

Even though our model is first and foremost concerned with how people manage their moods, we believe that it has some obvious implications for understanding issues more generally related to mood and processing. Not surprisingly, it shares many features with other models presented in this volume (e.g., context dependence of mood effects, interplay between motivated and systematic processing). Nonetheless, we also feel that our model is unique in many ways. For one thing, it takes into account the mounting evidence that negative moods by themselves do not automatically trigger a repair motive. This has led us to adopt a theoretical position denying that moods carry any sort of default mechanisms or processes. Instead, by considering context and motivation early on (i.e., when a potentially mood-eliciting stimulus is encountered), we were able to come up with a processing model that is considerably more parsimonious than models based on default-override principles. That we were able to integrate a number of diverse research findings attests to the model's theoretical power. In our headier moments we hope that others will find our model as helpful for the generation of hypotheses about mood and processing as we do.

REFERENCES

Allport, G. H. (1954). The historical background of social psychology. In G. Lindzey (Ed.), *The handbook of social psychology* (2nd ed., Vol. 1, pp. 3–56). Cambridge, MA: Addison-Wesley.

Bentham, J. (1789). *An introduction to the principles of morals and legislation*. Oxford, England: Clarendon Press.

Blaney, P. H. (1986). Affect and memory: A review. *Psychological Bulletin, 99,* 229–246.

Bless, H., Bohner, G., Schwarz, N., & Strack, F. (1990). Mood and persuasion: A cognitive response analysis. *Personality and Social Psychology Bulletin, 16,* 331–345.

Bodenhausen, G. V., Kramer, G. P., & Suesser, K. (1994). Happiness and stereotypic thinking in social judgment. *Journal of Personality and Social Psychology, 66,* 621–623.

Bower, G. H. (1981). Mood and memory. *American Psychologist, 36,* 12–48.

Bower, G. H., Gilligan, S. J., & Monteiro, K. P. (1981). Selectivity of learning caused by affective states. *Journal of Experimental Psychology: General, 110,* 451–473.

Campbell, J. D., Trapnell, P. D., Heine, S. J., Katz, I. M., Lavalle, L. F., & Lehman, D. R. (1996). Self-concept clarity, personality correlates, and cultural boundaries. *Journal of Personality and Social Psychology, 70,* 141–156.

Carlson, M., & Miller, N. (1987). Explanation of the relation between negative mood and helping. *Psychological Bulletin, 102,* 91–108.

Catanzaro, S. J., & Mearns, J. (1990). Measuring generalized expectancies for negative mood regulation: Initial scale development and implications. *Journal of Personality Assessment, 54,* 546–563.

Clark, M. S., & Isen, A. M. (1982). Toward understanding the relationship between feeling states and social behavior. In A. Hastorf & A. M. Isen (Eds.), *Cognitive social psychology* (pp. 73–108). New York: Elsevier North Holland.

Commons, M. J., & Erber, R. (1997, May). *Mood regulation in anticipation of social interaction: The case of strangers versus romantic partners.* Paper presented at the annual meeting of the Midwestern Psychological Association, Chicago, IL.

Eich, E., & Metcalfe, J. (1989). Mood dependent memory for internal versus external events. *Journal of Experimental Psychology: Learning, Memory, and Cognition, 15,* 443–455.

Erber, R. (1991). Affective and semantic priming: Effects of mood on category accessibility and inference. *Journal of Experimental Social Psychology, 24,* 79–88.

Erber, R. (1996). The self-regulation of moods. In L. L. Martin & A. Tesser (Eds.), *Striving and feeling: Interactions among goals, affect, and self-regulation* (pp. 251–275). Hillsdale, NJ: Lawrence Erlbaum Associates.

Erber, R., & Erber, M. W. (1994). Beyond mood and social judgment: Mood incongruent recall and mood regulation. *European Journal of Social Psychology, 24,* 79–88.

Erber, R., Erber, M. W., Therriault, N., & Onesto, R. (1999). *On the puzzling nature of the self-regulation of anxiety: Absorption, anxiety, and anagrams.* Manuscript in preparation.

Erber, R., & Tesser, A. (1992). Task effort and the regulation of mood: The absorption hypothesis. *Journal of Experimental Social Psychology, 28,* 339–359.

Erber, R., & Therriault, N. (1994, May). *Sweating to the oldies: The mood-absorbing qualities of exercise.* Paper presented at the annual meeting of the Midwestern Psychological Association, Chicago, IL.

Erber, R., Wegner, D. M., & Therriault, N. (1996). On being cool and collected: Mood regulation in anticipation of social interaction. *Journal of Personality and Social Psychology, 70,* 757–766.

Forgas, J. P. (1995). Mood and judgment: The affect infusion model (AIM). *Psychological Bulletin, 117,* 39–66.

Forgas, J. P., & Bower, G. H. (1987). Mood effects on person perception judgments. *Journal of Personality and Social Psychology, 53*, 53–56.

Forgas, J. P., Bower, G. H., & Krantz, S. (1984). The influence of mood on perceptions of social interactions. *Journal of Experimental Social Psychology, 20*, 497–513.

Forgas, J. P., Burnham, D., & Trimboli, C. (1988). Mood, memory, and social judgments in children. *Journal of Personality and Social Psychology, 54*, 697–703.

Forgas, J. P., Levinger, G., & Moylan, S. J. (1994). Feeling good and feeling close: Affective influences on the perception of intimate relationships. *Personal Relationships, 2*, 165–184.

Gilbert, D. T., Pinel, E. C., Wilson, T. D., Blumberg, S. J., & Wheatley, T. P. (1998). Immune neglect: A source of durability bias in affective forecasting. *Journal of Personality and Social Psychology, 75*, 617–638.

Gollwitzer, P. M., Heckhausen, H., & Steller, B. (1990). Deliberative and implemental mind-sets: Cognitive tuning toward congruous thoughts and information. *Journal of Personality and Social Psychology, 59*, 1119–1127.

Hirt, E. R., Melton, R. J., McDonald, H. E., & Harackiewicz, J. M. (1996). Processing goals, task interest, and the mood-performance relationship: A mediational analysis. *Journal of Personality and Social Psychology, 71*, 245–261.

Isen, A. M. (1984). Toward understanding the role of affect in cognition. In R. S. Wyer, Jr. & T. Srull (Eds.), *Handbook of social cognition* (pp. 179–236). Hillsdale, NJ: Lawrence Erlbaum Associates.

Isen, A. M. (1993). Positive mood and decision making. In M. Lewis & J. Haviland (Eds.), *Handbook of emotion* (pp. 261–277). New York: Guilford.

Isen, A. M., & Daubman, K. A. (1984). The influence of affect on categorization. *Journal of Personality and Social Psychology, 47*, 1206–1217.

Isen, A. M., & Levin, P. F. (1972). The effect of feeling good on helping: Cookies and kindness. *Journal of Personality and Social Psychology, 21*, 384–388.

Isen, A. M., Shalker, T., Clark, M. S., & Karp, L. (1978). Affect, accessibility of material in memory and behavior: A cognitive loop? *Journal of Personality and Social Psychology, 36*, 1–12.

Kaufmann, G., & Vosburg, S. K. (1997). "Paradoxical" mood effects on creative problem-solving. *Cognition and Emotion, 11*, 151–170.

Lambert, A. J., Khan, S. R., Lickel, B. A., & Fricke, K. (1997). Mood and the correction of positive versus negative stereotypes. *Journal of Personality and Social Psychology, 72*, 1002–1016.

Ludwig, A. M. (1994). Mental illness and creative activity in female writers. *American Journal of Psychiatry, 151*, 1650–1656.

Mackie, D. M., & Worth, L. T. (1989). Processing deficits and the mediation of positive affect in persuasion. *Journal of Personality and Social Psychology, 57*, 27–40.

Martin, L. L., Abend, T., Sedikides, C., & Greene, J. D. (1997). How would it feel if . . . ? Mood as input to a role fulfillment evaluation process. *Journal of Personality and Social Psychology, 73*, 242–253.

Martin, L. L. & Stoner, P. (1996). Mood as input: What we think about how we feel determines how we think. In L. L. Martin & A. Tesser (Eds.), *Striving and feeling: Interactions among goals, affect, and self-regulation* (pp. 279–301). Hillsdale, NJ: Lawrence Erlbaum Associates.

Martin, L. L., Ward, D. W., Achee, J. W., & Wyer, R. S. (1993). Mood as input: People have to interpret the motivational implications of their moods. *Journal of Personality and Social Psychology, 64*, 317–326.

Mayer, J. D., Gaschke, Y. N., Braverman, D. L., & Evans, T. (1992). Mood-congruent judgment is a general effect. *Journal of Personality and Social Psychology, 63*, 110–132.

McDougall, W. (1923). *Outline of psychology*. New York: Scribner's.

Murray, N., Sujan, H., Hirt, E. R., & Sujan, M. (1990). The influence of mood on categorization: A cognitive flexibility interpretation. *Journal of Personality and Social Psychology, 59*, 411–425.

Parrott, W. G., & Sabini, J. (1990). Mood and memory under natural conditions: Evidence for mood incongruent recall. *Journal of Personality and Social Psychology, 59*, 321–336.

Salovey, P. (1992). Mood-induced self-focused attention. *Journal of Personality and Social Psychology, 62*, 699–707.

Salovey, P., Hsee, C. K., & Mayer, J. D. (1993). Emotional intelligence and the self-regulation of affect. In D. M. Wegner & J. W. Pennebaker (Eds.), *Handbook of mental control* (pp. 258–277). Englewood Cliffs, NJ: Prentice-Hall

Schildkraut, J. J., & Otero, A. (1996). *Depression and the spiritual in modern art: Homage to Miro.* New York: Wiley.

Schwarz, N., & Clore, G. L. (1983). Mood, misattribution, and judgments of well-being: Informative and directive functions of affective states. *Journal of Personality and Social Psychology, 45*, 513–523.

Schwarz, N., & Clore, G. L. (1988). How do I feel about it? The information function of affective states. In K. Fiedler & J. P. Forgas (Eds.), *Affect, cognition, and social behavior* (pp. 44–62). Lewinston, NJ: Hogrefe.

Sinclair, R. C., & Mark, M. (1992). The influence of mood state on judgment and action: Effects on persuasion, categorization, social justice, person perception, and judgment accuracy. In L. L. Martin & A. Tesser (Eds.), *The construction of social judgments* (pp. 165–193). Hillsdale, NJ: Lawrence Erlbaum Associates.

Sinclair, R. C., & Mark, M. M. (1995). The effects of mood state on judgmental accuracy: Processing strategy and a mechanism. *Cognition and Emotion, 9*, 417–438.

Smith, S. M., & Petty, R. E. (1995). Personality moderators of mood effects on cognition: The role of self-esteem and negative mood regulation. *Journal of Personality and Social Psychology, 68*, 1092–1107.

Strack, F., Martin, L. L., & Stepper, S. (1988). Inhibiting and facilitating conditions of the human smile: A nonobtrusive test of the facial feedback hypothesis. *Journal of Personality and Social Psychology, 54*, 768–777.

Taylor, S. E. (1991). The asymmetrical effects of positive and negative events: The mobilization-minimization hypothesis. *Psychological Bulletin, 110*, 67–85.

Tesser, A., & Rosen, S. (1975). The reluctance to transmit bad news. In L. Berkowitz (Ed.), *Advances in experimental social psychology* (Vol. 8, pp. 193–232). New York: Academic Press.

Therriault, N., Erber, R., & Oktela, C. (1996, May). *Mood and self-perception in response to negative self-information: To ruminate or regulate.* Paper presented at the annual meeting of the Midwestern Psychological Association, Chicago, IL.

Wegener, D. T., Petty, R. E., & Smith, S. M. (1995). Positive mood can increase or decrease message scrutiny: The hedonic contingency view of mood and message processing. *Journal of Personality and Social Psychology, 69*, 5–15.

Wood, J. V., Saltzberg, J. A., & Goldsamt, L. A. (1990). Does affect induce self-focused attention? *Journal of Personality and Social Psychology, 58*, 899–908.

Chapter 4

Affective States Trigger Processes of Assimilation and Accommodation

Klaus Fiedler
University of Heidelberg

No theory can claim to explain everything. Theories are systematizations of sufficient conditions that can account for the occurrence of an effect, but hardly any psychological theory can exclude the possibility that the same effect may also originate from other causes or processes. Being aware of this methodological truism is important to avoid misunderstandings in any theoretical debate, and in particular for this book. Two theories are incompatible neither if they predict different phenomena nor if they predict the same phenomena for different reasons. A crucial test between two theories is only possible when they predict different outcomes under the very same conditions. When comparing theories of affect and cognition, it is thus essential to be specific about the domain and about the truly distinct predictions of different conceptions.

With this goal in mind, I present my own affect–cognition theory in a way that accentuates those implications and empirical findings that set it apart from other theories. To repeat, if my theory succeeds in making distinct predictions, it may, but need not, be incompatible with other theories. Conflicts only arise in a small subset of empirical findings to which both competing theories are applicable but which give rise to opposite preditions.

Which empirical questions are diagnostic for the comparison of theories? In my opinion, current approaches to affect and cognition differ mainly in their positions vis-à-vis the following crucial questions: (a) whether or not the cognitive consequences of affective states are mediated by resource or capacity limitations that accompany emotions, (b) whether affect causes genuine changes in internal cognitive processes or merely superficial response biases reflecting shallow heuristics, and (c) whether the theory emphasizes the associative learning history behind the current task or the motivational incentives before the task. The position of my theory within this three-dimensional cube is clear-cut: It refrains from assuming resource or capacity limitations, it predicts genuine cognitive effects, and it is a "because" theory rooted in antecedent learning factors rather than a "so that" theory drawing on consequent incentives.

TWO MOOD-DEPENDENT LEARNING SETS

The theory I advocate starts from two basic assumptions, one about the dual forces of cognitive processes (Fiedler, 1990, 1991) and the other about the basic distinction between appetitive and aversive states. Both assumptions can be made without much loss of generality.

1. Every cognitive process can be decomposed into two complementary functions, conservation of given input information and active generation of new output information on the basis of internal knowledge structures. Both functions complement each other in virtually every cognitive process. In order to be processed, input information first has to be captured and conserved for a moment; however, we would not speak of a cognitive process if that input were not actively transformed into something new. Thus visual perception involves the conservation of a visual image projected on the retina, which is then actively interpreted as representing a meaningful category. Risk assessment means to conserve input data on probabilities and payoffs and to generate prognostic inferences. Intelligent problem solving (e.g., in chess) requires the precise conservation of a problem state and the active generation of operators to achieve a goal state. Conservation is essentially a stimulus-driven function, whereas active generation is a knowledge-driven function of the individual's general knowledge structures. Although both functions coexist and interact (e.g., prior knowledge is used to interpret new stimuli), real tasks differ in the emphasis they place on conservation versus active generation.

2. With regard to emotional states, the theory does not address qualitatively different emotions but the primary dimension of positive versus negative mood states, or euphoric versus dysphoric moods, that are typically manipulated in virtually all experiments on affect and cognition (see Clark & Fiske, 1982; Fiedler & Forgas, 1988; Isen, 1984). There are good theoretical reasons for concentrating on positive versus negative states, which correspond directly to different learning sets that govern adaptive

learning in appetitive and aversive situations, respectively. Whereas appetitive settings encourage exploration and creativity, aversive learning maximizes the avoidance of mistakes. Avoidance behavior has to be perfectly reliable, attentive to potentially threatening stimuli, even in the absence of any reinforcement (e.g., a child must be cautious on the street without ever experiencing the unconditional stimulus of a traffic accident). In contrast, in positive, appetitive settings, the organism is freed from careful stimulus monitoring and can instead trust in internalized knowledge and behavioral routines.

This is the learning theoretical background from which my theory is derived. Positive and negative mood states are but special cases of, or affective cues to, appetitive and aversive settings, respectively. And, as I show subsequently, the adaptive influence of positive and negative moods on behavior is analogous to the differential learning sets that hold for appetitive and aversive situations in general. Whereas negative mood supports the conservative function of sticking to the stimulus facts and avoiding mistakes, positive mood supports the creative function of active generation, or enriching the stimulus input with inferences based on prior knowledge. For convenience, I use Piaget's (1952) terms *accommodation* (tuning the cognitive system to fit the stimulus environment) and *assimilation* (transforming external information to fit internal knowledge structures) for these two adaptive functions. Thus negative mood facilitates accommodation (avoiding mistakes, conserving input), whereas positive mood supports assimilation (inferences, interpretation). This is the core assumption supposed to explain and predict a variety of empirical findings.

EMPIRICAL VALIDATION

One asset of this theory is that it can explain the two major classes of empirical findings within the same framework, namely, mood effects on cognitive style and performance, as well as mood-congruent recall and judgment. With respect to performance, no global superiority but rather a crucial interaction effect is predicted for either positive or negative mood. Whether positive or negative mood facilitates performance depends crucially on the requirements of the task.

Performance on productive tasks that require a high degree of assimilation (e.g., creative inferences, active generation) should profit from positive moods. In contrast, negative moods should have a relative advantage on reproductive tasks that require accommodation (careful conservation and scrutiny). With respect to mood congruency and selective processing, it is important to understand an important source of asymmetry. Because the conservation component of cognitive tasks is by definition stimulus-driven and therefore nonselective, the accommodation function of negative mood supports the conservation of any input, whether mood congruent or not. In contrast, the active-generation component invites selective, mood-congruent influences because assimilation means to impose internal structure and states on the external stimulus world. Therefore, the selective activation of mood-congruent knowledge and information should mainly affect the creative or generative functions of the assimilation component. Consequently, the tendency to selectively process mood-congruent information should be most pronounced for positive mood. This does not imply, of course, that congruency effects are fully eliminated in negative mood, because some degree of assimilation is involved under any mood state in any task.

The remainder of this chapter is devoted to pertinent research evidence. The original and distinctive predictions of the assimilation–accommodation theory will be considered with reference to four classes of well-established phenomena that impose empirical constraints on any viable theory: (a) mood-congruent memory, (b) mood-congruent judgment, (c) systematic processing in negative mood, and (d) creativity and flexibility in positive mood. Topics (a) and (b) can be treated together, just as (c) and (d) will be considered as complementary sides of the same issue.

Mood-Congruent Memory and Judgment

Evidence from numerous studies shows that pleasant stimuli are more readily and more efficiently processed in positive moods, whereas unpleasant material has a relative advantage under negative moods (Bower, 1981; Clore, Schwarz, & Conway, 1994; Forgas & Bower, 1987). There is also wide agreement on the asymmetry of this effect; mood congruency is rather pronounced for positive mood but much weaker or even eliminated under negative mood (Isen, 1984).

To account for these findings, the assumptions about the assimilation and accommodation functions of mood states have only to be supplemented with a few ordinary principles of associative memory (Fiedler, 1990, 1991). From a broader cognitive perspective, the dependence of memory on affective states is but a special case of context effects. Just as mood–state dependency (i.e., the enhanced retrieval of information learned in the same mood; Bower, 1981; Bower, Monteiro, & Gilligan, 1978) fits the more general principle of encoding specificity (Tulving & Thompson, 1973), the phenomenon of mood congruency belongs to a more general congruity principle. Accordingly, the processing of information is facilitated by the presence of other, congruent information.

Another basic memory principle is that the degree of active involvement and elaboration during encoding provides a catalyst for associative processes, as is evident in the depth-of-processing effect (Craik & Tulving, 1975) or the generation effect (Slamecka & Graf, 1978). Mood influences come into play because the degree of active generation and elaboration is assumed to increase in an assimilation set under positive mood. Positive affective states should thus amplify the advantage of elaborative encoding. But due to the congruity principle, the benefit should mainly stem from pleasant, mood-congruent stimuli. People in positive moods should not only generate more associations and richer encoding contexts, but in doing so they should also rely on mood-congruent knowledge structures that facilitate the generation of congruent responses and possibly inhibit incongruent responses. Under negative moods, the congruency effect may not totally disappear (because the generative component is not totally eliminated), but the selective mood influence should decline markedly.

Several experiments confirm that positive mood states support generative, elaborative encoding in general and encoding of mood-congruent information in particular. For example, when pleasant and unpleasant words were presented either in complete format or as incomplete fragments to be completed by the participants themselves, positive mood enhanced the generation effect (i.e., better memory for self-generated than experimenter-provided information; Fiedler, Lachnit, Fay, & Krug, 1992). When evaluative stimuli were used, the facilitative effect of positive mood was confined to the generation of pleasant words, whereas memory for unpleasant words was slightly inhibited (Fiedler, 1991). The same three-way interaction between mood, valence, and generation showed that mood congruency was largely confined to self-generated information (i.e., tasks that emphasize the active component).

In another paradigm (Fiedler, 1991), the degree of active generation was manipulated by having participants form picture stories from subsets of positive and negative photographs. Again the mood-congruency effect was confined to the subsets of those pictures that were actively used for the self-generated stories and disappeared for the remaining pictures. What positive mood facilitates is the active construction of positively toned stories that in turn provide an efficient memory code for recalling mood-congruent pictures (as evident from the participants' generally better memory for pictures included in stories).

The generative processes under positive mood need not always improve accuracy. In another experiment (Fiedler, Asbeck, & Nickel, 1991), happy people's readiness to generate inferences beyond the given information led to an enhanced rate of constructive memory intrusions. This raises the interesting question of whether recall hits and false alarms are equally affected by mood states and the related question of whether mood congruency is a genuine memory effect or merely a response bias based on crude heuristics (Schwarz & Clore, 1988).

In a recent experiment (Fiedler, Nickel, Muehlfriedel, & Unkelbach, 2000), we applied signal-detection analyses to distinguish sensitivity (genuine memory advantage of congruent stimuli) and criterion (readiness to make mood- congruent guesses based on shallow heuristics) in a special type of recognition task. The results indicate a genuine sensitivity effect rather than a heuristic guessing bias. That is, participants in positive moods do not show a response set to endorse each and any positive item, stimulus or distractor, but show actually improved discrimination between mood-congruent stimuli and lures. Moreover, the genuine mood-congruent recognition effect reflects the familiar asymmetry; it is stronger for positive than negative mood.

All these findings are fully in line with our conception of mood congruency arising from ordinary rules of associative memory and with the notion that the assimilation set under positive mood supports the formation of effective memory codes. However, the aforementioned results cannot be explained by memory-independent heuristics. If there were no genuine advantage for mood-congruent retrieval and participants were merely using a judgment heuristic (i.e., endorsing positive stimuli while in a positive mood; Schwarz & Clore, 1988), why should these judgment heuristics affect only self-generated stimuli or only pictures included in stories? Why has mood-congruent information a sensitivity advantage in signal detection? Although heuristic approaches have their merits for explaining some superficial judgment effects, they hardly apply to the aforementioned memory data.

Note that these findings are not compatible with capacity theories of affect and cognition. Because the crucial moderator variables (i.e., self-generated vs. conserved information, included vs. excluded pictures) were typically manipulated within participants, it is hard to see why any capacity reduction should differentially affect only the generative subset of stimuli.

With regard to mood-congruent judgments, a good deal of evidence shows that judgment biases are not bound to biases in stimulus recall (Hastie & Park, 1986), because preformed (online) judgments may themselves be included as fixed modules in memory. Nevertheless, the activation of preformed judgment modules may follow the same associative principles that govern all memory contents. The only difference is that in the case of preformed judgments, associative influences directly act on the judgment module rather than on memorized raw data from which judgments are computed. In principle, then, the often-noted independence of judgment biases from recall biases (Mayer & Salovey, 1988; Schwarz & Clore, 1988) does not undermine an ordinary-memory approach to mood-congruent judgment.

Parenthetically, those ordinary principles of associative memory may be more adequately explained within modern connectionist frameworks

(Kashima & Kerekes, 1994; Kruschke, 1992) than within the old seman-tic-network framework suggested by Bower (1981) and others. Connec-tionist models have several advantages when applied to affect and cogni-tion (see Fiedler, 2000). They replace the storehouse metaphor of memory with the metaphor of a distributive-knowledge system in which both memory outputs and judgments are reconstructed from learned as-sociations rather than retrieved as fixed units. Such a flexible, ever-chang-ing system in which meaning does not reside in the individual units but only as patterns of connections between units is more suitable for under-standing the crucial role of active generation. Moreover, connectionist models are less rigid than traditional models in suggesting obviously false implications, such as the prediction that all mood-congruent items should appear in early positions of free recall protocols, whereas all incongruent items should cluster toward the end. Thus, in a connectionist, distributive memory model, it is easy to see that one positive item can be associatively very close to its negative opposite, produced by the inversion of one single feature value.

Careful Processing Versus Creativity

Positive affective states not only facilitate the active generation of mood-congruent (i.e., pleasant) encoding units but also support the assimilative processing mode in general, thus supporting diverse genera-tive and creative functions (Fiedler, 1988). When stimulus materials are neutral rather than evaluatively charged, positive mood will still enhance the generation effect on memory (Fiedler et al., 1992). In fact, the basic as-sumption of my theory (i.e., conservation under negative mood and active generation under positive mood) pertains immediately to predicting the different processing styles that characterize elated and depressed states.

If positive moods facilitate assimilative functions—that is, inferences, transformations, active generation, and knowledge-based elaboration—then it is clear that performance should improve on a number of tasks that require exactly these cognitive functions. There is convergent evidence for this contention showing that elated (as compared with neutral or de-pressed) mood leads to more productive problem solving (Isen, 1984), un-usual word associations (Isen, Johnson, Mertz, & Robinson, 1985), flexible decision and judgment strategies (Forgas & Fiedler, 1996; Hertel & Fiedler, 1994), higher segmentation rates (Lassiter, Koenig, & Apple, 1996), and more flexibility in responses to persuasive communication (Wegener, Petty, & Smith, 1995). That enhanced flexibility follows posi-tive mood can be derived from two assumptions: that multiple knowledge structures are available for assimilation and that external stimulus con-straints are low. The often-cited finding in persuasion research that people in good moods differentiate less between strong and weak arguments than people in bad moods need not mean that good mood leads to less effortful or more impoverished processing. From my perspective, strong arguments are essential for the conservative, stimulus-driven style of people in negative moods. In contrast, for people in positive mood states, even weak arguments can turn on active inferences and self-generated inferences that are not contingent on the quality of the original communication. As Bless and colleagues (Bless et al., 1996; Bless & Fiedler, 1995) have shown, this creative enrichment effect under positive mood arises from the productive use of generic knowledge structures and stereotypes (Bodenhausen, Kramer, & Suesser, 1994) and is not the consequence of decreasing cognitive capacity.

Several of these effects are also expected from other theoretical perspectives. For example, the mood-as-information approach (Schwarz, 1990) assumes that positive affective states signal the absence of dangers and obstacles so that the individual can take the risk of unusual, creative, exploratory behaviors. However, such an account appears to be confined to predicting volitional, motivated behaviors at the molar level. In contrast, the present model extends to more molecular functions of assimilation that are not amenable to voluntary, strategic control. For example, in a cued recognition task with degraded presentation, Fiedler et al. (2000) found that participants in positive moods used semantic cue words more readily for inferring mood-congruent stimuli that slowly appeared subliminally behind a mask. However, this effect was confined to fast responses driven by creative inferences from the cue words and disappeared for the slow responses that were already based on sufficient stimulus details. It is hard to see why the mood-as-information principle should selectively affect only the fastest, hardly controllable responses. Within my conception, the pattern of findings makes perfect sense, because only the fast responses are driven by active inferences from the cue words, whereas the slower responses rely on an increasing proportion of already visible stimulus details.

For a similar demonstration, Bless and Fiedler (1995) found that positive mood led to stronger priming effects (i.e., reduced latencies to judge a behavior when preceded by a semantically matched trait), but only when the task involved an active inference (i.e., judging whether behaviors and traits apply to a target person). When the same stimulus series was embedded in a conservative task (i.e., judging whether a word of similar meaning had been presented in the previous five trials), the response latencies revealed a priming advantage for participants in negative moods. Again, it is hardly plausible that such molecular, almost automatic priming effects are brought about by motivated, strategic processes.

The reversal reported in the last experiment once more highlights the contention that neither mood state will generally produce better performance or richer output. Using a constant stimulus series, the priming effect is either stronger in positive or in negative mood, depending on whether the task calls for active inferences (assimilation) or careful stimulus tracking (accommodation). Similar interactions are predicted for other performance aspects. For instance, considering flexibility as an aspect of performance, the prediction of enhanced flexibility under positive mood only holds when knowledge is rich enough to allow for variation in assimilative functions. However, if knowledge is impoverished, as may be the case with group stereotypes, then the reliance on prior knowledge in positive mood leads to reduced flexibility.

ADDRESSING THE QUESTIONS RAISED
BY COMMENTATORS

In this section, I briefly address the questions that were raised by commentators regarding the theoretical approach presented here. Altogether, the feedback I received revolves around three issues that appear to be less than perfectly clear, although the answers to these open questions are at least implicit in the preceding sections.

1. Why is it the case that positive and negative moods support assimilation and accommodation, respectively? What is the reason for this basic assumption?

The answer is straightforward. Assimilation and accommodation are conceived as characteristic aspects of two generalized learning sets, for appetitive and aversive situations, respectively. So the explanation of the basic assumption is in terms of long-term learning history. Over a long period of (ontogenetic or even phylogenetic) learning, organisms acquire different generalized learning sets for positive versus negative situations that emphasize either exploration and curiosity or avoidance and vigilance. Note that such a learning-based account is clearly distinct from functionalist or motivational accounts that try to explain affective influences in terms of future goals or incentives. Thus it is not assumed that people in good or bad moods change their performance or cognitive style in order to reach some hedonic or functional goal (mood repair, conservation of pleasure), but because past learning has linked positive and negative settings to different sets. One noteworthy implication of this position is that one needs no emotions proper to induce the typical "mood" effects; superficial and transitory affective cues may be as effective in eliciting the learning sets as enduring mood states or genuine emotions (cf. Fiedler, 1991).

2. Why should the use of prior knowledge be confined to the domain of active generation (assimilation)? Doesn't prior knowledge also help to evaluate stimulus facts under the conservation (accommodation) function?

Answering this question provides an opportunity to clarify a common source of misunderstanding. It is important to distinguish between real tasks involving active generation or conservation on the one hand and the idealized theoretical constructs of active generation and conservation on the other. At the theoretical level, using prior knowledge to actively transform the stimulus input is by definition equated with the term *active generation*. Likewise, the construct of stimulus conservation means to carefully retain the original input and not to confuse it with prior knowledge. However, at the operational level, it was stated from the beginning that pure conservation or pure active generation can hardly ever be observed. Virtually every real task involves both components to some degree. The research trick is to figure out those task conditions for experimentation that can be ordered unequivocally on a dimension describing the relative weight of conservation and active generation.

In attempting to test my theory, I have thus designed experiments in which the entire stimulus series was held constant and only one element was manipulated (e.g., an active-generation task of whether a trait applies to a target person vs. a conservation task of whether a trait appeared within the last five items) that can be clearly ordered on the conservation–generation continuum. There are many other real tasks in which both components are intertwined and positively correlated, as, for example, when extended processing increases both careful conservation and rich generation. It is also possible that knowledge-based encoding may be used to facilitate stimulus conservation (yielding a blend of assimilation and accommodation) or that knowledge structures serve the function of simplifying and pigeonholing rather than enriching stimulus input. However, these more complex cases or alternative outcomes do not invalidate the theory; they are simply ill suited for testing the theory.

3. How can the model account for flexible shifts in processing mode when there is no change in the nature of the task?

Of course, there is no logical reason for excluding the possibility that other factors not covered by this theoretical approach can also affect the cognitive-processing style. So why should this theory be incompatible with the demonstration that individuals can change their cognitive processes as a function of hedonic goals or processing demands from one moment to the other? The problem with several studies that intend to demonstrate such flexible changes is that they rarely ever diagnose the processing mode. What they measure is how long individuals continue on a task, or how much information they attend to, or whether they distinguish between strong and weak arguments in persuasion. But these crude measures can hardly be considered as experimentally sound evidence for processing styles. Nevertheless, if an experiment succeeds in making a strong point for flexible changes between processing styles, this would not be incompatible with my point of view.

Furthermore, it should be repeated that switching between appetitive learning and aversive learning sets does not necessarily require different tasks. Affective cues or signals within a task may have an effect similar to enduring mood manipulations. For example, in an experiment reported in Fiedler (1991), changing the positive versus negative tone of a background picture projected on the wall every few seconds caused a mood-congruency effect on the learning of positive versus negative words that was similar to conventional mood treatments. However, to repeat, providing cogent evidence for short-time changes in cognitive processing mode is a very difficult and ambitious methodological task.

CONCLUSIONS

Returning to the three theoretical distinctions introduced at the outset, the reported findings have illustrated why the theory presented here (a) is not dependent on resource or capacity limitations, (b) predicts genuine cognitive process effects rather than shallow response tendencies, and (c) reflects antecedent learning sets rather than functional principles anchored in future goals. These conclusions were reached in an attempt to account for the four major classes of empirical findings: mood-congruent memory, mood-congruent judgment, creativity under positive mood, and systematic processing under negative mood. In dealing with congruency effects, this theory relies on ordinary memory principles: Efficient encoding and successful recall require that stimuli be embedded in older knowledge structures; memory improves if a stimulus meets a congruent encoding context. An asymmetric mood congruency effect follows from the assumption that knowledge-based encoding is mood-sensitive and that this assimilative function increases under positive mood. Such an explanation is clearly different from accounts in terms of capacity restrictions or heuristic-judgment tendencies.

Capacity theories are devised to explain mood influences on effortful processing but have difficulty in explaining selective mood effects (mood-dependent congruency on demanding generation tasks). The degree of cognitive effort is rarely measured directly. A lack of cogent evidence for capacity constraints is also shown in the ironical fact that different authors postulate reduced capacity for positive mood (Mackie & Worth, 1989) and for negative mood (Ellis & Ashbrook, 1988). The rigidity of the capacity concept makes it impossible to explain disordinal interactions showing that the same mood states can either increase or decrease processing depth (Bless & Fiedler, 1995; Lassiter et al., 1996; Wegener et al., 1995).

On the other hand, heuristic-response approaches (Clore et al., 1994; Schwarz & Clore, 1988) were primarily developed for direct mood effects on social judgment and cognitive problem-solving styles. They are not readily applicable to mood-congruent memory and to involuntary, uncontrollable memory effects (e.g., priming) or flexible shifts of processing modes within the same constant mood (Forgas & Fiedler, 1996; Lassiter et al., 1996; Wegener et al., 1995).

Unlike heuristic approaches, the theory I present here explains mood congruency and mood effects on cognitive style in terms of genuine memory processes rather than mere response tendencies or heuristic strategies, such as the "How-do-I-feel-about-it?" heuristic, when judging a person or decision option. To be sure, this does not mean that such heuristic tools (see also Martin, Ward, Achee, & Wyer, 1993) may not sometimes influence judgments or decisions. However, if they do, these effects are simply of a different kind than the genuine, learning-based effects of assimilation versus accommodation on mood congruency and cognitive processing styles. Regarding the other pair of findings, creativity under positive mood and systematic processing under negative mood, my theory is compatible with challenging interactions. The flexibility, cooperation, and self-efficacy (Kavenagh & Bower, 1985) resulting from the assimilative processing mode under positive mood can explain that people differentiate or integrate depending on what is called for (Murray, Sujan, Hirt, & Sujan, 1990), stop or continue working depending on what the desired goal is (Martin et al., 1993), cooperate or compete in dilemma games (Hertel & Fiedler, 1994), and exhibit fairness or unfairness toward outgroups (Forgas & Fiedler, 1996).

At the same time, the assumption that negative mood facilitates conservative functions can explain the relative advantage of negative mood on many tasks that call for scrutiny and careful processing of stimulus input. Within this theory, these differential influences of positive and negative affective states are not assumed to be confined to strategic behaviors, hedonic self-regulation (Cialdini & Kenrick, 1976; Isen, 1984; Wegener et al., 1995), and heuristic guessing effects. Rather, they are supposed to reflect genuine memory effects and distinct internal adaption processes, referred to as assimilation and accommodation.

Other phenomena—such as mood repair (Isen, 1984) and motivated distortions (Wegener et al., 1995)—are simply outside the domain of this theory but not incompatible with it (see Forgas', 1994, affect-infusion model for an integrative account of a wider range of different effects). As I emphasized at the beginning of this chapter, no single theory can claim to explain everything.

REFERENCES

Bless, H., Clore, G. L., Schwarz, N., Golisano, V., Rabe, C., & Woelk, M. (1996). Mood and the use of scripts: Does happy mood make people really mindless? *Journal of Personality and Social Psychology, 71*, 665–679.

Bless, H., & Fiedler, K. (1995). Affective states and the influence of activated general knowledge structures. *Personality and Social Psychology Bulletin, 21*, 766–778.

Bodenhausen, G. V., Kramer, G. P., & Suesser, K. (1994). Happiness and stereotypic thinking in social judgment. *Journal of Personality and Social Psychology, 66*, 621–632.

Bower, G. H. (1981). Mood and memory. *American Psychologist, 36*, 129–148.

Bower, G. H., Monteiro, K. P., & Gilligan, S. G. (1978). Emotional mood as a context for learning and recall. *Journal of Verbal Learning and Verbal Behavior, 17*, 573–585.

Cialdini, R. B., & Kenrick, D. T. (1976). Altruism and hedonism: A social developmental perspective on the relationship of negative mood state and helping. *Journal of Personality and Social Psychology, 34*, 907–914.

Clark, M. S., & Fiske, S. T. (Eds.). (1982). *Affect and cognition*. Hillsdale, NJ: Lawrence Erlbaum Associates.

Clore, G. L., Schwarz, N., & Conway, M. (1994). Cognitive causes and consequences of emotion. In R. S. Wyer & T. K. Srull (Eds.), *Handbook of social cognition* (2nd ed., pp. 323–418). Hillsdale, NJ: Lawrence Erlbaum Associates.

Craik, F. I. M., & Tulving, E. (1975). Depth of processing and the retention of words in episodic memory. *Journal of Experimental Psychology: General, 104*, 268–294.

Ellis, H. C., & Ashbrook, P. W. (1988). Resource allocation model of the effects of depressed mood states on memory. In K. Fiedler & J. P. Forgas (Eds.), *Affect, cognition, and social behavior* (pp. 25–43). Toronto, Ontario, Canada: Hogrefe.

Fiedler, K. (1988). Emotional mood, cognitive style, and behavior regulation. In K. Fiedler & J. P. Forgas (Eds.), *Affect, cognition, and social behavior* (pp. 100–119). Toronto, Ontario, Canada: Hogrefe.

Fiedler, K. (1990). Mood-dependent selectivity in social cognition. In W. Stroebe & M. Hewstone (Eds.), *European Review of Social Psychology* (Vol. 1, pp. 1–32). New York: Wiley.

Fiedler, K. (1991). On the task, the measures, and the mood in research on affect and social cognition. In J. P. Forgas (Ed.), *Emotion and social judgments* (pp. 83–104). New York: Cambridge University Press.

Fiedler, K. (2000). Towards an integrative account of affect and cognition phenomena using the BIAS computer algorithm. In J. P. Forgas (Ed.), *Feeling and thinking: The role of affect in social cognition* (pp. 223–252). New York: Cambridge University Press.

Fiedler, K., Asbeck, J., & Nickel, S. (1991). Mood and constructive memeory effects on social judgment. *Cognition and Emotion, 5*, 363–378.

Fiedler, K., & Forgas, J. P. (Eds.) (1988). *Affect, cognition, and social behavior*. Toronto, Ontario, Canada: Hogrefe.

Fiedler, K., Lachnit, H., Fay, D., & Krug, C. (1992). Mobilization of cognitive resources and the generation effect. *Quarterly Journal of Experimental Psychology, 45A*, 149–171.

Fiedler, K., Nickel, S., Muehlfriedel, T., & Unkelbach, C. (2000). *Is mood congruency a matter of discrimination or response bias?* Unpublished manuscript, University of Heidelberg.

98 FIEDLER

Forgas, J. P. (1994). Mood and judgment: The affect infusion model (AIM). *Psychological Bulletin, 116,* 39–66.

Forgas, J. P., & Bower, G. H. (1987). Mood effects on person perception judgments. *Journal of Personality and Social Psychology, 53,* 53–60.

Forgas, J. P., & Fiedler, K. (1996). Mood effects on intergroup discrimination: The role of affect in reward allocation decisions. *Journal of Personality and Social Psychology, 70,* 28–40.

Hastie, R., & Park, B. (1986). The relationship between memory and judgment depends on whether the judgment task is memory-based or on-line. *Psychological Review, 93,* 258–268.

Hertel, G., & Fiedler, K. (1994). Affective and cognitive influences in a social dilemma game. *European Journal of Social Psychology, 24,* 131–145.

Isen, A. M. (1984). Toward understanding the role of affect in cognition. In R. S. Wyer & T. K. Srull (Eds.), *Handbook of social cognition* (2nd ed., Vol. 3, pp. 179–236). Hillsdale, NJ: Lawrence Erlbaum Associates.

Isen, A. M., Johnson, M. M. S., Mertz, E., & Robinson, G. (1985). The influence of positive affect on the unusualness of word association. *Journal of Personality and Social Psychology, 48,* 1413–1426.

Kashima, Y., & Kerekes, A. R. Z. (1994). A distributed memory model of averaging phenomena in person impression formation. *Journal of Experimental Social Psychology, 30,* 407–455.

Kavenagh, D. J., & Bower, G. H. (1985). Mood and self-efficacy: Impact of joy and sadness on perceived capabilities. *Cognitive Therapy and Research, 9,* 507–525.

Kruschke, J. K. (1992). ALCOVE: An exemplar-based connectionist model of category learning. *Psychological Review, 99,* 22–44.

Lassiter, G. D., Koenig, L. J., & Apple, K. J. (1996). Mood and behavior perception: Dysphoria can increase or decrease effortful processing of information. *Personality and Social Psychology Bulletin, 22,* 794–810.

Mackie, D. M., & Worth, L. T. (1989). Cognitive deficits and the mediation of positive affect in persuasion. *Journal of Personality and Social Psychology, 57,* 27–40.

Martin, L. M., Ward, D. W., Achee, J. W., & Wyer, R. S. (1993). Mood as input: People have to interpret the motivational implications of their moods. *Journal of Personality and Social Psychology, 64,* 317–326.

Mayer, J. D., & Salovey, P. (1988). Personality moderates the interaction of mood and cognition. In K. Fiedler & J. P. Forgas (Eds.), *Affect, cognition, and social behavior* (pp. 87–99). Toronto, Ontario, Canada: Hogrefe.

Murray, N., Sujan, H., Hirt, E. R., & Sujan, M. (1990). The influence of mood on categorization: A cognitive flexibility interpretation. *Journal of Personality and Social Psychology, 59,* 411–425.

Piaget, J. (1952). *The origins of intelligence in children.* New York: International Universities Press.

Schwarz, N. (1990). Feelings as information: Informational and motivational functions of affective states. In R. M. Sorrentino & E. T. Higgins (Eds.), *Handbook of motivation and cognition: Foundations of social behavior* (Vol. 2, pp. 527–561). New York: Guilford.

Schwarz, N., & Clore, G. L. (1988). How do I feel about it? The informative function of affective states. In K. Fiedler & J. P. Forgas (Eds.), *Affect, cognition, and social behavior* (pp. 44–62). Toronto, Ontario, Canada: Hogrefe.

Slamecka, N. J., & Graf, P. (1978). The generation effect: Delineation of a phenomenon. *Journal of Experimental Psychology: Learning, Memory and Cognition, 4,* 592–604.

Tulving, E., Thompson, D. N. (1973). Encoding specificity and retrieval processes in episodic memory. *Psychological Review, 80,* 352–373.

Wegener, D. T., Petty, R. E., & Smith, S. S. (1995). Positive mood can increase or decrease message scrutiny: The hedonic contingency view of mood and message processing. *Journal of Personality and Social Psychology, 69,* 5–15.

Chapter 5

The Affect Infusion Model (AIM): An Integrative Theory of Mood Effects on Cognition and Judgments

Joseph P. Forgas
University of New South Wales

Research on affect and social cognition has been one of the most active areas of exploration in psychology during the 1980s and the 1990s (Forgas, 2000). This interest started with the discovery, documentation, and theoretical explanation of affect congruence phenomena is the early 1980s. The associative network model (Bower, 1981) provided perhaps the first truly integrative theoretical treatment of these effects. However, by the mid-1980s there was a clear recognition that affect congruence in cognition and judgments is a context-dependent phenomenon, and several competing theoretical explanations for affect congruence or its absence in cognition were proposed. By the late 1980s, the information-processing consequences of affective states also received growing attention. The third period, still continuing today, is marked by the emergence of integrative theoretical models seeking to account for both the informational and processing consequences of affect and for both affect congruence and incongruence within a comprehensive framework.

The Affect Infusion Model (AIM) to be discussed here is such a third-generation theory. The AIM was developed as a comprehensive, integrative theory seeking to explain both the presence and the absence of affect infusion into cognition and taking account of both the informational and the processing consequences of affect for social thinking. The AIM argues that people's tendency to adopt different processing strategies in response to different contextual requirements is the key to understanding why affect infusion sometimes occurs and sometimes does not. The existing literature offers strong evidence for affect-congruency in cognition and judgments; however, there are also numerous studies that either reveal no effects or show an opposite affect-incongruent pattern. I argue here that the commonly reported effects of mood-congruency, mood-incongruency, and no mood effects are not necessarily incompatible.

Rather, these findings can be reconciled within a single theoretical framework, if we make the reasonable assumptions that (a) situational and contextual variables do have a significant impact on how people approach a social cognitive task and (b) the adoption of different processing strategies plays a crucial role in mediating different mood effects. Specifying the circumstances under which congruency, incongruency, or no effects should occur is one major objective of the AIM. The AIM also links the dual, informational, and processing consequences of affect on cognition and judgments within an integrated framework. Informational effects occur because affect may influence the content of cognition (what people think). Processing effects occur because affect also has an impact on the process of cognition (how people think).

The AIM assumes that affective states, although distinct from cognitive processes, do interact with and inform cognition and judgments through influencing processing strategies, as well as the availability of cognitive constructs used in the constructive processing of information. This interactionist view is based on functionalist definitions of affect that characterize most contemporary affect–cognition theorizing (cf. Bower, 1991; Forgas, 2000; Frijda, 1988; Isen, 1987; Salovey & Mayer, 1990) and assumes that "the experience of an emotion *is* a cognition" (Laird & Bresler, 1991, p. 24).

The main objective of the model is thus to offer a systematic framework within which the interaction between different processing strategies and ensuing mood effects or their absence can be understood. The AIM then seeks to provide answers to a variety of intriguing questions recently posed in the literature, such as: What is the reason for the apparent context sensitivity of many mood effects on cognition? What sorts of processing strategies are most likely to be influenced by affect? How can we reconcile the informational and processing consequences of affect? Thinking about what kinds of tasks are most and least likely to be open to affective distortions? What is the role of affect in the processing of complex or otherwise problematic information? Is more prolonged, systematic processing more or less likely to be subject to affect infusion? The model can also deal with some intriguing and nonobvious results, such as recent evidence that more prolonged and extensive processing often increases, rather than decreases, the degree of affect infusion (Fiedler, 1991; Forgas, 1992b, 1992c, 1993, 1994, 1998a, 1998b).

THE AFFECT INFUSION MODEL (AIM)

Affect infusion will be defined here as the process whereby affectively loaded information exerts an influence on, and becomes incorporated into, cognitive and judgmental processes, entering into a person's deliberations and eventually coloring the outcome. The AIM predicts that affect infusion is most likely to occur in the course of constructive processing that involves the substantial transformation rather than the mere reproduction of existing cognitive representations, requiring a relatively open information search strategy and a significant degree of generative elaboration of the available stimulus details (Fiedler, 1991).

By postulating multiple processing strategies to mediate mood effects, the AIM represents a further stage in the recent development of social cognition theories, going beyond existing dual-process formulations. The model involves two major assumptions. The assumption of process mediation implies that affect infusion is conditional on the kind of processing strategy adopted by a person and is most likely to occur in conditions that recruit more constructive and generative rather than predetermined processing strategies (Fiedler, 1991; Forgas, 1992a). A taxonomy of processing strategies and the circumstances leading to their adoption is thus a major component of the model. This is in marked contrast to the "single process" assumptions of many traditional information-processing models that emphasize robust, universal, and relatively context-insensitive cognitive mechanisms. The second assumption of the AIM is that people are effort-minimizing information processors who adopt the simplest and least effortful processing strategy as long as it satisfies the minimal contextual requirements.

The Four Processing Strategies

What are the various strategies a person might employ to solve a social cognitive task, and what determines their use? The AIM proposes a distinction between four basic cognitive strategies: direct access, motivated, heuristic, and substantive processing. The theory predicts that the direct access and motivated processing strategies involve relatively closed, directed information search processes, limiting the opportunity for incidental affect infusion. In contrast, heuristic and substantive processing are more open-ended and constructive strategies, allowing greater scope for affect infusion to occur.

The Direct Access Strategy. The direct access strategy is the simplest method of responding, based on the direct retrieval of preexisting stored information. The assumption of effort minimization suggests that people should use this strategy whenever possible, drawing on their repertoire of crystallized, preformed responses rather than computing an online response. Direct access processing is most likely when the target is familiar and has prototypical features that cue an available response, when personal involvement is low, and when no contextual forces mandate more elaborate processing. This is clearly a low-affect-infusion strategy, because it involves little or no constructive elaboration. The strongly cued retrieval of an already stored response should thus be quite robust and resistant to affective distortions (Fiedler, 1991). Although direct access processing should be impervious to current mood, responses may of course contain stored affective components. It is interesting that this simple and common strategy is largely ignored in theories of social cognition. However, several studies do report an absence of affect infusion precisely in conditions in which, according to the AIM, a direct access strategy should be used (Salovey & Birnbaum, 1989, Exp. 3; Sedikides, 1995; Srull, 1983, 1984).

The Motivated Processing Strategy. The motivated processing strategy is characterized by strong and specific motivational pressures for a particular outcome to be achieved. In these circumstances, people are likely to engage in highly selective, guided, and targeted information search strategies to support a motivational objective. Motivated processing is thus also a low-infusion judgmental strategy, because little open and constructive information search occurs. Emotions, replete with cognitive content and appraisal qualities, may often trigger motivated processing (Berkowitz, 1993). The motivational consequences of moods tend to be more subtle and indirect (Martin, Ward, Achee, & Wyer, 1993). However, motivated processing may often be used to achieve mood maintenance as well as mood repair (Clark & Isen, 1982; Erber & Erber, 1994). It seems that merely directing participants' attention to their affective states is often sufficient to trigger deliberate, motivated strategies and has the paradoxical effect of reducing rather than enhancing affect infusion (Berkowitz, 1993). Similarly, we found that affect infusion is also constrained when people are motivated to achieve a rewarding outcome in their affiliative choices (Forgas, 1989, 1991b).

Motivated processing as understood here involves more than just a generic motivation to be careful and accurate or to avoid cognitive effort. Rather, it assumes the imposition of a specific, preexisting preference to guide information search and processing. There are numerous specific goals that have been found to direct this kind of processing, such as mood repair and mood maintenance, self-evaluation maintenance, ego enhancement, achievement motivation, affiliation, and the like. Some enduring personality differences also predispose people to adopt motivated processing leading to the reduction of affect infusion (Ciarrochi & Forgas,

1999, in press; Forgas, 1998a; Rusting, 1998). Despite the obviously motivated character of many social cognitive tasks, the precise processing consequences of this kind of thinking have received insufficient attention so far. Because many experimental studies employ artificial and uninvolving tasks, motivated processing is also rarely demonstrated in the literature. There are several studies that show an absence of priming effects (including affect-priming effects) under conditions that are conducive to motivated processing, such as high level of awareness about the primed material when attention is directed to the mood state in tasks requiring deliberate processing or when participants compensate for unbalanced information by "resetting" the input array (Erber & Erber, 1994; Forgas, 1991b; Forgas & Fiedler, 1996; Martin, 1986). Normative pressures arising in a group interaction may also lead to motivated processing and the elimination of affect infusion (Forgas, 1990). Affect itself may be crucial in triggering motivated processing (Fig. 5.2), as people engage in targeted information search and retrieval to alleviate dysphoria (Forgas, 1989; Forgas, 1991b).

The Heuristic Processing Strategy. When people have neither a stored evaluation nor a strong motivational goal to rely on, they often seek to compute a response with the least amount of effort, considering only a limited range of information and using whatever shortcuts or simplifications are readily available. Such a heuristic processing strategy has been identified in several domains of social cognition research in recent years (Brewer, 1988; Petty, Gleicher, & Baker, 1991). In terms of the AIM, heuristic processing is most likely when the target is simple or highly typical, there are no specific motivational objectives, when the judge has limited cognitive capacity and is in a positive mood, and when the situation does not demand accuracy or detailed consideration. Several past studies created conditions consistent with these assumptions. Thus judgments may be based on irrelevant associations with environmental variables (Griffitt, 1970), or respondents may simply infer a judgment from their prevailing affective state (cf. Clore & Parrott, 1991; Schwarz & Clore, 1988).

The affect-as-information account appears to be the primary mechanism for affect infusion under heuristic processing. The view that affect may have a direct, immediate influence on thinking and judgments was first suggested by conditioning theories (Clore & Byrne, 1974). In an elaboration of this idea, the recent affect-as-information model suggests that

> rather than computing a judgment on the basis of recalled features of a target, individuals may . . . ask themselves: "How do I feel about it?" [and] in doing so, they may mistake feelings due to a preexisting state as a reaction to the target. (Schwarz, 1990, p. 529)

Thus affect can only function as a heuristic cue due to mistaken inferences, suggesting that heuristic processing that relies on affect is an ineffective and dysfunctional strategy most likely to be adopted when judges lack the involvement, motivation, or capacity to engage in more substantive processing. Although heuristic processing can account for some affect-infusion effects, it has difficulty explaining mood effects on judgments that are produced as a result of more elaborate and generative processing.

The Substantive Processing Strategy. The most demanding strategy for producing a judgment requires judges to select, learn, and interpret novel information about a target and to relate this information to preexisting knowledge structures. We may call this the *substantive processing strategy.* Substantive processing is more likely when the task is complex or atypical, when the judge has no specific motivation to pursue and has adequate cognitive capacity, and when there are explicit or implicit situational demands for more elaborate processing. In terms of the AIM, substantive processing is adopted only when simpler and less effortful processing strategies prove inadequate to the judgmental task. Because substantive processing involves the use of a preexisting representational system to interpret and assimilate novel information, it is most commonly analyzed in terms of memory principles in recent social cognition research (Bower, 1991).

Affect priming offers a parsimonious mechanism to explain affect infusion during substantive processing. Because social cognition and judgments are fundamentally constructive, the ideas, memories, and interpretations of the judge are of prime importance in determining how complex and often ambiguous social stimuli are perceived, learned, and interpreted. The affect-priming principle suggests that affect can indirectly inform social judgments through facilitating access to related cognitive categories (Bower, 1981; Isen, 1987), as "activation of an emotion node also spreads activation throughout the memory structures to which it is connected" (Bower, 1981, p. 135). According to the AIM, affect-priming can influence selective attention, encoding, associations, and retrieval processes during substantive processing (Bower, 1991; Forgas, 1992a). Further, the AIM suggests that affect infusion should be greater the more extensive and constructive the processing strategy used, a counterintuitive prediction that has received empirical support in recent years (Fiedler, 1991; Forgas, 1992b, 1993, 1994).

As predicted by the AIM, there is strong evidence for affect infusion in many social cognitive tasks that require substantive processing. Affect may thus influence the outcome of simple behavior interpretation tasks (Forgas, Bower, & Krantz, 1984), person perception judgments (Baron, 1987; Forgas, 1992b; Forgas & Bower, 1987), perceptions of health and illness (Salovey & Birnbaum, 1989), reactions to persuasive messages (Petty et al., 1991), and the planning and performance of strategic social behaviors (Forgas, 1998a, 1998b, 1999a, 1999b). Similar results were obtained in studies of mood effects on stereotype judgments, showing greater mood effects linked to more constructive, extensive processing, "consistent with the affect-priming explanation" (Haddock, Zanna, & Esses, 1994, p. 203). In the course of substantive processing, affect may also influence the processing of nonevaluative judgments, such as causal inferences, where the "how do I feel about it" heuristic is unlikely to be relevant (Forgas, Bower, & Moylan, 1990). Greater mood effects on judgments about self versus others may also be explained in terms of the AIM as due to the greater complexity and more extensive processing received by self-referent information (Forgas et al., 1984). Consistent with the AIM model, Sedikides (1995) predicted and found that highly consolidated, central self-conceptions were processed using the direct access strategy and showed no mood effects, whereas peripheral self-conceptions that required more elaborate, substantive processing were influenced by an affect-priming effect.

Evidence from Processing Latency Data. Given the strong prediction of process mediation by the model, the analysis of processing latency and memory data is of particular importance (Forgas & Bower, 1987). Consistent with the AIM, during substantive processing people do take longer to process and encode mood-congruent information but are faster in producing a mood-congruent judgment (Forgas & Bower, 1987, Fig. 3). An important and counterintuitive implication of the AIM is that the longer and more extensively a person needs to think to compute a response, the more likely that affect infusion should occur due to the operation of the affect-priming mechanism. Atypical, unusual, or complex tasks should selectively recruit longer and more substantive processing strategies and correspondingly greater affect infusion effects. This has been confirmed in several recent studies using more or less complex people (Forgas, 1992b, 1992c), relationships (Forgas, 1993; Forgas, Levinger, & Moylan, 1994; Forgas & Moylan, 1991), and conflict episodes (Forgas, 1994) as stimuli. Mood effects on perceptions of real-life intimate relationships and explanations for more or less serious interpersonal conflicts (Forgas, 1994) showed a similar pattern: Greater mood effects were consistently associated with longer processing times, a pattern uniquely predicted by the AIM.

Variables Determining Processing Choices

Because different kinds of processing strategies imply different kinds of affect infusion effects, the variables determining processing choices are an integral part of the model (see Figs. 5.1 and 5.2). According to the AIM,

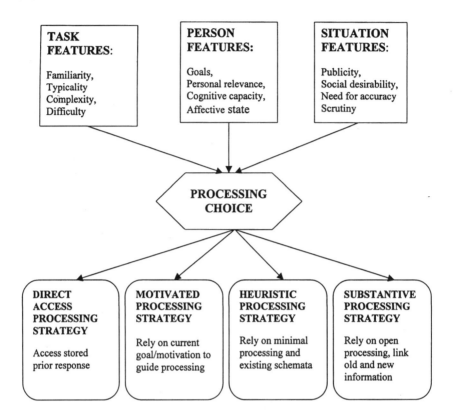

FIG. 5.1. Outline of the multiprocess Affect Infusion Model (AIM). Affect infusion in social judgments depends on which of four alternative processing strategies is adopted in response to target, judge, and situational features—direct access and motivated processing are low-infusion strategies with little mood congruence in judgments, whereas heuristic and substantive processing are high-infusion strategies with marked mood congruence in judgments.

processing choices are determined by three sets of variables, associated with the target, the judge, and the judgmental situation, respectively (cf. Forgas, 1992a). Familiarity, typicality, and complexity are the main target features of interest. Judge features include personal relevance, motivational goals, cognitive capacity, and affective state. Finally, pragmatic situational features such as perceived need for accuracy, social desirability expectations,

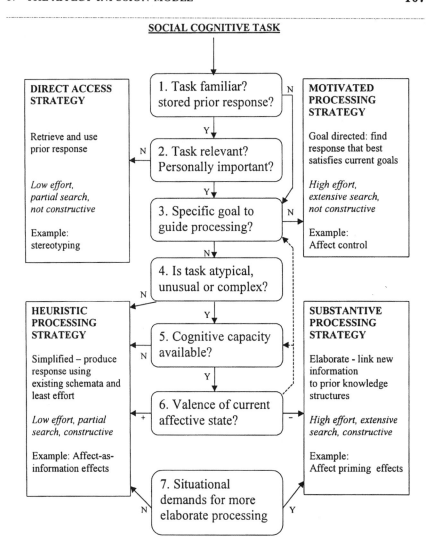

FIG. 5.2.   A flowchart illustrating the hierarchical relationship between various factors that determine processing choices and the multiple informational and processing effects of affect on judgments.

and the availability of objective criteria may also influence processing choices. The role of these predictor variables in processing choices is schematically depicted in Fig. 5.1, whereas Fig. 5.2 presents in a flowchart form the predicted hierarchical relationship between these variables. Several testable predictions may be derived from this general model.

Target Familiarity. When a target is highly familiar and the judgment has low personal relevance, a direct access strategy should be used unless further processing is recruited by other variables. Familiarity is used here not merely to denote a prior exposure to a stimulus but also to mean that the judge already possesses detailed and extensive information about the target. Consistent with the AIM, Srull (1983, 1984) found that affect had no influence on evaluations of familiar products that could be processed using a direct access strategy, yet judgments of unfamiliar products did show affect infusion. However, even highly familiar targets, such as intimate partners, may be processed substantively and show affect infusion when personal relevance is high (Forgas et al., 1994).

Target Complexity and Typicality. Targets that are more complex, atypical, or unusual should recruit more extensive processing strategies, increasing the scope of affect infusion during substantive processing. In contrast, typical, simple, and usual targets are more likely to be processed heuristically (assuming lack of familiarity and lack of specific motivation that may otherwise lead to direct access or motivated processing). Supporting this prediction, several recent studies found greater affect infusion when participants needed more time to judge complex, atypical, or otherwise demanding targets (Forgas, 1992b, 1992c, 1993, 1994).

Personal Relevance. All things being equal, judgments that are personally relevant are more likely to be processed substantively (if no prior motivation is present) or by the motivated processing strategy (if prior motivation does exist). Lack of personal relevance in turn should recruit direct access processing. There is ample evidence that even simple manipulations of personal relevance can result in quite profound changes in processing strategies (Brewer, 1988; Forgas & Fiedler, 1996). Recent studies showed for example that the combination of high personal relevance and sad mood leads to the selective adoption of a motivated, mood repair processing strategy (Forgas, 1989, 1991b).

Specific Motivation. When a person is influenced by a strong, preexisting motivation, little open and constructive processing is employed in interpreting the actual features of the target, limiting the scope for affect infusion. Affect itself, and negative affect in particular, may have strong motivational properties (e.g., mood repair), probably accounting for the more volatile affect infusion effects often associated with negative rather than positive moods (Forgas et al., 1984; Forgas & Bower, 1987). Motivated processing can not only eliminate affect infusion but can also produce mood-incongruent outcomes (Erber & Erber, 1994).

Cognitive Capacity. The cognitive capacity of the judge plays an important role in processing choices, with heuristic rather than substantive processing more likely when processing capacity is in some way impaired (Mackie & Worth, 1991). When judges suffer from information overload, need to pay attention to multiple inputs, are put under time pressure or are in other ways impaired, they typically adopt simplified, heuristic processing (Mackie & Worth, 1991).

Individual Differences. There is growing evidence that there are enduring differences between people in the ways they tend to approach a cognitive task, and many of these differences in habitual processing style are related to traditional personality measures (Rusting, 1998). We found recently that people who score high on personality measures such as social desirability or Machiavellianism are more likely to adopt a targeted, motivated processing strategy when planning and executing a bargaining encounter (Forgas, 1998a). As a result they show significantly less affect infusion in their thoughts, plans, and eventual negotiating strategies. In a similar way, people who score high on trait anxiety tend to use more motivated processing and to show reduced affect infusion in intergroup judgments (Ciarrochi & Forgas, 1999). In contrast, those who score high on Openness to Feelings were found to show significantly greater affect infusion in consumer judgments than do low scorers (Ciarrochi & Forgas, in press). The point is that individual differences are often related to habitual preferences in processing styles. High scorers on measures such as social desirability, anxiety, Machiavellianism, and the like are more inclined to adopt motivated thinking in social cognitive tasks and to show reduced affect infusion, according to the AIM.

Affect and Processing Choices. An important feature of the multiprocess judgmental model is the recognition that affect itself can play a dual processing and informational role in judgments, influencing both the processing choices judges make (how they think) and the kind of information they subsequently consider (what they think). Consistent with other models, the AIM also predicts that positive moods typically generate more superficial and heuristic and less systematic processing strategies, whereas negative moods trigger more vigilant, effortful processing styles.

The AIM recognizes that multiple mechanisms may produce this processing asymmetry. Capacity explanations suggest that less systematic processing in positive mood is due to the good mood taking up scarce processing capacity, reducing people's ability to deal with other information systematically (Mackie & Worth, 1991), although this explanation has been challenged by some recent findings (Bless, 2000, chapter 1, this volume). Functional, evolutionary accounts suggest that positive moods reduce processing effort because they signal a safe and unproblematic situation, whereas negative moods trigger more vigilant processing because they signal problematic situations requiring careful monitoring (Schwarz, 1990). Finally, motivational explanations suggest that people in a good mood process heuristically in order to safeguard their pleasant affective state by avoiding excessive effort (mood maintenance), whereas people in a negative mood process systematically in order to improve their mood (mood repair; Clark & Isen, 1982). More recent theories suggest that mood does not necessarily influence processing effort; rather, positive moods facilitate the use of general knowledge structures (Bless, 2000, chapter 1, this volume) and reliance on top-down, assimilative thinking styles (Fiedler, 2000). For the purposes of the AIM it is not necessary to clearly separate these alternative mechanisms that all produce processing asymmetry. Indeed, it may well be that several of these mechanisms operate in a parallel fashion in producing processing differences in good or bad moods.

Unlike in other affect–cognition theories, different processing strategies are central to the predictions of the AIM. The AIM clearly suggests that the processing consequences of good or bad moods are secondary to the processing requirements associated with target and judge features (see Fig. 5.2). Several experiments now confirm that more complex, demanding, or ambiguous targets do recruit more extensive, systematic processing by both happy and sad people, consistent with the subsidiary role of affect in the determination of processing strategies (Forgas, 1992b, 1993, 1995b).

Situational Pragmatics. Given the complex pragmatics of social situations, the judgmental context itself can also impose explicit and implicit processing demands (Forgas, 1981, 1982). Different situations call for different standards of accuracy, impose different expectations and social desirability pressures, and imply varying levels of scrutiny and publicity. For example, judgments that are made publicly, that are likely to be scrutinized and evaluated by others, or that are made to high-status others should elicit either motivated or substantive processing strategies.

Of course, these predictor variables may interact in determining processing choices. The processing effects of factors such as familiarity, complexity, typicality, and specific motivation are often straightforward and relatively robust, as suggested by recent empirical results. However, the processing consequences of affect are often indirect (Martin et al., 1993) and may operate through influencing other factors such as cognitive capacity or specific motivation, as shown in Fig. 5.2. The hierarchical sequence depicted in Fig. 5.2, although generally supported by the evidence so far, also need not be invariable.

Several of the variables may recruit either heuristic or substantive processing, with affect infusion predicted under either processing outcome (Fig. 5.2). For example, in the absence of familiarity and specific motivation, some degree of constructive processing is necessary. Depending on the availability of cognitive resources and situational requirements, mood congruence may then occur as a result of either substantive processing and affect-priming effects or of heuristic processing and affect-as-information effects. Because the prediction is mood congruence in both cases, does this make the model unfalsifiable? The answer is no, because heuristic or substantive processing can in fact be empirically distinguished through the analysis of memory, exposure latency, and processing latency data, making the specific predictions derivable from the AIM empirically testable.

HOW THE AIM DEALS WITH THE FOUR MOST TYPICAL FINDINGS IN THE FIELD

The model predicts the absence of affect infusion under conditions of direct access or motivated processing and the presence of affect infusion during heuristic and substantive processing. The AIM places particular emphasis on the need to measure processing variables (encoding and judgmental latencies, memory data) in order to distinguish between different processing mechanisms. Thus one fundamental difference between the AIM and other theories is its emphasis on processing differences and on the need to assess processing variables to determine what kinds of mechanisms produced a particular outcome. This section surveys the theoretical explanations offered by the AIM for some of the major empirical findings produced by the affect–cognition literature.

Mood-Congruent Memory

The model assumes that mood-congruent memory effects are most likely to occur in the course of substantive processing and are largely due to the operation of affect-priming mechanisms. The AIM also predicts that these memory effects should become weak or unreliable whenever conditions do not favor constructive, substantive processing. There are two major avenues by which mood-congruent memory effects occur, according to the AIM.

Mood-State-Dependent Retrieval. The AIM, consistent with affect-priming principles, also suggests that memory should be better whenever retrieval mood matches encoding mood, as implied by Tulving's encoding specificity principle. Numerous studies found that memory for word lists, autobiographical memories, and other information is better when recall mood matches encoding mood (Bower, 1981, 1991). Depressed people show a similar pattern, preferentially remembering aversive childhood experiences, a memory bias that disappears once depression is brought under control (Lewinsohn & Rosenbaum, 1987). Despite promising early results, mood-state-dependent retrieval effects proved to be rather volatile in impoverished contexts such as standard word-learning memory tasks (Blaney, 1986; Eich & Macauley, 2000).

Problems of obtaining reliable mood-state-dependent memory effects were variously explained as due to the lack of sufficiently intense mood manipulations, the lack of causal belonging between mood induction and the experimental task (Bower, 1991; Eich & Macauley, 2000), and the fact that mood-priming may be difficult to obtain in conditions that are "antithetical to self-referencing" (Blaney, 1986, p. 232). The AIM suggests a simpler and more parsimonious explanation: These problems seem to be confined to standard memory tasks, in which people try to learn and recall relatively meaningless word lists, a task that requires relatively little substantive, generative processing. In studies of person perception, impression formation, or similarly complex and demanding tasks, mood-state-dependent retrieval has been a very reliable phenomenon (cf. Bower, 1991; Fiedler & Forgas, 1988; Forgas, 1991a). These tasks require more extensive and substantive processing strategies and provide people with a richer and more elaborate set of encoding and retrieval cues, allowing mood to function more effectively as a relevant differentiating context (Bower, 1981; see Neisser, 1982, for a related argument). Similar conclusions were reached by Eich (1995; Eich & Macauley, 2000), who concluded that mood-dependent retrieval is a robust effect that best appears when constructive processing is required, when the moods induced are strong, when free recall rather than recognition is called for, and when the memories are self-generated rather than externally imposed.

Mood-Congruent Retrieval. Mood-congruent retrieval is a second mechanism that can explain mood-congruent memory effects during substantive processing, according to the AIM. This occurs when affective state facilitates the recall of affectively congruent material from memory. For example, depressed or anxious people selectively recall negative, unpleasant memories, whereas nondepressed individuals show the opposite pattern (Burke & Mathews, 1992; Lloyd & Lishman, 1975). Some of these studies may, however, confound mood-state-dependent retrieval with mood-congruent retrieval effects. A more convincing demonstration of mood-congruent retrieval due to affect-priming requires that participants experience no specific affect during encoding, yet they still show better retrieval for information that is consistent with the retrieval mood later on. Such results were obtained in several studies using implicit memory tasks such as word completion, stem completion, lexical decision, and sentence completion, which showed strong evidence for mood-congruent memory effects (Niedenthal & Showers, 1991; Ruiz-Caballero & Gonzalez, 1994).

As these effects occurred in conditions that should require substantive-processing strategies for a response to be computed, these results are also consistent with the AIM.

In terms of the AIM, then, affect-priming mechanisms provide a parsimonious and well-supported explanation for a wide variety of mood-congruent memory effects in the course of substantive processing. However, the AIM also predicts that these mood-congruent memory effects should be highly process-sensitive, occurring only in circumstances that are conducive to open, constructive information processing that allows the generative use of previously stored and affectively primed information. The AIM thus goes beyond affect-priming explanations by seeking to clearly define the boundary conditions for mood-congruent memory outcomes.

Mood-Congruent Judgments

The AIM predicts that mood-congruent judgments can be produced either as a result of affect-priming mechanisms in the course of substantive processing or as a result of affect-as-information mechanisms in the course of heuristic processing. Most of the research relevant to the AIM so far suggests that affect priming is the major mechanism responsible for mood-congruent judgmental effects (Forgas, 1994, 1995a; Mayer, Gaschke, Braverman, & Evans, 1992; Salovey & Birnbaum, 1989; Sedikides, 1995). However, mood congruence arising from the direct use by individuals of their affective states as information can also occur, mostly in situations in which people need to produce simple, personally uninvolving and superficial judgments in circumstances in which processing resources are impaired. As more than one processing strategy can lead to mood-congruent judgments, the AIM highlights the critical need to measure processing variables such as encoding latency, judgmental latency, and recall performance in order to determine whether heuristic or substantive processing produced a particular mood-congruent outcome.

Mood-Congruent Judgments During Substantive Processing. The AIM predicts that in circumstances in which substantive processing is required, affect-priming mechanisms should result in people paying selective attention to mood-congruent information, learning such details better, forming more mood-congruent associations, and remembering more mood-congruent material. The net result of these processes is mood congruence in judgments. In complex cognitive tasks such as social judgments people often experience information overload and tend to pay selective attention to mood-congruent information (Niedenthal & Showers, 1991). Several experiments show that as a result of the selective priming and greater availability of a mood-congruent associative base, people spend longer reading affect-congruent information, process such material more deeply, and as a result recall and use such details more extensively in constructing their judgments (Bower, 1981; Forgas, 1992b; Forgas & Bower, 1987). These effects occur because concepts, words, themes, and rules of inference that are associated with an affective state will become primed and highly available for use in top-down or expectation-driven processing, functioning as interpretive filters of reality (Bower, 1991).

In addition to its effects on information selectivity, mood also impacts on associations. Judgments require people to "go beyond the information given," and it is in the course of such constructive, elaborative processing that they are most likely to use primed associations and inferences to construct a response. In terms of the AIM, mood-congruent judgment is partly the result of the greater availability of mood-congruent ideas and associations when evaluating a target, which can influence the top-down, constructive interpretation of complex or ambiguous details (Bower, 1981, 1991). For example, in producing associations to an ambiguous word such as *life*, happy participants generate more positive associations (love, freedom), whereas sad participants think of such words as *struggle* and *death* (Bower, 1981). Similar effects occur when emotional participants daydream or produce associations to Thematic Apperception Test (TAT) pictures (Bower, 1981). These associative mood effects will also produce mood congruence in judgments in many real-life situations due to naturally occurring moods (Mayer et al., 1992).

Mood-primed associations can also play a role in clinical states. Anxious people tend to interpret spoken homophones such as *pane/pain* or *die/dye* in the more anxious, negative direction (Eysenck, MacLeod, & Mathews, 1987), consistent with the greater activation these affect-consistent concepts received. Associative mood effects can have a marked impact on many social judgments, such as perceptions of human faces, impressions about people (Forgas et al., 1984; Forgas & Bower, 1987), self-perceptions (Sedikides, 1995), and attributions (Forgas, 1994; Forgas et al., 1990). Several recent experiments provide specific evidence for the process mediation of these effects, as predicted by the AIM. For example, mood-congruent judgmental effects tend to be diminished as the targets to be judged become more clear-cut and thus require less constructive processing (Forgas, 1994, 1995b).

The Links Between Processing Strategy and Mood-Congruent Judgments. The AIM specifically predicts that mood congruence in judgments should be highly process-dependent, with more extensive, substantive processing producing greater affect infusion. Several studies measuring processing variables have provided evidence for this prediction. In one of the first investigations of mood effects on person perception judgments (Forgas & Bower, 1987), strong mood congruence in memory and judgments was found. As suggested by the AIM, participants were also slower in processing and encoding mood-congruent rather than mood-incongruent information into a richer activated associative base. In contrast, they were faster in producing mood-congruent rather than -incongruent judgments (Fig. 5.3). These results were among the first in which reaction-time data confirmed a direct link between the extended encoding of mood-congruent information and greater subsequent mood congruity in judgments as suggested by the AIM.

Unlike other models, the AIM does make the counterintuitive prediction that more complex or demanding cognitive tasks that require more extensive, substantive processing should also produce greater affect infusion effects. Several recent experiments support this prediction. In these studies, participants induced to feel happy or sad were asked to encode and later to recall and evaluate more or less typical other people (the "strange people" experiments; Forgas, 1992b, 1992c), to form impressions about more or less well-matched heterosexual couples (the "odd couples" experiments; Forgas, 1993, 1995b; Forgas & Moylan, 1991; Forgas et al., 1994), and to explain more or less serious interpersonal conflicts in their current intimate relationships (the "sad and guilty" experiments;

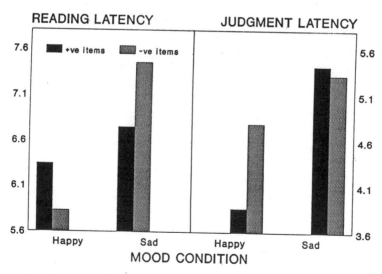

FIG. 5.3. Mood effects on processing latencies: time taken in seconds to read a positive or a negative item and to make a positive or a negative judgment by people in happy or sad moods. (Based on data from Forgas & Bower, 1987.)

Forgas, 1994). In the "strange people" experiments, happy, sad, or control participants read about, and formed impressions of, people who were either highly prototypical, highly atypical, or intermediate in prototypicality (Forgas, 1992b, Exp. 1). Judgments showed a clear mood-congruent bias, and these mood effects were significantly greater when the targets were atypical rather than prototypical. Consistent with the AIM, follow-up experiments found a direct link between affect infusion and processing latencies. Participants took longer to encode and judge atypical than typical targets and remembered such targets better, and it was these more substantively processed judgments that were also most influenced by affect (Forgas, 1992b, Exp. 3).

In order to control for the possibility of semantic-priming confounds, other experiments used pictures of well-matched or poorly matched couples as stimuli (Forgas, 1993, 1995b). Once again, results supported the AIM, indicating greater affect infusion into judgments about unusual, mismatched couples than well-matched couples. This effect was replicated using mixed-race rather than same-race dyads as targets (Forgas & Moylan, 1991). In another study that simultaneously manipulated physical attractiveness and race to create fully matched, partially matched, or mismatched couples, we found that the size of mood effects on judgments increased directly with the degree of visible mismatch between the partners (Forgas, 1995b, Exp. 3; see Fig. 5.4). Memory and processing latency data confirmed that greater mood effects consistently occurred because of the more extensive and prolonged processing recruited by these problematic, "odd" couples (Forgas, 1995b, Exp. 4). A path analysis also showed that processing strategy (as measured by encoding latency and latency of judgment) was a significant mediator of mood-congruency effects on memory and judgments. These experiments thus specifically support the AIM by showing that unusual targets recruit more substantive processing, take longer to encode, and are better remembered than more common ones and that judgments about these targets are significantly more mood congruent.

Would these counterintuitive findings also occur in more realistic, real-life judgments? The AIM suggests that as long as substantive processing is adopted, the answer should be yes. This prediction was supported in a series of experiments that examined the influence of mood on judgments and attributions about real-life intimate relationships (Forgas, 1994; Forgas et al., 1994). Mood had a significant influence on evaluations of intimate partners and relationships, and these effects were even more powerful in well-established, long-term relationships than in short-term, superficial liaisons. In terms of the AIM, personal relationships—and long-term relationships in particular—provide couples with a particularly rich and elaborate set of both positive and negative experiences, increas-

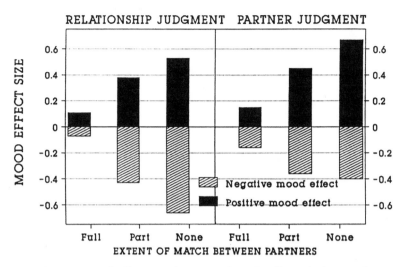

FIG. 5.4. Mood effects on the perception of well-matched, partially matched, and badly matched couples. The size of the mood effect on judgments of the relationship and judgments of the partners is proportional to the degree of mismatch between the couples. (Based on data from Forgas, 1995b).

ing the likelihood that temporary mood can selectively trigger the retrieval and use of mood-congruent evidence when formulating a relationship judgment. Our findings are also consistent with other evidence from the relationship literature suggesting that the same relationship can sometimes be seen as almost perfect and at other times as highly problematic following relatively minor changes in affect or other situational circumstances.

In other studies, specific explanations for different kinds of relationship conflicts also showed a strong mood-congruent pattern (Forgas, 1994, Exp. 1). Consistent with the affect-priming hypothesis, more self-deprecatory attributions were made by sad than by happy participants. In a nonobvious pattern, these mood effects were significantly stronger on attributions for serious, complex conflicts rather than simple, undemanding conflicts (Forgas, 1994, Exp. 2). Again, it seems that the more extensive processing recruited by these more complex tasks enhanced mood-congruity effects, even though judges were dealing with highly familiar and involving information. Measurements of processing latencies (Forgas, 1994, Exp. 3; see Fig. 5.5) confirmed that the longer and more constructively a person needs to think to compute a judgment, the greater the likelihood that affect infusion will significantly influence the outcome.

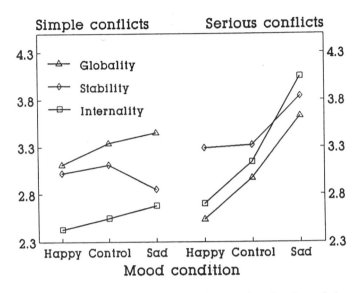

FIG. 5.5.   Mood effects on explanations about simple and serious relationship conflicts. Mood has a greater impact on judgments of the internality, stability, and globality of serious, complex conflicts, requiring longer, more substantive processing. (Based on data from Forgas, 1994).

The AIM implies that these effects should apply not only to judgments about others but also to judgments about the self. In a review of mood effects on self-perception, Sedikides (1992) concluded that "self-valence is affected by mood in a congruent manner" (1992, p. 301). However, according to the AIM, mood effects on self-perception should also be greatest in conditions in which people need to engage in substantive processing rather than to use direct access or motivated processing to produce a response. Just such a pattern was recently reported by Sedikides (1995). Happy, sad, or control participants were asked to complete a series of self-descriptions, and their processing latencies were recorded. Consistent with the AIM, Sedikides (1995) confirmed that mood effects were significantly greater on peripheral, less salient self-descriptions that required more constructive and substantive processing to be computed. In contrast, salient and central self-descriptions were less influenced by mood, as these judgments were more likely to be processed using low-infusion strategies such as direct access or motivated processing. Sedikides (1995) concluded that these four experiments were "consistent with the AIM . . . [that] predicted the absence of mood effects in reference to central self-conceptions, but the presence of a mood-congruency bias in reference to peripheral self-conceptions" (p. 39).

   Thus the AIM predicts that mood-congruent judgments should occur as long as circumstances favor either a substantive or a heuristic processing strategy. In contrast, mood congruence is unlikely when motivated or direct-access processing is used. Evidence for mood congruity during heuristic processing using the affect-as-information heuristic is discussed elsewhere in this volume (see Clore et al., chapter 2, and Schwarz, chapter 7). The AIM suggests that this mechanism should operate only when there are no pressures calling for a more considered, substantive processing style. According to the AIM, the affect-as-information mechanism can only account for a small subset of mood-congruent judgmental outcomes. Affect is most likely to be misattributed this way only when the judgment is of little importance and judges lack the cognitive resources and/or motivation to deal with the task more exhaustively. For example, the affect-as-information mechanism may operate in circumstances in which people are asked to respond to an unfamiliar question asked by a stranger who expects a quick reply, thereby placing the respondent under some time pressure. This is just the kind of situation described in the telephone survey "weather study" by Schwarz and Clore (1988). In another conceptually similar study, we asked some one thousand moviegoers who had just seen a happy, sad, or violent film to respond to a "street survey" after the performance. Results showed clear mood-congruent effects, which could be best explained in terms of affect-as-information mechanisms operating under conditions conducive to a rapid, heuristic processing strategy. One of the main contributions of the AIM is thus that it places the affect-priming and affect-as-information accounts of mood congruence within a single integrated theoretical framework, specifying with some precision the kinds of conditions likely to favor one or the other of these mechanisms.

Mood Effects on Planning and Executing Strategic Social Behaviors

In addition to explaining mood effects on memory and judgments, in recent years we have also applied the AIM to understanding affective influences on strategic social behaviors. As most social behaviors require actors first to judge and interpret a situation and to plan their responses using constructive thinking, the AIM predicts that positive affect should facilitate more confident, friendly, and cooperative "approach" behaviors, whereas negative affect should prime more avoidant, defensive, or unfriendly behaviors. Surprisingly, the behavioral consequences of affect infusion have received very little attention so far. The role of different processing strategies in mediating these behavioral effects was a particular focus in some of our recent experiments (Forgas, 1998a, 1998b, 1999a, 1999b).

In one unobtrusive paradigm, mood was induced by leaving positively or negatively valenced material on students' desks in a library (Forgas,

1998a). Behavioral responses to a subsequent unexpected request showed significant affect infusion. Further, as predicted by the AIM, these mood effects were significantly greater when a more unconventional, impolite request elicited more extensive and substantive information processing. Results showed that evaluations and recall of and compliance with an impolite request showed significantly greater affect congruence than did responses to polite requests. Could affect also have a similar process-mediated influence on more deliberate and consciously planned social behaviors? This possibility was examined in another series of studies looking at affective influences on negotiator cognition and bargaining behaviors (Forgas, 1998b). As bargaining is by definition a complex and indeterminate event, substantive processing is required to plan an appropriate strategy. In these experiments, participants received a mood induction before they planned and participated in either an interpersonal, informal, or formal intergroup bargaining encounter. In all three experiments, positive affect produced more cooperative, integrative thoughts and plans, and participants actually used more constructive, cooperative bargaining behaviors. Those in positive moods also obtained significantly better results due to their more integrative approach.

There was also evidence for the process mediation of these effects. People who scored high on measures likely to predict a habitually motivated approach to interpersonal tasks (such as high need for approval and high Machiavellianism) were significantly less influenced by affect infusion when planning and executing the negotiation task than were low scorers on these measures. These results support the AIM and the key argument proposed here, that affect infusion into social thinking and behavior is also highly process-sensitive and tends to be constrained whenever more targeted, motivated information processing is adopted.

Other recent experiments investigating the generation of strategic social behaviors such as the formulation of requests provide additional support for these theoretical arguments (Forgas, 1999a, 1999b). Formulating a request is an intrinsically complex and demanding behavioral task, characterized by uncertainty and ambiguity. Requesters need to formulate their messages to be sufficiently direct so as to maximize compliance yet be sufficiently polite so as to avoid giving offense. To the extent that open, substantive processing is required to perform this task, positive affect should produce a more confident, direct strategy, and negative affect should result in a more cautious, polite, and elaborate strategy due to the greater availability of mood-congruent thoughts and associations. As expected, the first set of studies (Forgas, 1999a, 1999b) found that happy participants preferred more direct, impolite request forms and sad persons used more indirect, polite, and elaborate requests. Further, as predicted by the AIM, these affective influences on requesting behavior were

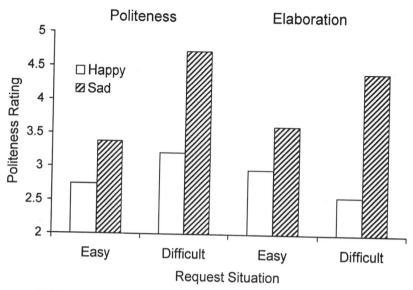

FIG. 5.6. The effects of happy and sad mood on producing a request in easy or difficult social situations. Positive mood results in less polite and less elaborate requests, and negative mood leads to more polite and more elaborate requests. These mood effects are significantly greater in a more difficult, demanding social situation that requires more substantive processing. (Based on data from Forgas, 1998, 1999a).

significantly greater in more difficult, demanding request situations that were likely to require more extensive substantive processing strategies (Fig. 5.6). Affect also had a relatively greater influence on decisions about using unconventional, impolite, and direct requests that deviated from the norm and thus required more substantive processing (Forgas, 1999a, 1999b). These results show that mood effects on social behaviors are indeed process-dependent, with affect infusion enhanced when more constructive processing is required to deal with more difficult and demanding interpersonal tasks.

Similar mechanisms also operate when naturalistic requests are made, according to an unobtrusive study designed to elicit and observe spontaneous requests by happy and sad people in a real-life situation (Forgas, 1999a, 1999b). In this study, participants received an audiovisual mood induction. They were then asked by the experimenter to get a file from a neighboring office while the next part of the experiment was being set up. Their words were surreptitiously recorded by a concealed tape recorder. There was a significant affect infusion into these naturally produced requests. Negative mood produced significantly more polite, elaborate, and hedging requests, whereas happy people employed more direct and less polite forms. Negative affect also increased the latency (delay) in posing the request, consistent with the more cautious, defensive strategies primed by negative mood. These experiments confirm that affect infusion also influences the planning and execution of real-life strategic behaviors, as long as constructive, substantive processing is required to perform a task, as suggested by the AIM.

Mood Effects on Processing Style

The AIM clearly recognizes that positive and negative moods have asymmetrical processing consequences, with less systematic and more creative and flexible processing strategies in positive moods. Several recent experiments have confirmed this effect. For example, in one series of studies we found that positive mood increased and negative mood decreased the incidence of the fundamental attribution error. Those in a positive mood were more likely to disregard information suggesting that an actor's behavior was coerced. Thus happy persons were inclined to form a unit relation between the actor and his behavior, inferring internal causation despite the presence of coercion (Forgas, 1998c). In contrast, negative mood produced greater attention to situational information and a significant decrease in the fundamental attribution error. Such mood-induced processing differences could also have significant applied consequences. For example, we found in recent experiments that eyewitness testimony is significantly more likely to be corrupted when misleading information about a witnessed event is presented while people are experiencing a positive mood rather than a negative mood (Forgas, 1998d). The AIM predicts that these processing differences can be due to any of three possible causes, as suggested by Fig. 5.2.

1. *Capacity effects.* The AIM allows for the possibility that affectively primed thoughts and associations may take up scarce attentional and memory resources, impairing attention and cognitive processing capacity both in negative and in positive moods. However, the evidence for such mood-induced processing impairment remains somewhat equivocal (Bless, 2000). Although some theorists argue that negative mood should reduce attentional and processing resources (Ellis & Ashbrook, 1988), others suggest that positive mood should produce similar effects (Mackie & Worth, 1991).

2. *Functional effects.* In addition to capacity effects, the AIM incorporates the prediction that positive affect should generally facilitate a loose, creative, and heuristic processing style, whereas negative mood should recruit more careful and substantive processing (Fiedler, 1991; 2000; Forgas, 1992b; Forgas & Bower, 1987; Schwarz, 1990). According to functionalist theories, affects "exist for the sake of signaling states of the world that have to be responded to" (Frijda, 1988, p. 354). Good mood may in a

sense inform us that the situation is favorable and that little monitoring and processing effort is required. Bad moods in turn signal incipient danger, recruiting vigilant, systematic, and even ruminative processing strategies (Schwarz, 1990). Although there is some evidence for such mood effects on processing styles, these effects are themselves often indirect and context-dependent (Martin et al., 1993). The AIM predicts that mood effects on processing should be secondary to the more dominant processing requirements associated with the target, the judge, or the situation (Forgas, 1993, 1994). Thus demanding targets will be processed more substantively even by happy individuals (Forgas, 1992b; 1993; 1994).

   3. *Motivational effects.* The AIM predicts (Fig. 5.2) that in some conditions (such as high personal relevance) affect itself may also be the source of a specific motivation, recruiting controlled, motivated processing in the service of mood maintenance (in positive moods) or mood repair (in negative moods), thus reducing the likelihood of affect infusion occurring. In terms of the AIM, the commonly found asymmetry between positive and negative mood effects may often be due to the greater propensity of negative moods to recruit motivated processing, thus constraining affect infusion in dysphoria (Forgas, 1990, Forgas et al., 1984).

   What determines processing strategy and subsequent affect infusion when mood and task characteristics are pitted against each other and seem to call for conflicting processing styles? For example, what happens when a happy person (inclined to process heuristically) is asked to perform a complex social judgment that requires substantive processing? The AIM makes the clear hierarchical prediction that the processing consequences of mood are subsequent to and dependent on the processing requirements of other contextual variables (Fig. 5.2). Several experiments now confirm the prediction that affect plays a secondary role in determining processing choices. Thus happy participants will adopt a substantive and not heuristic processing strategy when this is required by a complex or an atypical target, allowing positive mood to infuse the judgment due to affect-priming effects (Forgas, 1992b, 1993, 1994; 1998a, 1998b).

   The AIM also highlights the importance of considering mood effects on processing style in conjunction with the processing requirements of the particular task or situation. Several experiments suggest that the processing consequences of mood significantly interact with the processing requirements of the target in producing a particular outcome. For example, in one study (Forgas, 1992b, Exp. 2) we found an intriguing asymmetric mood effect on memory. Recall was comparatively better for atypical targets for participants in negative moods but was comparatively better for typical targets for participants in positive moods (Fig. 5.7). In this instance

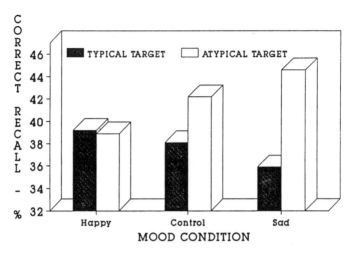

FIG. 5.7.   Affective influences on the recall of typical and atypical persons. Mood and target typicality interact in influencing recall performance. (Based on data from Forgas, 1992b).

encoding and remembering information about atypical people was selectively facilitated by the kind of careful substantive processing strategy usually associated with dysphoria (Schwarz, 1990). In contrast, learning and remembering information about "easy," prototypical characters was facilitated by positive mood that usually cues heuristic, schematic processing styles. These asymmetric mood effects suggest an interaction between moods and target features in recruiting contrasting or matching processing strategies as specifically predicted by the AIM (Fig. 5.2). That is, best recall performance seems to occur in circumstances in which both target typicality and mood call for similar, rather than conflicting, styles of information processing. This experiment also showed that mood effects on judgments were greatest when more substantive processing was used. In conclusion, consistent with other theories, the AIM can explain processing differences between good moods and bad moods in terms of cognitive capacity and functional and motivational principles. In addition, the AIM also predicts a clear hierarchical relationship between mood and other variables in triggering different processing strategies, with mood predicted to play a subsidiary role to other influences, such as task characteristics.

Mood Effects on Creative and Flexible Processing Styles

In addition to suggestions that positive moods facilitate heuristic processing, some theorists also claim that good moods specifically generate a more creative, inclusive, and flexible overall processing style (Hertel &

Fiedler, 1994; Isen, 1987). One of the main theoretical explanations for the claimed processing benefits of good mood comes from the work of Isen (1987), who emphasized the beneficial consequences of good mood for retrieving information from memory. As positively valenced information represents a large, heterogenous, and more diverse set of representations in memory than does negatively valenced information, positive mood is likely to prime more unusual, creative, and flexible associations than does negative mood. Such priming effects are also an integral component of the Affect Infusion Model. Others, such as Hertel and Fiedler (1994), suggest that positive moods also produce greater processing flexibility, with happy persons more likely to vary their responses in reaction to shifting requirements. From the perspective of the AIM, however, no strong distinction can be made between the degree of creativity and flexibility associated with simplified heuristic processing strategies and with more elaborate, substantive processing strategies.

In fact, the model suggests that creative processing, at least in the limited sense of "going beyond the information given," is as much a feature of the substantive processing strategy as of heuristic processing. Predictions and evidence for greater affect infusion as a result of a more elaborate and substantive processing style show that people are processing creatively and flexibly, allowing mood-primed thoughts and associations to infuse their thoughts and judgments. The AIM thus implies that both the heuristic- and the substantive processing strategies can involve an element of constructive, creative thinking that makes direct, categorical (affect-as-information) or indirect, memory-based (affect-priming) affect infusion possible. The AIM suggests that we may need to distinguish between the kind of creativity that is associated with heuristic thinking (e.g., using simpler, more inclusive and higher level categories and information) and a different kind of creativity that is involved in substantive processing (using more generative, elaborate, and heterogenous primed information).

Perhaps we may refer to these two kinds of "creativities" as *inductive* creativity (most characteristic of substantive processing), and *deductive* creativity (most likely to occur in the course of heuristic processing). Unlike other models, the AIM does not make a strong valence-based prediction about creativity. Rather, it implies that different moods and different contextual requirements can combine to facilitate either a heuristic or a substantive processing style. Both of these processing strategies can produce creativity, either in the sense of elaborating and going beyond the specific information given (inductive creativity) or in the sense of generating responses based on external, often heuristic, information (deductive creativity). The empirical testing of these predictions requires a clearer definition and operationalization of different kinds of creativities than has been available in the literature. Exploring how mood and heuristic or substantive processing affect different kinds of creativities is one of the objectives of our current research program.

ADDRESSING CONTRIBUTORS' QUESTIONS

With a comprehensive model such as the AIM, which seeks to account for a wide variety of research findings within an integrative framework, there are clearly a number of issues that may require additional elaboration. Several such questions will be addressed here in what is by no means an exhaustive discussion.

1. AIM relegates the heuristic use of affect to artificial, rarefied, and personally irrelevant situations. How can this assumption be reconciled with evidence showing that even experts use heuristics and that they do so while processing information of high personal importance?

It was suggested here that reliance on the heuristic processing strategy and the affect-as-information mechanism represent a truncated and incomplete judgmental strategy that should be adopted only when people lack interest, motivation, or capacity to adequately compute a response. This is so because, when relying on their mood as the sole source of information, people are likely to ignore other relevant features of the stimulus and their interpretation of it. How can we reconcile this argument with evidence from the social judgmental literature indicating that reliance on heuristic cues is often a highly efficient and appropriate strategy for producing an adaptive judgment?

Whether heuristic processing is functional or not in a given situation depends of course on what is used as a heuristic. The judgmental literature suggests many kinds of heuristics (representativeness, availability, etc.) that can produce highly adaptive outcomes in the right circumstances. However, most of the evidence so far available suggests that affect is rarely an adaptive or functional heuristic cue. Indeed, the affect-as-information theory explicitly argues that it is only irrelevant, misattributed affect that is responsible for affect infusion effects in the course of heuristic processing (Schwarz & Clore, 1988). When affect is correctly attributed to its source, it should cease to have heuristic informational value according to this model. In a sense, the affect-as-information model is not so much a theory of judgment but rather a theory of *mis*-judgment: It describes what happens when people ignore all relevant information and instead rely on one irrelevant source of information only, their misattributed affect. Thus the AIM suggests that heuristic processing that relies solely on affect as the information is not likely to be a functional and adaptive processing strategy. The empirical evidence also suggests that the affect-as-information heuristic is most likely to be adopted by people when they have little interest and involvement in the task and lack cognitive resources and/or motivation to properly and substantively deal with stimulus information available.

2. You discuss several studies in which affect has a greater impact when substantive processing is high. It is not clear, though, how this fits with AIM. Doesn't the model predict affect infusion through heuristic mechanisms when substantive processing is low? Is there some reason why affect infusion due to heuristics is smaller than affect infusion due to priming?

We discussed several studies in this chapter that demonstrated that affect has a greater impact on judgment when more substantive processing is required. For example, judgments about unusual rather than typical people (Forgas, 1994), badly matched rather than well-matched couples (Forgas, 1993, 1995b), and serious rather than simple conflicts (Forgas, 1994) were all processed more constructively and substantively and as a result were more infused by affect. However, the AIM also predicts the possibility of affect infusion through a fast, heuristic mechanism. Given that the processing of complex stimuli leads to high substantive processing and high affect infusion due to affective priming and that the processing of simple stimuli may lead to heuristic processing and affect infusion through the "How do I feel about it?" mechanism, why do we see a difference in affect infusion in these studies?

In fact, there is no evidence that heuristic processing played any role in these results. These experiments sought to contrast conditions requiring different levels of substantive processing in terms of their affect infusion potential. According to the model, affect infusion due to heuristic processing is characterized by a reliance on misattributed affect as information and by the absence of substantive processing of the actual stimulus details provided. In the studies described here, people did spend some time substantively processing the actual stimulus details and did report remembering this information later on, even when the task was relatively easy (judging typical people, well-matched couples, and easy conflicts). Thus these experiments make the point that as substantive processing becomes more extensive and constructive to deal with more demanding stimulus details, affect infusion also increases due to the greater opportunity to use affectively primed information. In other words, these studies sought to compare two levels of substantive processing, not heuristic processing with substantive processing.

3. Are the four different processing strategies identified here mutually exclusive, or is it possible that they operate simultaneously and that what

varies is the weight given to each strategy in different situations? Also, what is your rationale for assuming that individuals process systematically only after finding heuristic processing lacking?

As it stands, the AIM clearly suggests that each of the four processing strategies identified should be the dominant strategy used in a particular situation and that its use should determine the affect infusion potential in that context. However, there is no reason to assume that the four processing strategies need always be mutually exclusive. For example, the adoption of a predominantly substantive and memory-based processing style need not imply that some heuristic information may not also be incorporated into this process. The key point is that the dominant processing style should determine the presence and the extent of affect infusion, as was found in several of the studies reported here (Forgas, 1994, 1995b, 1998a, 1998b).

A related issue is that there are only limited empirical means available to document the coexistence of multiple processing strategies. Measures of encoding latency, judgmental latency, and recall rates were routinely collected in most of our experiments. These measures can tell us how long a person spent on a task and to what extent the stimulus information was learned and remembered. Thus we can establish that some degree of substantive processing has occurred. However, these measures are unlikely to be appropriate to detect the coexistence of multiple processing strategies. Indeed, past claims for the coexistence of multiple processing strategies have not been based on any such direct processing measures. Rather, what is shown is that information a priori identified as a heuristic cue may also have some impact when systematic processing is used and vice versa. However, the use of a heuristic cue need not mean that a heuristic processing style was necessarily used, and the use of systematic information may not mean that it was necessarily processed systematically (Chaiken & Maheswaran, 1994). There is a difference between what kind of information is used and how it is used. The best we can say on the basis of the available evidence is that people use a variety of information sources in performing a social cognitive task but tend to rely on one dominant strategy as they do so. The AIM argues that the dominant strategy they use should determine the presence and extent of affect infusion. The evidence reviewed here clearly supports this assertion.

SUMMARY AND CONCLUSIONS

As this chapter argues, the infusion of affect into social thinking and judgments is now a well-established phenomenon supported by a large number of studies. However, these effects are highly context-sensitive, with several experiments failing to find affect infusion in conditions characterized by highly restrictive, targeted information processing. The Affect Infusion Model (AIM) seeks to account for these effects in terms of the different processing strategies adopted by people in response to contextual variables.

The available evidence suggests that people may choose from several alternative processing strategies when dealing with a social cognitive task. The AIM represents a further evolution of the recent trend toward dual-process theories in the social cognition literature. In terms of the model, mood effects on social cognition are most likely when constructive processing is used, with affect-priming (during substantive processing), and affect-as-information (during heuristic processing) as the two major affect infusion mechanisms. The choice between processing strategies is determined by a combination of judge, target, and situational characteristics that can be summarized in the form of a series of testable links and predictions (Fig. 5.2). An interesting, if counterintuitive, prediction of the Affect Infusion Model, now confirmed by several experiments, is that more extensive and substantive processing recruited by unusual or complex targets will paradoxically increase rather than decrease affect infusion effects, as such strategies offer greater scope for affectively valenced information to be incorporated in a judgment.

A range of empirical studies demonstrated either the absence (following direct access and motivated processing) or the presence (during heuristic and substantive processing) of affect infusion in circumstances that fit the predictions of the AIM. An analysis of processing times and judgmental latencies in several of the studies specifically supports affect-priming as a major mechanism of affect infusion in realistic situations. Under conditions conducive to heuristic processing, affect-as-information mechanisms can also play an important role in producing mood congruency in judgments (Clore & Parrott, 1991; Schwarz & Clore, 1988). At the most general level, the evidence suggests that there is a pervasive tendency for people to process social cognitive tasks in terms of their feelings at the time under conditions in which heuristic or substantive processing strategies are adopted.

The AIM paves the way toward a more dynamic, interactive conceptualization of the affect–cognition relationship in the future. For one thing, the rapid development of research in neuropsychology and neurophysiology is likely to shed new light on the close interdependence between affective and cognitive phenomena (Damasio, 1994). We are also likely to see more precise explorations of how affective states and different information-processing strategies interact. Most research up to now was concerned with unidirectional relationships—how affect influences cognition and how cognition affects emotional experience. We may be approaching the stage at which theories can begin to look at affect and cognition in a genuinely interactive, dynamic way. For example, we suggested recently that continuous and gradual shifts in information-processing style (producing affect congruence or affect incongruence) could be the key mechanism that people use to control and manage their everyday mood fluctuations (Forgas, Johnson, & Ciarrochi, 1998). We do already know that different affective states facilitate different processing strategies, and we also know that different processing strategies produce different levels of affect infusion and affect congruence. If we put these two ideas together, we may be on the way toward developing genuinely interactive, dynamic theories about cognition and emotion. Such an interactive conceptualization of the cognition–emotion system has some important evolutionary, functional implications that are only just beginning to be explored.

In conclusion, we have good cause to be pleased with what has been achieved in research on affect and cognition, and we have every reason to be optimistic about the future. During the past twenty years, this field has been characterized by a steady progression of interesting empirical findings, an exemplary development of ever-more sensitive and inclusive theories, and the discovery of important and reliable effects that have widespread practical implications. We now have a better understanding of the delicate interplay between affect and social cognition than at any time before. The Affect Infusion Model is offered here as an integrative theory that recognizes the complex, constructive character of social cognition and integrates the different roles of affect in social information processing. The model also seeks to link several of the theoretical explanations now available in the literature and offers a comprehensive framework for specifying the boundary conditions under which each processing mechanism is most likely to operate. By advocating a flexible and process-sensitive framework as a means of integrating the heterogenous literature on affect and cognition, the AIM should help to stimulate further interest in this fascinating research domain.

ACKNOWLEDGMENTS

The preparation of this chapter was facilitated by financial support from an Australian Research Council Special Investigator Award and the Alexander von Humboldt Research Prize, Germany. I am grateful to Stephanie Moylan, Joseph Ciarrochi, Patrick Vargas, and Roland Neumann for their contribution to the work reported here.

REFERENCES

Baron, R. (1987). Interviewers' moods and reactions to job applicants: The influence of affective states on applied social judgments. *Journal of Applied Social Psychology, 16,* 16–28.

Berkowitz, L. (1993). Towards a general theory of anger and emotional aggression. In T. K. Srull & R. S. Wyer (Eds.), *Advances in social cognition* (Vol. 6, pp. 1–46). Hillsdale, NJ: Lawrence Erlbaum Associates.

Blaney, P. H. (1986). Affect and memory: A review. *Psychological Bulletin, 99*, 229–246.

Bless, H. (2000). The interplay of affect and cognition: The role of general knowledge structures. In J. P. Forgas (Ed.), *Feeling and thinking: The role of affect in social cognition* (pp. 201–222). New York: Cambridge University Press.

Bower, G. H. (1981). Mood and memory. *American Psychologist, 36*, 129–148.

Bower, G. H. (1991). Mood congruity of social judgments. In J. P. Forgas (Ed.), *Emotion and social judgments* (pp. 31–53). Oxford, England: Pergamon Press.

Brewer, M. (1988). A dual-process model of impression formation. In T. K. Srull & R. S. Wyer (Eds.), *Advances in social cognition* (Vol. 1, pp. 1–36). Hillsdale, NJ: Lawrence Erlbaum Associates.

Burke, M., & Mathews, A. M. (1992). Autobiographical memory and clinical anxiety. *Cognition and Emotion, 6*, 23–35.

Chaiken, S., & Maheswaran, D. (1994). Heuristic processing can bias systematic processing: Effects of source credibility, argument ambiguity, and task importance on attitude judgment. *Journal of Personality and Social Psychology, 66*(3), 460–473.

Ciarrochi, J. V., & Forgas, J. P. (1999). On being tense yet tolerant: The paradoxical effects of trait anxiety and aversive mood on intergroup judgments. *Group Dynamics: Theory, Research and Practice, 3*, 227–238.

Ciarrochi, J. V., & Forgas, J. P. (in press). The pleasure of possessions: Affect and consumer judgments. *European Journal of Social Psychology.*

Clark, M. S., & Isen, A. M. (1982). Towards understanding the relationship between feeling states and social behavior. In A. H. Hastorf & A. M. Isen (Eds.), *Cognitive social psychology* (pp. 73–108). New York: Elsevier-North Holland.

Clore, G. L., & Byrne, D. (1974). The reinforcement affect model of attraction. In T. L. Huston (Ed.), *Foundations of interpersonal attraction* (pp. 143–170). New York: Academic Press.

Clore, G. L., & Parrott, G. (1991). Moods and their vicissitudes: Thoughts and feelings as information. In J. P. Forgas (Ed.), *Emotion and social judgments* (pp. 107–123). Oxford, England: Pergamon.

Damasio, A. R. (1994). *Descartes' error.* New York: Grosset/Putnam.

Eich, E. (1995). Searching for mood dependent memory. *Psychological Science, 6*, 67–75.

Eich, E., & Macauley, D. (2000). Fundamental factors in mood dependent memory. In J. P. Forgas (Ed.), *Feeling and thinking: The role of affect in social cognition* (pp. 109–130). New York: Cambridge University Press.

Ellis, H. C., & Ashbrook, T. W. (1988). Resource allocation model of the effects of depressed mood state on memory. In K. Fiedler & J. P. Forgas (Eds.), *Affect, cognition and social behavior* (pp. 25–43). Toronto, Ontario, Canada: Hogrefe.

Erber, R., & Erber, M. W. (1994). Beyond mood and social judgment: Mood incongruent recall and mood regulation. *European Journal of Social Psychology, 24*, 79–88.

Eysenck, M. W., MacLeod, C., & Mathews, A. M. (1987). Cognitive functioning in anxiety. *Psychological Research, 49*, 189–195.

Fiedler, K. (1991). On the task, the measures and the mood in research on affect and social cognition. In J. P. Forgas (Ed.), *Emotion and social judgments* (pp. 83–104). Oxford, England: Pergamon.

Fiedler, K. (2000). Towards an integrative account of affect and cognition phenomena using the BIAS computer algorithm. In J. P. Forgas (Ed.), *Feeling and thinking: The role of affect in social cognition* (pp. 223–252). New York: Cambridge University Press.

Fiedler, K., & Forgas, J. P. (Eds.). (1988). *Affect, cognition and social behavior.* Toronto, Ontario, Canada: Hogrefe.

Forgas, J. P. (Ed.). (1981). *Social cognition: Perspectives on everyday understanding.* London and New York: Academic Press.

Forgas, J. P. (1982). Episode cognition: Internal representations of interaction routines. In L. Berkowitz (Ed.), *Advances in experimental social psychology* (Vol. 15, pp. 59–100). New York: Academic Press.

Forgas, J. P. (1989). Mood effects on decision-making strategies. *Australian Journal of Psychology, 41,* 197–214.

Forgas, J. P. (1990). Affective influences on individual and group judgments. *European Journal of Social Psychology, 20,* 441–453.

Forgas, J. P. (Ed.). (1991a). *Emotion and social judgments.* Oxford, England: Pergamon.

Forgas, J. P. (1991b). Mood effects on partner choice: Role of affect in social decisions. *Journal of Personality and Social Psychology, 61,* 708–720.

Forgas, J. P. (1992a). Affect in social judgments and decisions: A multi-process model. In M. Zanna (Ed.), *Advances in experimental social psychology* (Vol. 25, pp. 227–275). New York: Academic Press.

Forgas, J. P. (1992b). On bad mood and peculiar people: Affect and person typicality in impression formation. *Journal of Personality and Social Psychology, 62,* 863–875.

Forgas, J. P. (1992c). Mood and the perception of unusual people: Affective asymmetry in memory and social judgments. *European Journal of Social Psychology, 22,* 531–547.

Forgas, J. P. (1993). On making sense of odd couples: Mood effects on the perception of mismatched relationships. *Personality and Social Psychology Bulletin, 19,* 59–71.

Forgas, J. P. (1994). Sad and guilty? Affective influences on the explanation of conflict episodes. *Journal of Personality and Social Psychology, 66,* 56–68.

Forgas, J. P. (1995a). Mood and judgment: The affect infusion model (AIM). *Psychological Bulletin, 117,* 1–28.

Forgas, J. P. (1995b). Strange couples: Mood effects on judgments and memory about prototypical and atypical targets. *Personality and Social Psychology Bulletin, 21,* 747–765.

Forgas, J. P. (1998a). On feeling good and getting your way: Mood effects on negotiation strategies and outcomes. *Journal of Personality and Social Psychology, 74,* 565–577.

Forgas, J. P. (1998b). Asking nicely? The effects of mood on responding to more or less polite requests. *Personality and Social Psychology Bulletin, 24,* 173–185.

Forgas, J. P. (1998c). On being happy and mistaken: Mood effects on the fundamental attribution error. *Journal of Personality and Social Psychology, 75,* 318–331.

Forgas, J. P. (1998d). *Mood effects on eyewitness accuracy.* Unpublished manuscript, University of New South Wales, Sydney, Australia.

Forgas, J. P. (1999a). Feeling and speaking: Mood effects on verbal communication strategies. *Personality and Social Psychology Bulletin, 25,* 850–863.

Forgas, J. P. (1999b). On feeling good and being rude: Affective influences on language use and request formulations. *Journal of Personality and Social Psychology, 76,* 928–939.

Forgas, J. P. (Ed.). (2000). *Feeling and thinking: The role of affect in social cognition.* New York: Cambridge University Press.

Forgas, J. P., & Bower, G. H. (1987). Mood effects on person perception judgements. *Journal of Personality and Social Psychology, 53,* 53–60.

Forgas, J. P., Bower, G. H., & Krantz, S. (1984). The influence of mood on perceptions of social interactions. *Journal of Experimental Social Psychology, 20,* 497–513.

Forgas, J. P., Bower, G. H., & Moylan, S. J. (1990). Praise or blame? Affective influences on attributions for achievement. *Journal of Personality and Social Psychology, 59,* 809–818.

Forgas, J. P., & Fiedler, K. (1996). Us and them: Mood effects on intergroup discrimination. *Journal of Personality and Social Psychology, 70,* 36–52.

Forgas, J. P., Johnson, R., & Ciarrochi, J. (1998). Affect control and affect infusion: A multi-process account of mood management and personal control. In M. Kofta, G.

Weary, & G. Sedek (Eds.), *Personal control in action. Cognitive and motivational mechanisms* (pp. 155–189). New York: Plenum.

Forgas, J. P., Levinger, G., & Moylan, S. (1994). Feeling good and feeling close: Mood effects on the perception of intimate relationships. *Personal Relationships, 2,* 165–184.

Forgas, J. P., & Moylan, S. J. (1991). Affective influences on stereotype judgments. *Cognition and Emotion, 5,* 379–397.

Frijda, N. (1988). The laws of emotion. *American Psychologist, 43,* 349–358.

Griffitt, W. (1970). Environmental effects on interpersonal behavior: Ambient effective temperature and attraction. *Journal of Personality and Social Psychology, 15,* 240–244.

Haddock, G., Zanna, M. P., & Esses, V. M. (1994). Mood and the expression of intergroup attitudes: The moderating role of affect intensity. *European Journal of Social Psychology, 24,* 189–206.

Hertel, G., & Fiedler, K. (1994). Affective and cognitive influences in a social dilemma game. *European Journal of Social Psychology, 24,* 131–146.

Isen, A. (1987). Positive affect, cognitive processes and social behavior. In L. Berkowitz (Ed.), *Advances in experimental social psychology* (Vol. 20, pp. 203–253). New York: Academic Press.

Laird, J. D., & Bresler, C. (1991). The process of emotional experience: A self-perception theory. In M. Clark (Ed.), *Review of Personality and Social Psychology* (Vol. 14, pp. 213–234). Beverly Hills, CA: Sage.

Lewinsohn, P. M., & Rosenbaum, M. (1987). Recall of parental behavior by acute depressives, remitted depressives, and nondepressives. *Journal of Personality and Social Psychology, 52,* 611–619.

Lloyd, G. G., & Lishman, W. A. (1975). Effect of depression on the speed of recall of pleasant and unpleasant experiences. *Psychological Medicine, 5,* 173–180.

Mackie, D., & Worth, L. (1991). Feeling good, but not thinking straight: The impact of positive mood on persuasion. In J. P. Forgas (Ed.), *Emotion and social judgments* (pp. 201–220). Oxford, England: Pergamon.

Martin, L. L. (1986). Set/reset: Use and disuse of concepts in impression formation. *Journal of Personality and Social Psychology, 51,* 493–504.

Martin, L. L., Ward, D. W., Achee, J. W., & Wyer, R. S. (1993). Mood as input: People have to interpret the motivational implications of their moods. *Journal of Personality and Social Psychology, 64,* 317–326.

Mayer, J. D., Gaschke, Y. N., Braverman, D. L., & Evans, T. W. (1992). Mood congruent judgment is a general effect. *Journal of Personality and Social Psychology, 63,* 119–132.

Niedenthal, P., & Showers, C. (1991). The perception and processing of affective information and its influences on social judgments. In J. P. Forgas (Ed.), *Emotion in social judgments* (pp. 125–143). Oxford, England: Pergamon.

Petty, R. E., Gleicher, F., & Baker, S. (1991). Multiple roles for affect in persuasion. In J. P. Forgas (Ed.), *Emotion and social judgments* (pp. 181–200). Oxford, England: Pergamon.

Ruiz-Caballero, J. A., & Gonzalez, P. (1994). Implicit and explicit memory bias in depressed and non-depressed subjects. *Cognition and Emotion, 8,* 555–570.

Rusting, C. L. (1998). *Personality, mood and cognitive processing of emotional information: Three alternative models.* Manuscript submitted for publication.

Salovey, P., & Birnbaum, D. (1989). Influence of mood on health-related cognitions. *Journal of Personality and Social Psychology, 57,* 539–551.

Salovey, P., & Mayer, J. D. (1990). Emotional intelligence. *Imagination, Cognition and Personality, 9,* 185–211.

Schwarz, N. (1990). Feelings as information: Informational and motivational functions of affective states. In E. T. Higgins & R. Sorrentino (Eds.), *Handbook of motivation and cognition: Foundations of social behavior* (Vol. 2, pp. 527–561). New York: Guilford.

Schwarz, N., & Clore, G. L. (1988). How do I feel about it? The informative function of affective states. In K. Fiedler & J. P. Forgas (Eds.), *Affect, cognition, and social behavior* (pp. 44–62). Toronto, Ontario, Canada: Hogrefe.

Sedikides, C. (1992). Changes in the valence of self as a function of mood. *Review of Personality and Social Psychology, 14,* 271–311.

Sedikides, C. (1995). Central and peripheral self-conceptions are differentially influenced by mood: Tests of the differential sensitivity hypothesis. *Journal of Personality and Social Psychology, 69*(4), 759–777.

Srull, T. K. (1983). Affect and memory: The impact of affective reactions in advertising on the representation of product information in memory. In R. Bagozzi & A. Tybout (Eds.), *Advances in Consumer Research* (Vol. 10, pp. 244–263). Ann Arbor, MI: Association for Consumer Research.

Srull, T. K. (1984). The effects of subjective affective states on memory and judgment. In T. Kinnear (Ed.), *Advances in Consumer Research* (Vol. 11, pp. 530–533). Provo, UT: Association for Consumer Research.

Chapter 6

Mood as Input: A Configural View of Mood Effects

Leonard L. Martin
University of Georgia

One empirical generalization that has virtually taken on the status of a truism in social psychology is that context can have a profound impact on a person's thoughts, feelings, and behavior. We know, for example, that ordinary, kind, caring individuals may, under the right conditions, perform behaviors that are harmful to others (Milgram, 1974) or fail to perform behaviors that would be helpful to others (Darley & Latané, 1968). We also know that personality traits (Asch, 1946) and behaviors (Higgins, Rholes, & Jones, 1977) can take on different meanings in different contexts and that evaluations of a target stimulus can be significantly affected by the contextual stimuli with which the target is judged (Manis, Biernat, & Nelson, 1991). Observations such as these, showing that different contexts can significantly influence a wide range of phenomena, form the basis of the mood-as-input model (Martin, Abend, Sedikides, & Greene, 1997; Martin, Achee, Ward, & Harlow, 1993; Martin & Davies, 1998; Martin & Stoner, 1996; Martin, Ward, Achee, & Wyer, 1993). The core assumption of the model is that the effects of mood on evaluation and motivation are, by their very nature, context-dependent.

Of course, other theoretical models of mood allow for different mood effects in different contexts. The mood-as-input model differs from these models, however, in that it does not assume that one effect (e.g., mood-congruent judgment) is basic, whereas other effects (e.g., mood-incongruent judgment) are exceptions to the basic rule. This basic/exception orientation toward explaining mood effects was captured succinctly by

Mayer, Gaschke, Braverman, and Evans (1992) when they described mood-congruent judgment as a general effect that "automatically occurs for every judgment for which there is a class of legitimate responses that can be distinguished according to their mood congruence. The effect would fail to occur only when a second process interferes" (p. 119). The mood-as-input model, by comparison, makes no reference to a second interfering process because, according to the model, there is no default effect with which to interfere. It is inherent in moods to produce different effects in different contexts.

Confusion/Congruence Versus Configurality

The mood-as-input model starts with the same basic assumption as the mood-as-information model (see Bless, chapter 1; Clore et al., chapter 2; Schwarz, chapter 7, this volume). Namely, both models assume that a person's phenomenal experiences (e.g., a mood) can provide that person with information and that this information, in turn, can influence the person's evaluations and motivation. Beyond this commonality, however, the mood-as-input model and the mood-as-information model are quite different. For example, the mood-as-information model assumes that moods influence evaluations when people confuse aspects of their mood for aspects of their appraisal of the target. The specific mechanism through which this confusion (i.e., misattribution) is said to occur is the "How do I feel about it?" heuristic. The argument is that, in lieu of computing a judgment through systematic processing, individuals simply assess how they feel while thinking about the target and add this assessment to their judgment. The result is a mood-congruent judgment. Schwarz and Clore (1996) summarized the "How do I feel about it?" process as follows: "As we have only one window on our immediate experience, however, we may mistake feelings due to a pre-existing mood state as part of our reaction to the target stimulus, resulting in more positive evaluations under positive than under negative moods" (p. 438).

By comparison, the mood-as-input model assumes that moods operate much like any other piece of information. They serve as input into a configural processing system. Individuals do not ask merely, "How do I feel about it?" They ask, "What does it mean that I am feeling this way in this context?" With the latter question, it is possible for either negative or positive feelings to convey either negative or positive implications. It depends on the context. For example, what does it mean if you experience positive feelings at the funeral of a friend? Are these feelings a sign that you are coping well or a sign that you are repressing? Alternatively, might the positive feelings suggest that you were not particularly close to the deceased or that you are generally not a sensitive, emotional person? Without additional information, we cannot decide between these alternate interpretations. This is why the mood-as-input model suggests that the evaluative and motivational implications conveyed by a given mood depend on the broader context in which the mood is experienced.

Another implication of the mood-as-input model is that it should be possible for moods to influence judgment of a target even when individuals do not interpret their moods as their reaction to the target. This possibility runs counter to the mood-as-information hypothesis that mood "effects should be eliminated, however, when individuals are aware that their current feelings are due to some other source and hence do not reflect their reaction to the target of judgment" (Schwarz & Bohner, 1996, p. 140). Consider the case of Professor Jones. He is in a negative mood because his paper was rejected. Will this negative mood lead Jones to render a negative evaluation of a lunch invitation from some colleagues? It might, but it might not, and even if it does it need not be because Jones confused his rejection-induced negative mood for his appraisal of the lunch invitation. From a mood-as-input perspective, Jones would evaluate the lunch invitation by taking into consideration both his mood and some features of the situation and doing this configurally. For example, Jones might consider how long the lunch would take him away from his work, who else would be present at the lunch, the tone and amount of conversation in which he would be expected to participate, and the likelihood that he would be distracted from the food and the social interactions by his negative mood. In this way, Jones might decline the lunch invitation, knowing full well that he did so because of his negative mood and that this mood was due to the rejection of his paper. To put this hypothesis in everyday language, Jones did not accept the lunch invitation because he was simply not in the mood for a social lunch. The fact that he was still brooding over the rejection of his paper was part of the information he took into consideration while evaluating the lunch invitation.

To summarize, both the mood-as-information model and the mood-as-input model start with the assumption that subjective experiences convey information. The models differ, however, in the mechanism by which this is assumed to occur. The mood-as-information model suggests that individuals mistake aspects of their mood for aspects of their appraisal of the target, resulting in more favorable evaluations under positive mood than under negative. The mood-as-input model, on the other hand, suggests that mood is one piece of information in a configural processing system. In this system either a negative or a positive mood can convey either negative or positive implications, and moods can influence judgments even when individuals do not mistake these moods for their appraisal of the target.

Mood Can Be Processed Configurally

What does it mean to say that moods are input to a configural processing system? It means in essence that individuals process information in parallel (e.g., Rumelhart, McClelland, and the PDP Research Group, 1986). They do not evaluate each piece of information separately and then add (Clore, 1992) or average (Abele & Petzold, 1994) the pieces together. They evaluate various pieces of information as a unit (Anderson & Ortony, 1975; Asch, 1946; Higgins & Rholes, 1976; Pusateri & Latané, 1982; Woll, Weeks, Fraps, Pendergrass, & Vanderplas, 1980). One consequence of this type of processing is that the implications of any one piece of information, including a mood, can change with the other information with which it is considered. This configural, context-dependent view of mood follows naturally from the assumption that moods function as information. Other information is context-dependent in its implications (e.g., the word *bank* in the context of *river* vs. *money*). Why should it be any different for moods?

More generally, the mood-as-input model assumes that positive moods, by definition, feel better than negative moods in any context but that this experiential difference need not convey the same evaluative or motivational implications in every context. A sad mood experienced at a friend's funeral might imply that one is a sensitive person who cared about the deceased (a positive implication), whereas a sad mood experienced at one's own birthday party might imply that one is concerned about his or her inability to age gracefully (a negative implication). Moreover, to the extent that it is more socially appropriate to respond with sadness to the loss of a loved one than to the loss of our youth, a sad mood at a birthday party might trigger attempts at mood repair and increase systematic processing as the person attempts to ascertain why he or she is feeling sad in a situation in which he or she should be happy. These same motivations are less likely to be aroused when the sad mood is experienced as appropriate (i.e., at a funeral). Thus it is not mood that conveys evaluative and motivational implications. It is mood in the context in which it occurs.

Configural Rules and the Role-Fulfillment Hypothesis

The assumption that evaluative and motivational implications of a mood are context-dependent allows the mood-as-input model to explain a wide range of mood effects, including mood-congruent evaluations, mood-incongruent evaluations, and even no effect of mood on evaluation. Moreover, the model explains these effects with a single theoretical mechanism. It does not need to resort to outside, interfering processes (e.g., mood-repair motivations). Of course, an ability to explain all possible outcomes could be a weakness if the model were unable to generate predictions on an a priori basis. We would have a model that could explain everything but predict nothing. Fortunately, configual models can generate a priori predictions when the rules governing the configural processing are articulated (see Rosenberg, Carnot, & Vivekananthan, 1968; Wishner, 1960). The mood-as-input model is no exception.

To make specific predictions, the mood-as-input model has relied on a role-fulfillment process. This process is a variant of the process proposed by Higgins and Rholes (1976; see also Mandler, 1984; Wyer, 1970) to account for the impressions people form on the basis of trait and role information. According to Higgins and Rholes (1976), when people are exposed to a verbal description composed of a role and a descriptor (e.g., *cruel mother*), people call to mind stored information about the target to which the description as a whole refers (e.g., an exemplar). Then they use this information to make two judgments: (a) whether the target's role (i.e., mother) generally has positive or negative social value, and (b) whether the descriptor (i.e., cruel) allows the target to fulfill its expected role (i.e., the role of mothers is to be kind rather than cruel). A person presented with the target *careful surgeon*, for example, may judge the role of surgeon to have positive social value and may feel that being careful is a feature of a good surgeon. Thus the person would render a positive evaluation of a careful surgeon. A person asked to evaluate a *casual surgeon*, on the other hand, may feel that the role of surgeon has positive social value but that being casual, despite being positive in and of itself, is not a feature of a good surgeon. As a result, this person would render a negative evaluation of a casual surgeon—even though both casual and surgeon are individually positive. The mood-as-input model assumes that mood is functionally equivalent to the descriptor in the examples. It provides information regarding the extent to which the target has fulfilled its role.

As a case in point, consider the studies in which participants have been asked to rate their satisfaction with their lives as a whole (Schwarz & Clore, 1983). Presumably, most people want happy rather than unhappy lives. If so, then how would a person feel if his or her life were fulfilling its role? The person would feel happy. It is not surprising, therefore, that people in positive moods report greater life satisfaction than people in negative moods. A similar point can be made with regard to studies in which participants were asked to evaluate their progress toward their goals (Cervone, Kopp, Schaumann, & Scott, 1994), decisions they have made (Isen, 1993), their household products (Isen, Shalker, Clark, & Karp, 1978), or their liking for a target person (Sinclair, 1988). People typically strive to attain positively valenced goals, make decisions they hope will lead to favorable outcomes, buy products they hope will work satisfactorily, and like pleasant as opposed to unpleasant people. Thus, in each of these studies, there was a tacit association between positive mood and role fulfillment. It is not surprising, therefore, that in each study participants in positive moods rendered more favorable evaluations than participants in negative moods.

Had the relation between mood valence and role fulfillment been reversed in these studies, then the effects of mood on evaluation would have been reversed. For example, individuals can consider themselves to be empathetic if they experience the feelings of another person. So, if something unpleasant happens to another person and we feel sad, then we can rate ourselves as caring and empathetic, both positive traits. We would not rate ourselves as favorably in terms of empathy if we felt happy after observing something unpleasant happen to another person. So, in this situation, we would have mood-incongruent judgments that were produced by a role-fulfillment process. In this situation, negative feelings suggest the presence of a more positive trait than positive feelings do (Martin et al., 1997).

More generally, the mood-as-input model assumes that when individuals make evaluations they act as if they were asking themselves the question, "What would I feel if . . . ?". For example, what would I feel if the sad story I just read was a good sad story? Sadness. What would I feel if my life as a whole were going well? Happiness. What would I feel if I were an assertive individual who had just been wronged? Righteous anger. An evaluation is then rendered subjectively when a person compares his or her current feelings with the expected feelings. Favorable evaluations arise to the extent that the person's feelings (positive or negative) are congruent with what would be expected if the target had fulfilled a positive role, whereas unfavorable evaluations arise to the extent that the person's feelings are incongruent with what would be expected if the target had fulfilled a negative role.

Configural Processing Is Easy

The configural processing suggested by the mood-as-input model may seem very time consuming and effortful. Individuals consider not only their moods but also some target information and some context information, and they do all of this concurrently. Would anyone ever really engage in such a complicated process? Yes, for the simple reason that configural processing is not complicated. In fact, configural processing is very efficient and seems to reflect the natural operating characteristics of the human information-processing system. Evidence for this assertion can be seen not only in the early work on perceptual Gestalts (e.g., Wertheimer, 1923) but also in the more recent work in parallel distributed processing (e.g., Rumelhart & McClelland, 1986). Compelling examples of configural processing can also be seen in research on word recognition (Allen, Wallace, & Weber, 1996; Cosky, 1976). For example, when Jacewicz (1979) asked participants to determine whether or not a letter had been present in a tachistoscopically exposed word, he found that participants identified the target letter faster if it was clearly sounded in the word (*g* in the word *tiger*) than if it was not (*g* in the word *right*). These results suggest that participants first recognized the word as a whole, then transformed the word from a visual to an acoustic code, and only then analyzed its component letters.

The mood-as-input model suggests that moods are processed in an analogous holistic way. People do not consider each piece of target, context, and mood information separately and then combine them into an overall judgment. Rather, people process this information in parallel (Rumelhart & McClelland, 1986), asking, in essence, "What is the meaning of my feelings given the context in which I am experiencing them?" This is a basic operation that people can perform quickly, spontaneously, and effortlessly.

ADDRESSING THE FOUR MAJOR FINDINGS

The four effects of mood that have been demonstrated most frequently are (a) mood-congruent recall, (b) mood-congruent judgment, (c) the greater likelihood of negative moods than positive moods fostering a systematic processing style, and (d) the greater likelihood of positive moods than negative moods fostering flexible, creative processing. In the following sections, I discuss how the mood as input model addresses each of these major findings.

Mood-Congruent Recall

It should be noted that the mood-as-input model was not developed to address the role of mood in recall. The model, in essence, is a model of mood and evaluation. Nevertheless, the mechanisms specified in the mood-as-input model might have some implications for our understanding of the effects of mood on memory. For example, if the effects of mood are really context-dependent, then mood-congruent recall need not be the default outcome. It should be possible to find conditions in which moods lead naturally (i.e., without a second, interfering process) to the recall of mood-incongruent information. Although this general idea has not been tested yet, it is possible to lay out a mood-as-input mechanism that is consistent with this idea. First, because the mood-as-input model relies on the assumption that moods operate as information (Schwarz & Clore, 1988), the model would address memory phenomena through a mechanism other than spreading activation (e.g., Bower, 1981). We could assume, for example, that individuals use their moods as a direct cue (Isen, 1987). Unlike other cueing models, however, the mood-as-input model would suggest that either a positive or a negative mood could cue either positive or negative memories. This is because a mood by itself is not an effective retrieval cue (Gunther, Ferraro, & Kirchner, 1996). An instantiated mood, on the other hand, (i.e., a mood in the context in which it occurs) could make an effective compound cue (cf., McKoon & Ratcliff, 1992). Consider the following analogy. The word *bank* could refer to a financial institution, the side of a river, the turn of an airplane, a shot in pool, and more. As such, it cannot operate as an efficient cue for any one of these memories. But the compound cues of bank/money or bank/water, on the other hand, could unambiguously direct one to financial institution and river, respectively. So it is with mood. Mood in context, but not mood in isolation, makes an effective retrieval cue.

Thus a sad mood experienced at a funeral may cue positive memories, whereas a sad mood experienced at a birthday party may cue sad memories. After all, the reason we feel sad at a funeral is because we lost someone close to us. We do not feel sad at the death of someone not close to us. Because of this, feeling sad at a funeral may lead us to reminisce about the good times we had with the deceased (mood-incongruent recall). Feeling sad at a birthday party, on the other hand, may suggest that we are regretting the aging process. These feelings may lead us to examine our current life situation and may lead us to ruminate about missed opportunities, broken dreams, and so on. So mood by itself does not cue specific memories. Mood in context does.

An additional consideration that follows from the mood-as-input model is that moods may influence processing motivation, which, in turn, may increase or decrease the duration or intensity of a memory search (Martin et al., 1993). For example, suppose individuals ask themselves, "Have I recalled enough?" With this question, individuals in positive moods may feel satisfied with the amount they have recalled and cease their memory search, whereas individuals in negative moods may feel dissatisfied and continue their memory search. So if individuals begin by recalling predominantly mood-congruent memories, then the total recall of those in positive moods would reflect mood congruence (because they would stop with the initial, congruent memories), but no effect of mood might be reflected among those in negative moods (because these individuals would retrieve memories beyond the initial, congruent ones). It is interesting to note that this asymmetry has often been observed in the literature and has traditionally been interpreted in terms of mood regulation (e.g., Clark & Isen, 1982).

Of course, if the mood-as-input model is correct, then it should be possible to find conditions in which a recall asymmetry would naturally favor positive moods. For example, if people were concerned not about whether they had recalled enough but about whether they could recall more, then those in positive moods might be optimistic and continue their memory search, whereas those in negative moods might be pessimistic and terminate their memory search (Martin et al., 1993). Under these conditions, those in negative moods might be less likely to continue their recall beyond the initial mood-congruent memories. Thus a negative mood would induce greater mood-congruent recall than a positive mood. (Of course, these predictions are based on the assumption that people begin by recalling mood-congruent information. This need not always be the case.)

Mood-Congruent Evaluation

From a mood-as-input perspective, what is important in determining one's evaluation is not the valence of the mood per se but the degree of match between that valence and the valence one could expect to experience if the target had fulfilled its role (i.e., the target's standing compared with the exemplar or standard relative to which it is being evaluated). Positive evaluations arise when the evaluator's mood (positive or negative) signals that the target has fulfilled a positive role, whereas negative evaluations arise to the extent that the evaluator's mood (positive or negative) signals that the target has not fulfilled a positive role. From this perspective, mood-congruent evaluations are observed so frequently because people typically evaluate targets for which positive moods signal positive role fulfillment (e.g., people tend to want happy lives, reliable household products, and decisions that lead to positive outcomes). But the congruent relation between mood valence and evaluation valence is an actuarial one, not a necessary one. If people pursue outcomes the attainment of which entails unpleasant feelings (e.g., dieting, revenge, motivating empathy), then people will render what are, in essence, mood-incongruent judgments (Martin et al., 1997). Such judgments, however, are still reflective of the role-fulfillment process and do not necessarily suggest the operation of an interfering process (such as mood repair).

In a straightforward test of the role-fulfillment hypothesis, Martin et al. (1997, Exp. 1) placed participants into either a happy or sad mood by having them view happy or sad video clips. Then participants read either a happy or sad story and rated themselves along dimensions such as empathy, sensitivity, and ability to put oneself in another person's shoes. These dimensions reflect a positive trait (e.g., empathy) that a person can be said to have if he or she feels what another person is feeling. So if participants feel good after reading a story with a happy ending, then they can infer that they are empathetic. Interestingly, individuals can also rate themselves favorably in terms of empathy if they feel sad after reading a story in which something sad happens to a person. In short, the mood-as-input model would lead us to predict that participants would rate themselves most favorably in terms of empathy if they were experiencing the same mood (positive or negative) as the person in the story. Less favorable evaluations would come from participants whose video-induced moods did not match the emotions experienced by the person in the story. These were precisely the results obtained by Martin et al. (1997).

These results demonstrate that when people's moods serve as evidence of role fulfillment, what is important is not the valence of the mood per se but rather the match between the mood the person is experiencing and the mood the person could expect to experience if the target had fulfilled its role. Positive moods led to more favorable evaluations than negative moods when people evaluated a target for which a positive mood signaled fulfillment of a desirable role, whereas negative moods led to more favorable evaluations when people evaluated a target for which a negative mood signaled role fulfillment of a desirable role (Martin et al., 1997).

A second point to consider when trying to understand the mood-as-input approach to evaluation is that the effects of mood on evaluation are a function of what a person does with his or her mood, not a function of what the mood does to the person. What this means is that being in a mood is likely to have no effect on an evaluation unless that person takes the mood into consideration during the evaluation. This can be seen in a study by Strack, Martin, and Stepper (1988). In that study, participants in positive or negative moods (manipulated through facial expressions) were asked to make two evaluations of a cartoon: How amused did the cartoon make you feel? How funny was the cartoon relative to an objective standard? Participants in positive moods reported being more amused than those in negative moods, but the two groups did not differ in their rating of the cartoon relative to an objective standard. These results suggest that the question of how amused they were made participants' subjective experiences (i.e., their moods) relevant to the evaluation, whereas the objective-standard question did not. So the finding that participants' moods influenced evaluation of the amusement question but not the objective-standard question suggests that merely being in a mood is insufficient for that mood to influence evaluations. The mood must also be taken into consideration. Thus mood effects on evaluation are a function of processing objectives and are not reflective of passive processes.

Negative Moods and Systematic Processing

A general assumption of the mood-as-input model is that motivational processes are engendered when there is a discrepancy between a person's standards and the person's perception of their status relative to those standards (Carver & Scheier; 1990; Martin & Tesser, 1996; Wicklund, 1979). Research has shown that the experience of such a discrepancy elicits negative affect (Hsee & Abelson, 1991) and that people in negative moods feel farther from their standards than do people in positive moods (Cervone et al., 1994). Together, these findings make it plausible to assume that negative moods generally foster systematic processing that is more or less in the service of reducing discrepancies (Schwarz, chapter 7, this volume). If the implications of moods are as context-dependent as the mood-as-input model suggests, however, then this relation is not a necessary one. Under some conditions, positive moods may induce systematic processing, whereas negative moods may induce heuristic processing.

Evidence that mood operates in accordance with a role-fulfillment rule in determining the motivational implications of a mood was obtained by Martin et al. (1993; see also Hirt, Melton, McDonald, & Harackiewicz, 1996; Sanna, Turley, & Mark, 1996). They began by distinguishing between objective and subjective stop rules. Individuals may stop eating, for example, when their plates are empty (objective) or they may stop when they feel full (subjective). With cognitive tasks such as forming an impression or responding to a persuasive message, however, there are typically only subjective stop rules. Individuals stop processing when they feel they have processed enough. As Chaiken, Liberman, and Eagly (1989) noted, when people feel confident that heuristic processing will provide them with a satisfactory answer, they stop there. When individuals do not feel confident with heuristic processing, they move beyond heuristic processing to systematic processing. It follows that if mood can influence one's confidence, then mood can influence the likelihood that an individual will engage in heuristic or systematic processing. Moreover, according to the mood-as-input model, one's mood may influence one's confidence in a configural way. Thus under some conditions either a positive or a negative mood may stop a person at heuristic processing, whereas under other conditions either mood may induce a person to continue beyond heuristic processing to systematic processing.

To test this hypothesis, Martin, Ward, et al. (1993) instructed participants who were in either positive or negative moods to generate a list of birds. Half of the participants were told to stop generating the birds when they no longer enjoyed doing so, whereas half were asked to stop when they thought they had generated enough. What are the signs of role fulfillment in these two conditions? Or, more precisely, how would a participant feel if he or she enjoyed generating birds or felt satisfied with the number of birds he or she had generated? The answer in both cases is the same. The person would feel good. In other words, in both cases a positive mood signals role fulfillment. The motivational implications of this role fulfillment, however, are different in the two contexts.

If the person is enjoying the task, then he or she should continue. If the person feels that he or she has generated enough, then the person should stop. The end result would be that positive moods would induce more systematic processing than negative moods when the moods were input relative to an "enjoyment" rule, but the reverse should be true when the moods were input relative to an "enough" rule. The results of Martin, Ward, et al. (1993) were consistent with this interpretation. When participants were asked to stop generating the birds when they no longer enjoyed it, those in negative moods stopped sooner than those in positive moods, whereas when participants were asked to stop when they thought they had generated enough, those in positive moods stopped sooner than those in negative moods.

In sum, the mood-as-input model suggests that although there may be actuarial relations between certain moods and certain styles of processing, there is no necessary relation between the two. There are two reasons for this: (a) Negative moods signal a discrepancy only when individuals are in pursuit of a goal the attainment of which is accompanied by a positive mood. When individuals are in pursuit of a goal the attainment of which is accompanied by a negative mood, positive moods signal a discrepancy. (b) Even when a mood (positive or negative) signals a discrepancy, it is likely to predispose a person toward systematic processing only when such processing is instrumental to progress toward the goal (e.g., Have I processed enough?).

Positive Moods and Flexible and Creative Processing

When compared along a systematic–heuristic dimension, people in negative moods typically come out as the better thinkers in the sense that they are more systematic and more accurate. When compared in terms of creativity, flexibility, and efficiency, however, people in positive moods often appear to be the better thinkers. Relative to people in negative moods, those in positive moods have been shown to be more creative (Isen & Daubman, 1984), more flexible (Murray, Sujan, Hirt, & Sujan, 1990), and more efficient (Isen, 1993). One way to interpret such results from a mood-as-input perspective is to assume that people often use their moods to evaluate the quality of their output or their confidence in their output.

This result is perhaps best demonstrated in a study by Martin and Stoner (1996). Participants in positive or negative moods were presented with a cue word (e.g., *cat*) and given three seconds to come up with the first associate they could think of (e.g., *dog*). After participants gave this first response, some were asked whether they thought they had come up with a good response. If they felt they had, then they were to keep that response. If they felt they had not, then they were to come up with an alternate response. The remaining participants were asked whether they thought they could come up with a response that was better than their initial one. If they felt they could, then they were to do so. If they felt they could not, then they were to keep the first one.

When given only three seconds, people in positive moods generated the same number of creative responses as did people in negative moods. When asked if their initial response was a good one, however, people in negative moods were more likely to feel that it was not. Hence, they were more likely to generate an alternate response, and, ultimately, they were more likely to generate creative responses. On the other hand, when asked if they could come up with a better response, those in positive moods were more likely to feel that they could. Hence they were more likely to generate an alternate response and ultimately more likely to generate creative responses.

As can be seen, in this one study, all three possible results were obtained (i.e., no difference in creativity for positive and negative moods, greater creativity in positive than negative, and greater creativity in negative than positive). This pattern makes it clear that there is no inherent relation between being in a given mood and being open, flexible, and creative. A given mood is likely to foster flexible, creative responding only when it is used as input in a way that leads people to move beyond their initial mundane responses. In the right context, either positive or negative mood can do this.

ADDRESSING CONTRIBUTORS' QUESTIONS

Regardless of how well we, as chapter authors, think we have communicated our ideas, there are always points that remain unclear. In this section, I attempt to address three questions about the mood-as-input model raised by the other contributors to this volume.

1. The mood-as-input model admittedly involves the same starting assumption as the mood-as-information model. Specifically, both models assume that moods produce their effects by conveying information through subjective experience (rather than through spreading activation). Because of this commonality, a question can be raised regarding the extent to which the mood-as-input model is really a unique, independent model. Why have you portrayed your model as an independent model rather than as an add-on or qualification of the mood-as-information model?

The key to answering this question is understanding the distinction between the hypothesis that moods are used as information and the mood-as-information model. The two are not synonymous. The former suggests that moods influence judgments and processing through their subjective experience, whereas the latter suggests more specifically that moods influence judgments through the "How do I feel about it?" heuristic. The mood-as-input model incorporates the former but not the latter. In short, the mood-as-input model and the mood-as-information model propose different mechanisms through which moods can operate as information.

Consider the way in which the two mechanisms address the effects of mood on evaluation. According to the mood-as-information model, moods influence evaluations when individuals mistake aspects of their moods for aspects of their appraisal of the target. One implication of this confusion process is that the valence of an evaluation must necessarily be congruent with the valence of the mood. There is no way for an individual to mistake a positive mood for his or her appraisal of a target yet render a negative evaluation of that target. As Schwarz and Bohner (1996) put it, "Reliance on a 'How do I feel about it?' heuristic (Schwarz & Clore, 1988), however, is bound to result in more positive evaluation of the [target] under elated than under depressed moods" (p. 130). The mood-as-input model, by comparison, suggests that moods operate as a piece of information in a configural processing system. In this system, moods can influence evaluations even when the moods are not mistaken for the appraisal of the target, and either a positive or a negative mood can lead to either a positive or a negative evaluation.

The difference between the two models might be seen more clearly when one examines the way in which each model addresses mood-incongruent evaluations such as those obtained in the mood-as-input research. According to the mood-as-information model (Schwarz, chapter 7, this volume), mood-incongruent evaluations do not involve changes in the evaluative implications of the feelings. Rather, they "require mood-congruent evaluations of the target in the first place" (p. 162). In this explanation, an individual's mood leads the individual to render a mood-congruent evaluation, and it is this evaluation (rather than the mood) that subsequently conveys mood-incongruent implications when the individual considers the imposed standard (e.g., a sad movie, empathy). From the mood-as-input perspective, however, it is the mood (the actual subjective experience) that takes on different evaluative implications in different contexts and that gives rise to an evaluation that is inconsistent with the valence of the mood.

How would each of these views explain the finding of Martin et al. (1997) that the sadder participants felt while watching a sad movie, the more they liked that movie? If mood-incongruent evaluations "require mood-congruent evaluations in the first place" (Schwarz, chapter 7, this volume, p. 162), then we would have to assume that the participants' sad moods initially caused the participants to dislike the movie. After taking into consideration that the movie was supposed to be sad, however, participants would change their initial dislike for the movie into liking (for reasons not specified in the mood-as-information model).

From the mood-as-input perspective, on the other hand, when participants evaluated the sad movie, they used their moods to gauge the extent to which the movie fulfilled its role (i.e., made them feel sad). The sadder participants felt, the more the movie fulfilled its role, and the more favorably participants rated the movie. In this way, it was the participants' sad mood, not an initial negative evaluation, that contributed to the participants' subsequent positive evaluation of the movie. Participants liked the sad movie not because they initially disliked it (i.e., an initial mood-congruent evaluation) but because the movie made them experience sadness (which is a good thing in the context of evaluating a sad movie).

The mood-as-information model and the mood-as-input model also differ in their treatment of the motivational effects of moods. The mood-as-information model assumes that there are invariant associations between certain moods and certain motivational predispositions. Specifically, negative moods signal a problem with the environment, and "in response to that signal, individuals employ a detail-oriented, bottom-up processing strategy with close attention to information that is relevant to the task at hand" (Schwarz, chapter 7, this volume, pp. 171-172). Positive moods, on the other hand, signal a nonproblematic environment, and in response to that signal, individuals feel free to maintain a generally low level of motivation with regard to processing. Although these different motivational predispositions are the invariable outcome of being in a positive or a negative mood, they are not invariably reflected in an individual's behavior (e.g., level of processing). Other currently active goals can override the predispositions. An override is more likely with a positive than a negative mood, however, because individuals are more willing to process in a detail-oriented way in a safe (i.e., positive) environment than they are to process in a shallow way in an unsafe (i.e., negative) environment.

The mood-as-input model, by comparison, does not assume that certain moods are invariantly associated with certain motivational predispositions. According to the model, an individual's mood may indeed communicate information about the status of the environment, but this information need not lead invariably to certain motivational predispositions. From the mood-as-input perspective, either a positive or a negative mood can motivate increased or decreased processing, depending on the context. Because of this, no outside, interfering process (e.g., a current goal) is needed to overcome an initial motivational predisposition. There is no initial predisposition to overcome. Moods naturally convey different motivational implications in different conditions.

Consider how these two approaches address the role of a positive mood in an individual who is engaged in enjoyable cognitive activity, such as solving a crossword puzzle. According to the mood-as-information model, the positive mood grants the individual the freedom to process either heuristically or systematically. Because the environment feels safe, the individual would not experience any particular processing demand coming from the environment. So the individual would feel free to process according to the demands of the specific task (i.e., the crossword puzzle). From the mood-as-input perspective, however, a positive mood does more than merely allow an individual performing an enjoyable task to process systematically—it motivates the individual to do so. When performing an enjoyable task, the individual may interpret his or her positive mood as a sign that he or she is enjoying the task, and this is likely to foster continued performance of and greater involvement in the task (Hirt et al., 1996; Sansone & Harackiewicz, 1996). In other words, from the mood-as-input perspective, the individual would process systematically during the enjoyable task not because he or she felt free to do so but because he or she wanted to do so.

In summary, the mood-as-input model and the mood-as-information model are very different from one another once one moves past the common starting assumption that subjective experiences communicate information. Because of this, portraying the mood-as-input model as a variant or extension of the mood-as-information model would be misleading. It would hide a number of important and consequential theoretical differences.

2. The determination of mood meanings in your model appears to reflect sophisticated processing that involves a great deal of higher level, inferential thinking. How do you reconcile this kind of complex processing with the suggestion (e.g., Damasio, DeSousa, Zajonc) that affective states produce their effects through simple, precognitive, evolutionarily basic processes?

There is no disagreement between the two positions if one acknowledges that a process can be evolutionarily basic yet still be complex. Even the prototype of the evolutionarily basic process, the fixed action pattern, is sensitive to configural information. When a baby gull, for example, is presented with various models of its parent, the gull does not respond merely to the size of a model's head. It responds to the size of the head in relation to the body. This is why the baby may respond more favorably to a model that is twice the size of its parent than to a model that is the same size, provided the former maintains the same body–head ratio as the parent and the latter does not (Tinbergen & Perdeck, 1950).

The possibility of a process being both complex and evolutionarily basic makes sense when one considers that evolution selects for reproductive advantage, not for simplicity. If a simple process increases inclusive fitness, then this simple process will be represented in the subsequent generation. If a more complex process leads to greater inclusive fitness, however, then a more complex process will be represented in the subsequent generation. In either case, though, the processing will occur quickly and reliably. What this means is that there is no reason to believe that configural responding is not evolutionarily basic. On the contrary, there is reason to believe that it is evolutionarily basic.

Configural responding has been observed across the phylogenetic spectrum. It has been observed in monkeys (Delgado, 1983; Gaffan & Harrison, 1993), rats (Capaldi, 1985), pigeons (Pearce & Wilson, 1990), frogs and toads (Ingle, 1983), lizards (Hertz, Huey, & Nevo, 1982), salamanders (Roth, 1987), and insects (Prete, 1990; Rilling, Mittelstaedt, & Roeder, 1959). Hertz et al. (1982), for example, found that the fight-or-flight response of ground-dwelling lizards depended not merely on the lizards' body temperature nor on the presence or absence of a predator but on both. Because these lizards live on the ground, they depend on running speed to escape approaching predators. The lizards, however, are also cold-blooded. This means that they cannot run fast when their body temperature is low. If a lizard with a low body temperature tried to run from a predator, then the lizard might be eaten. It is more adaptive, therefore, for a lizard with a low body temperature to stay and fight. Because of this, we might expect that evolution would have built into these lizards a temperature-dependent response to predators. It has. When their body temperature is high, these ground-dwelling lizards run from an approaching predator. When their body temperature is low, the lizards stand their ground and fight. In short, the lizard does not respond merely to body temperature nor merely to the presence of a predator. It responds to the configuration of both. In terms of this chapter, we might refer to the lizard's fight-or-flight response as being dependent on temperature as input.

Another particularly compelling example of configural responding in nonhumans comes from the work of Delgado (1983). He allowed a troop of monkeys to interact naturally, and he noted each monkey's place in the social hierarchy. Then he implanted electrodes in the thalamus of several of the middle-ranked monkeys. He found that radio stimulation of the thalamus led to aggressive behavior when these monkeys were in the company of lower ranked monkeys but led to submissive behavior when the same monkeys were in the presence of higher ranked monkeys. In summarizing this work, Delgado (1983) wrote, "These experiments showed that stimulation of the same monkey in the same brain locus and with the same parameters induced aggressive or submissive responses depending on the subject's social rank" (p. 335). In short, even among nonhuman animals, stimuli can mean different things in different contexts.

Not only do we know that configural responding is present across the phylogenetic spectrum, but we are also beginning to learn which brain mechanisms govern configural responding in organisms such as rats and monkeys. Configural responding in these organisms entails significant participation of the hippocampus (e.g., Gaffan & Harrison, 1993; Rudy & Sutherland, 1995; Whishaw & Tomie, 1991). This finding is consistent with the mood-as-input conjecture that configural responding need not involve lengthy, effortful processing in higher order brain structures.

In sum, configural responding is seen across the phylogenetic spectrum, it takes place quickly and reliably, and it involves significant participation of subcortical regions of the brain. There is no reason to believe, therefore, that the configural processing depicted in the mood-as-input model necessarily involves conscious, deliberate, time-consuming processing in higher order brain structures. In fact, everything in evolution theory and a wealth of evidence from research on lower organisms leads us to the opposite conclusion. Configural responding is basic, adaptive, widespread, and efficient.

3. The use of mood in your model seems to involve more "executive" processing than most models, and the model seems to allow for any mood effect in any context. This raises two problems. How can researchers decide what the stimulus configuration or mood meaning is on any given occasion? Also, who decides what the stimulus information or mood meaning is on any given occasion? In other words, how does the mood-as-input model avoid the homunculus problem?

I start with the "Who decides?" part of the question. As just noted, configural responding need not be a conscious, deliberate, higher order process. After all, such responding has been observed in organisms as simple as insects (Prete, 1990). In fact, the configural processing of moods suggested in the mood-as-input model is perfectly compatible with connectionist thinking (Rumelhart & McClelland, 1986). In connectionist models, meaning is conveyed in the pattern of stimulation rather than in isolatable pieces of information. This is why a phrase such as "man eating shark" takes on different meanings in the sentence, "While swimming, I saw a man eating shark" compared to the sentence "While in a restaurant, I saw a man eating shark." The cognitive system is capable of processing multiple meanings simultaneously, with the particular meaning ultimately settled on being determined by the multiple, mutual, simultaneous constraints. In other words, each piece of information influences the meaning of the others, while at the same time its meaning is also influenced by the others. Moreover, the cognitive system can perform this constraint operation in the absence of an executive or a homunculus. As Rumelhart, Hinton, and McClelland (1986) described it, "There is no executive or other overseer. There are only relatively simple units, each doing its own relatively simple job" (p. 47).

This is essentially the argument of the mood-as-input model. Individuals process the mood, target, and context information in parallel, and each of these constrains the meaning of the other. Moreover, all of this can happen quickly, easily, and without the intervention of an executive or homunculus.

The second part of the question asks how we, as researchers, can decide on any given occasion what the meaning of a mood is. Is it possible to tell a priori if a positive mood will convey positive or negative implications? Of course. The answer is the same as it is with any theory. We use pilot testing and normative data. One particularly clear example of this practice comes from Green, Sedikides, and Martin (1997). They explored the conditions under which participants in negative moods would evaluate themselves more favorably than would participants in positive moods. From a mood-as-input perspective, positive evaluations should arise when a mood (positive or negative) signals fulfillment of a positive role. So to predict when a negative mood might lead to favorable self-ratings, we need to find a role that is positive yet that is fulfilled by being in a negative mood. Green and colleagues (1997) asked participants to rate various traits in terms of their desirability and also to indicate whether a positive or a negative mood signaled fulfillment of each trait (i.e., would make them feel as though they possessed each trait). The researchers found that the traits *deep, reflective,* and *thoughtful* were rated favorably but that their presence was signaled by a negative mood. What this means is that if participants are asked to rate themselves in terms of these traits, then those in negative moods should rate themselves more favorably than those in positive moods. These were in fact the results obtained (Green, Sedikes, & Martin, 1997).

More generally, one can make specific predictions using the mood-as-input model by ascertaining in any given situation (a) whether the role relative to which the target is being evaluated is positive or negative, (b) whether a positive or negative mood signals fulfillment of that role, and (c) whether the individual is in a positive or negative mood. Positive evaluations arise when individuals experience the mood (positive or negative) that signals fulfillment of a positive role, whereas negative evaluations arise when individuals experience the mood (positive or negative) that signals fulfillment of a negative role. Mood-congruent evaluations are obtained so often in the literature because the conditions of most experiments are those in which a positive mood signals fulfillment of a positive role (e.g., liking, life satisfaction).

CLOSING COMMENTS

In sum, the mood-as-input model is a unique theoretical model that can account for a number of different mood effects with a single mechanism. Without recourse to outside, interfering processes, the model can account for mood-congruent evaluations, mood-incongruent evaluations, and no effect of mood on evaluations. Although the model relies on the assumption that moods operate as information, it does not assume that they do so only through the "How do I feel about it?" heuristic. Rather, moods are processed in parallel with the target and contextual information in such a way that the meaning of the mood influences and is influenced by the meaning of the other information. Although this process is more complex than the hedonistic, associative processes proposed in most models of mood, there is reason to believe that the process is evolutionarily basic and that it can occur quickly, reliably, and without the intervention of an executive or a homunculus. Of course, the ultimate fate of the mood-as-input model rests in additional research. At this point, however, it may be better to assume that humans are sophisticated processors of mood information and to look for such processing than to assume that humans process mood information in primitive ways and thus fail to look for sophisticated processing.

REFERENCES

Abele, A., & Petzold, P. (1994). How does mood operate in an impression formation task? An information integration approach. *European Journal of Social Psychology, 24,* 173–187.

Allen, P. A., Wallace, B., & Weber, T. A. (1996). Influence of case type, word frequency, and exposure duration on visual recognition. *Journal of Experimental Psychology: Human Perception and Performance, 21,* 914–934.

Anderson, R. C., & Ortony, A. (1975). On putting apples into bottles: A problem of polysemy. *Cognitive Psychology, 7,* 167–180.

Asch, S. E. (1946). Forming impressions of personality. *Journal of Abnormal and Social Psychology, 67,* 258–290.

Bower, G. H. (1981). Mood and memory. *American Psychologist, 36,* 129–148.

Capaldi, E. J. (1985). Anticipation and remote associations: A configural approach. *Journal of Experimental Psychology: Learning, Memory, and Cognition, 11,* 444–449.

Carver, C. S., & Scheier, M. F. (1990). Origins and functions of positive and negative affect: A control process view. *Psychological Review, 97,* 19–35.

Cervone, D., Kopp, D. A., Schaumann, L., & Scott, W. D. (1994). Mood, self-efficacy, and performance standards: Lower moods induce higher standards for performance. *Journal of Personality and Social Psychology, 67,* 499–512.

Chaiken, S., Liberman, A., & Eagly, A. H. (1989). Heuristic and systematic information processing within and beyond the persuasion context. In J. S. Uleman & J. A. Bargh (Eds.), *Unintended thought* (pp. 212–252). New York: Guilford.

Clark, M. S., & Isen, A. M. (1982). Toward understanding the relationship between feeling states and social behavior. In A. Hastorf & A. M. Isen (Eds.), *Cognitive social psychology* (pp. 73–108). New York: Elsevier/North-Holland.

Clore, G. L. (1992). Cognitive phenomenology: Feelings and the construction of judgment. In L. L. Martin & A. Tesser (Eds.), *The construction of social judgments* (pp. 133–163). Hillsdale, NJ: Lawrence Erlbaum Associates.

Cosky, M. J. (1976). The role of letter recognition in word recognition. *Memory and Cognition, 4*, 207–214.

Darley, J. M., & Latané, B. (1968). Bystander intervention in emergencies: Diffusion of responsibility. *Journal of Personality and Social Psychology, 8*, 377–383.

Delgado, J. M. R. (1983). Dominance, hierarchy, and brain stimulation. *Behavioral and Brain Sciences, 2*, 334–335.

Gaffan, D., & Harrison, S. (1993). Role of the dorsal prestirate cortex in visuospatial configural discrimination by monkeys. *Behavioural Brain Research, 56*, 119–125.

Green, J. D., Sedikides, C., & Martin, L. L. (1997). [Assessing role fulfillment in mood incongruent evaluations]. Unpublished data. University of North Carolina.

Gunther, D. C., Ferraro, F. R., & Kirchner, T. (1996). Influence of emotional state on irrelevant thoughts. *Psychonomic Bulletin and Review, 3*, 491–494.

Hertz, P. E., Huey, R. B., & Nevo, E. (1982). Fight versus flight: Body temperature influences defensive responses of lizards. *Animal Behavior, 30*, 676–679.

Higgins, E. T., & Rholes, W. S. (1976). Impression formation and role fulfillment: A "holistic reference" approach. *Journal of Experimental Social Psychology, 12*, 422–435.

Higgins, E. T., Rholes, W. S., & Jones, C. R. (1977). Category accessibility and impression formation. *Journal of Experimental Social Psychology, 13*, 141–154.

Hirt, E. R., Melton, R. J., McDonald, H. E., & Harackiewicz, J. M. (1996). Processing goals, task interest, and the mood performance relationship: A mediational analysis. *Journal of Personality and Social Psychology, 71*, 245–261.

Hsee, C. K., & Abelson, R. P. (1991). Velocity relations: Satisfaction as a function of the first derivative of outcome over time. *Journal of Personality and Social Psychology, 60*, 431–347.

Ingle, D. (1983). Brain mechanisms of visual localization by frogs and toads. In J. P. Ewert, R. R. Capranica, & D. J. Ingle (Eds.), *Advances in vertebrates neurothology* (pp. 177–226). New York: Plenum.

Isen, A. M. (1987). Positive affect, cognitive processes, and social behavior. In L. Berkowitz (Ed.), *Advances in experimental social psychology* (Vol. 20, pp. 203–253). New York: Academic Press.

Isen, A. M. (1993). Positive mood and decision making. In M. Lewis & J. Haviland (Eds.), *Handbook of emotion* (pp. 261–277). New York: Guilford.

Isen, A. M., & Daubman, K. A. (1984). The influence of affect on categorization. *Journal of Personality and Social Psychology, 52*, 1122–1131.

Isen, A. M., Shalker, T. E., Clark, M. S., & Karp, L. (1978). Affect, accessibility of material in memory, and behavior: A cognitive loop? *Journal of Personality and Social Psychology, 36*, 1–12.

Jacewicz, M. M. (1979). Word context effects on letter recognition. *Perceptual and Motor Skills, 48*, 935–942.

Mandler, G. (1984). *Mind and body: Psychology of emotion and stress.* New York: Norton.

Manis, M., Biernat, M., & Nelson, T. F. (1991). Comparison and expectancy processes in human judgment. *Journal of Personality and Social Psychology, 61*, 203–211.

Martin, L. L., Abend, T., Sedikides, C., & Greene, J. D. (1997). How would I feel if . . . ? Mood as input to a role fulfillment evaluation process. *Journal of Personality and Social Psychology, 73*, 242–253.

Martin, L. L., Achee, J. W., Ward, D. W., & Harlow, T. F. (1993). The role of cognition and effort in the use of emotions to guide behavior. In R. S. Wyer & T. K. Srull (Eds.), *Advances in social cognition* (Vol. 6, pp. 147–157). Hillsdale, NJ: Lawrence Erlbaum Associates.

Martin, L. L., & Davies, B. (1998). Beyond hedonism and associationism: A configural view of the role of affect in evaluation, processing, and self-regulation. *Motivation and Emotion, 22*, 33–51.

Martin, L. L., & Stoner, P. (1996). Mood as input: What people think about how they feel moods determines how they think. In L. L. Martin & A. Tesser (Eds.), *Striving and feeling: Interactions between goals, affect, and self-regulation* (pp. 279–301) Hillsdale, NJ: Lawrence Erlbaum Associates.

Martin, L. L., & Tesser, A. (1996). Some ruminative thoughts. In R. S. Wyer (Ed.), *The handbook of social cognition* (Vol. 9, pp. 1–48). Mahwah, NJ: Lawrence Erlbaum Associates.

Martin, L. L., Ward, D. W., Achee, J. W., & Wyer, R. S. (1993). Mood as input: People have to interpret the motivational implications of their moods. *Journal of Personality and Social Psychology, 64*, 317–326.

Mayer, J. D., Gaschke, Y. N., Braverman, D. L., & Evans, T. (1992). Mood-congruent judgment is a general effect. *Journal of Personality and Social Psychology, 63*, 119–132.

McKoon, G., & Ratcliff, R. (1992). Spreading activation versus compound cue accounts of priming: Mediated priming revisited. *Journal of Experimental Psychology: Learning, Memory, & Cognition, 18*, 1155–1172.

Milgram, S. (1974). *Obedience to authority.* New York: Harper & Row.

Murray, N., Sujan, H., Hirt, E. R., & Sujan, M. (1990). The influence of mood on categorization: A cognitive flexibility interpretation. *Journal of Personality and Social Psychology, 59*, 411–425.

Pearce, J. M., & Wilson, P. N. (1990). Configural associations in discrimination learning. *Journal of Experimental Psychology: Animal Behavior Processes, 16*, 250–261.

Prete, F. R. (1990). Configural prey recognition by the praying mantis, *Sphodromantic lineola* (Burr.): Effects of size and direction of movement. *Brain, Behavior, and Evolution, 36*, 300–306.

Pusateri, T. P., & Latané, B. (1982). Respect and admiration: Evidence for configural information integration of achieved and ascribed characteristics. *Personality and Social Psychology Bulletin, 8*, 87–93.

Rilling, S. H., Mittelstaedt, K. D., & Roeder, K. D. (1959). Prey recognition in the praying mantis. *Behaviour, 14*, 164–184.

Rosenberg, S., Carnot, N., & Vivekananthan, P. S. (1968). A multidimensional approach to the structure of personality impressions. *Journal of Personality and Social Psychology, 9*, 283–294.

Roth, G. (1987). *Visual behaviour in salamanders.* New York: Springer.

Rudy, J. W., & Sutherland, R. J. (1995). Configural association theory and the hippocampal formation: An appraisal and reconfiguration. *Hippocampus, 5*, 375–389.

Rumelhart, D. E., Hinton, G. E., & McClelland, J. L. (1986). In D. E. Rumelhart & J. L. McClelland (Eds.), *Parallel distributed processing* (Vol. 1, pp. 45–76). Cambridge, MA: MIT Press.

Rumelhart, D. E., & McClelland, J. L. (Eds.). (1986). *Parallel distributed processing* (Vol. 1). Cambridge, MA: MIT Press.

Sanna, C. J., Turley, K. J., & Mark, M. M. (1996) Expected evaluation, goals, and performance: Mood as input. *Personality and Social Psychology Bulletin, 22*, 323–335.

Sansone, C., & Harackiewicz, J. M. (1996). "I don't feel like it": The function of interest in self-regulation. In L. L. Martin & A. Tesser (Eds.), *Striving and feeling* (pp. 203–228). Mahwah, NJ: Lawrence Erlbaum Associates.

Schwarz, N., & Bohner, G. (1996). Feelings and their motivational implications: Moods and the action sequence. In P. M. Gollwitzer & J. A. Bargh (Eds.), *The psychology of action: Linking cognition and motivation to behavior* (pp. 119–145). New York: Guilford.

Schwarz, N., & Clore, G. L. (1983). Mood, misattribution, and judgements of well-being: Informative and directive functions of affective states. *Journal of Personality and Social Psychology*, *45*, 513–523.

Schwarz, N., & Clore, G. L. (1988). How do I feel about it? The information function of affective states. In K. Fiedler & J. Forgas (Eds.), *Affect, cognition and social behavior* (pp. 44–62). Lewinston, NY: Hogrefe.

Schwarz, N., & Clore, G. L. (1996). Feelings and phenomenal experiences. In E. T. Higgins & A. W. Kruglanski (Eds.), *Social psychology: Handbook of basic principles* (pp. 433–465). New York: Guilford Press.

Sinclair, R. C. (1988). Mood, categorization breadth, and performance appraisal: The effects of order of information acquisition and affective state on halo, accuracy, information retrieval and evaluation. *Organizational Behaviors and Human Decision Processes*, *42*, 22–46.

Strack, F., Martin, L. L., & Stepper, S. (1988). Inhibiting and facilitating conditions of the human smile: A nonobtrusive test of the facial feedback hypothesis. *Journal of Personality and Social Psychology*, *54*, 768–777.

Tinbergen, N., & Perdeck, A. C. (1950). On the stimulus situation releasing the begging response in the newly hatched Herring Gull chick (*Larus argentatus argentatus Pont.*), *Behaviour*, *3*, 1–39.

Wertheimer, M. (1923). Untersuchungen zur Lehre von der Gestalt, II [Investigations on the theory of the Gestalt]. *Psychologische Forschung*, *4*, 301–350.

Whishaw, I. Q., & Tomie, J. (1991). Acquisition and retention by hippocampal rats of simple, conditional, and configural tasks using tactile and olfactory cues: Implications for hippocampal function. *Behavioral Neuroscience*, *105*, 787–797.

Wicklund, R. A. (1979). The influence of self-awareness on human behavior. *American Scientist*, *67*, 187–193.

Wishner, J. (1960). Reanalysis of "Impressions of Personality." *Psychological Review*, *67*, 96–112.

Woll, S. B., Weeks, D. G., Fraps, C. L., Pendergrass, J., & Vanderplas, M. A. (1980). Role of sentence context in the encoding of trait descriptors. *Journal of Personality and Social Psychology*, *39*, 59–68.

Wyer, R. S. (1970). The prediction of evaluations of social role occupants as a function of the favorableness, relevance and probability associated with attributes of these occupants. *Sociometry*, *33*, 79–96.

Chapter 7

Feelings as Information: Implications for Affective Influences on Information Processing

Norbert Schwarz
University of Michigan

Many theories of emotion share the assumption that affective experiences serve a signaling function (see Frijda, 1986, 1988, for reviews). Consistent with this notion, Wyer and Carlston (1979) suggested that mood effects on social judgment may reflect the use of one's feelings as a source of information. Elaborating on this widely shared premise in various ways, Gerald Clore and I developed an approach to mood effects on judgment that became known as the "mood as information" model (Schwarz & Clore, 1983, 1988). We later extended the model to feelings other than mood, including nonaffective phenomenal experiences such as ease or difficulty of recall or perceptual fluency (for a review, see Schwarz, 1998), and accordingly changed the label to "feelings as information" (Clore, 1992; Schwarz, 1990). In another extension, I suggested that the information provided by our feelings may trigger different processing strategies (Schwarz, 1990) and explored this hypothesis in collaboration with Herbert Bless and Gerd Bohner (Schwarz & Bless, 1991; Schwarz, Bless, & Bohner, 1991). As the contributions to this volume indicate, these lines of theorizing stimulated considerable research activity and resulted in a number of closely related conceptualizations.

Extensive reviews of this work are available (Clore, Schwarz, & Conway, 1994; Schwarz, 1987, 1990; Schwarz, Bless, & Bohner, 1991; Schwarz & Clore, 1988, 1996), and I only highlight the key assumptions of the feelings-as-information approach in this chapter. This approach bears most directly on the impact of feelings on evaluative judgment and processing style and is relatively silent on mood effects on memory. Accordingly, I first address these core areas and introduce the theoretical assumptions in the respective context to avoid unnecessary redundancy.

MOOD AND JUDGMENT

Key Assumptions

The mood-as-information model was initially developed to account for mood effects on evaluative judgments. Rather than engaging in a detailed review and integration of relevant information, people may simplify the judgmental task by holding the target of judgment in mind, asking themselves, "How do I feel about it?" In doing so, they may misread preexisting mood states as affective reactions to the target, resulting in more positive judgments under happy rather than sad moods. If so, mood effects on evaluative judgments should be eliminated when the informational value of one's mood for the judgment at hand is called into question. Importantly, the opposite of this hypothesis does not hold, in contrast to what some interpreters (e.g., Forgas, 1995) suggested. That is, the use of our feelings as a source of information does not require that we consciously attribute these feelings to the target. Much as we use the declarative information that happens to come to mind, we use the experiential information that happens to come to mind. In either case, we assume that the information is relevant to what we think about, or else why would it come to mind? Higgins (1998) has recently discussed this pervasive tendency as the "aboutness" principle of human inference. Yet we do not rely on the information that comes to mind when its relevance to the target is called into question, for example, because we attribute our mood to an irrelevant source (Schwarz & Clore, 1983) or because we are aware that the declarative information was brought to mind by a preceding priming task (e.g., Lombardi, Higgins, & Bargh, 1987; Strack, Schwarz, Bless, Kübler, & Wänke, 1993). In short, what comes to mind seems relevant by default—or else, why would I have these thoughts or feelings in apparent response to the target? In contrast, assessments that highlight the irrelevance and low diagnosticity of the input need to be triggered by salient features of the situation (cf. Schwarz & Bless, 1992).

Evidence and Issues

In a first experimental test of the basic logic of the feelings-as-information hypothesis, Schwarz and Clore (1983) observed that the impact of sad moods on judgments of general life satisfaction was eliminated when participants were induced to attribute their moods (either correctly or incorrectly) to a transient external source, such as rainy weather (Experiment 2) or alleged side effects of a soundproof experimental room (Experiment 1). The impact of happy moods, however, was not significantly affected by (mis)attribution manipulations. At the time, we accounted for this asymmetry by suggesting that most people feel good most of the time. Hence, sad moods are deviations from the normal state of the organism and require explanation. In contrast, happy moods do not require explanation, unless being in a happy mood is inconsistent with situational expectations. As a result, we argued, sad moods are more likely to trigger attributional efforts (e.g., Bohner, Bless, Schwarz, & Strack, 1988) and to direct attention to the likely sources of one's bad feelings, which is a prerequisite for obtaining (mis)attribution effects. I return to this issue later.

The assumption that moods may serve as a source of information in forming evaluative judgments has fared well in subsequent research (see Clore et al., 1994; Schwarz, 1987, 1990; Schwarz & Clore, 1988, 1996, for reviews), and it is now widely accepted that mood effects on evaluative judgment do not necessarily reflect mood-congruent recall, in contrast to the dominant perspective in the early 1980s (Bower, 1981; Isen, Shalker, Clark, & Karp, 1978). Moreover, the influence of specific emotions (e.g., Keltner, Locke, & Audrain, 1993; Schwarz, Servay, & Kumpf, 1985), physical arousal (e.g., Zillman, 1978), and phenomenal experiences such as ease of recall (e.g., Schwarz et al., 1991; Winkielman, Schwarz, & Belli, 1998) on subsequent judgments is also eliminated under (mis)attribution conditions, supporting the viability of the model as a general account of how people use experiential information in forming a judgment.

Under many conditions, reliance on one's feelings or phenomenal experiences reflects a heuristic strategy, as initially suggested by Schwarz and Clore (1988). Accordingly, the strength of feelings-as-information effects depends on variables commonly assumed to influence the degree of heuristic versus systematic processing, including the presence of time pressure (e.g., Siemer & Reisenzein, 1998), the amount (e.g., Schwarz, Strack, Kommer, & Wagner, 1987) and relative salience (e.g., Strack, Schwarz, & Gschneidinger, 1985) of competing information, and related variables (see Schwarz, 1990; Schwarz & Clore, 1996). Again, variables known to influence the use of heuristic versus systematic processing strategies also influence reliance on nonaffective feelings, such as experienced ease of recall (e.g., Grayson & Schwarz, 1999; Rothman & Schwarz, 1998; see Schwarz, 1998, for a review). Note, however, that reliance on one's feelings does not always reflect a heuristic strategy. When asked how we feel about Lenny, for example, our feelings may be the most relevant source of information available under a systematic judgment strategy. Accordingly, the assumption that feelings will only serve as information when individuals adopt a heuristic processing style (as suggested by Forgas, 1995) is mistaken.

In recent discussions of mood effects on evaluative judgments, Martin and his colleagues (e.g., Martin, Abend, Sedikides, & Green, 1997; Martin, chapter 6, this volume) emphasized that the informational implications of one's mood are context-dependent. This is certainly correct, as demonstrated in the initial Schwarz and Clore (1983) experiments: If the information conveyed by one's mood were not context-dependent, (mis)attribution effects would not be obtained. Martin et al.'s (1997) argument, however, goes beyond the perceived diagnosticity of one's feelings and entails that a positive mood, for example, may convey positive as well as negative information about a target, depending on the context of judgment. To use an example from their ingenious experiments, when I am asked how successful a story was at making me feel bad, but I feel good anyway, I am likely to conclude that the story was not successful—a condition under which feeling good leads to a negative judgment. In my reading, findings of this type do not indicate that the same mood may convey information of different valence. Instead, I propose that these findings simply reflect changes in the criterion: In the story example, my positive feelings inform me that the story was enjoyable (a positive, mood-congruent assessment of the target), consistent with numerous earlier findings. This positive assessment of the target, however, has negative implications for the imposed criterion of judgment, namely whether the story was successful at making me feel bad. From this perspective, the obtained findings illustrate that the same input has different implications for different criteria of judgment, yet this does not imply a change in the meaning of the input itself. Much as a sweet cookie makes for a poor salty snack, a story that maintains happy feelings is a poor sad story—yet the meaning of my happy feelings themselves changes as little as the sweet taste of the cookie. In my reading, Martin et al.'s (1997) findings require mood-congruent evaluations of the target in the first place, and therefore confirm rather than challenge the "How do I feel about it?" logic outlined previously.

In summary, the feelings-as-information model explains mood-congruent judgment as a result of the use of one's mood as a source of information. Its major strength is its general applicability across a wide range of different sources of experiential information that are not addressed by approaches that treat moods as highly unique phenomena. The model does not imply, however, that reliance on one's mood as a source of information is the only process that can drive mood-congruent judgment. However, conclusive demonstrations of other processes need to rule out the present assumptions by introducing the relevant (mis)attribution conditions, a step that is usually missed. As a result, many studies remain inherently ambiguous with regard to the underlying processes.

MOOD AND PROCESSING STYLE

As noted previously, Schwarz and Clore (1983) addressed the asymmetric impact of (mis)attribution manipulations by suggesting that sad moods are more likely than happy moods to deviate from one's "usual" feelings, which are mildly positive for most people most of the time (e.g., Matlin & Stang, 1979). Accordingly, sad moods may need explanation. If so, we initially assumed, being in an unexplained sad mood may interfere with other cognitive tasks, reflecting the competing demands of explaining one's mood. This hypothesis led to many surprises (see Schwarz, 1987). In an initial test, we exposed participants in a happy or sad mood to strong or weak persuasive arguments and assumed that sad moods would reduce systematic message elaboration (Bless, Bohner, Schwarz, & Strack, 1986; later published as Experiment 1 of Bless, Bohner, Schwarz, & Strack, 1990). In contrast to expectations, however, sad participants engaged in message elaboration, whereas happy participants did not, a now familiar finding that is reliably replicable (for reviews see Mackie, Asuncion, & Rosselli, 1992; Schwarz, Bless, & Bohner, 1991). At about the same time, research in person perception (most notably Sinclair, 1988) indicated that being in a sad mood reduced halo effects in impression formation.

Key Assumptions

To account for findings of this type, I suggested that the informative function of moods is more general than had been captured in our initial research, which focused solely on evaluative judgments. Specifically, I suggested (Schwarz, 1990) that the relationship between one's mood and the state of one's environment is bidirectional. We usually feel bad when we encounter a threat of negative or a lack of positive outcomes and feel good when we obtain positive outcomes and are not threatened by negative ones. Hence our moods reflect the state of our environment. If so, being in a bad mood signals a problematic situation, whereas being in a good mood signals a benign situation. I further proposed that our thought processes are tuned to meet the situational requirements signaled by our feelings:

> If negative affective states inform the individual about a lack of positive, or a threat of negative, outcomes, the individual may be motivated to change his or her current situation. Attempts to change the situation, however, initially require a careful assessment of the features of the current situation, an analysis of their causal links, detailed explorations of possible mechanisms of change, as well as an anticipation of the potential outcomes of any action that might be initiated. Moreover, individuals may be unlikely to take risks in a situation that is already considered problematic, and may therefore avoid simple heuristics as well as novel solutions. (Schwarz, 1990, p. 544)

Conversely,

> If positive affective states inform the individual that his or her personal
> world is currently a safe and satisfactory place, the individual may see little
> need to engage in cognitive effort, *unless* this is required by other currently
> active goals. In pursuing these goals, the individual may also be willing to
> take some risk, given that the general situation is considered safe. Thus, sim-
> ple heuristics may be preferred to more effortful, detail oriented judgmental
> strategies; new procedures and possibilities may be explored; and unusual,
> creative associations may be elaborated. (Schwarz, 1990, p. 544)

Meanwhile, numerous studies across a wide range of social judgment
tasks have obtained a higher degree of systematic processing under
bad-mood conditions and heuristic processing under good-mood conditions, consistent with the preceding suggestions (see Clore et al., 1994;
Schwarz, Bless, & Bohner, 1991; Schwarz & Clore, 1996, for reviews).
Most important, undermining the informational value of one's mood
through (mis)attribution manipulations has been found to eliminate the
otherwise observed impact of moods on strategies of information processing (Sinclair, Mark, & Clore, 1994), much as it has been found to eliminate
the impact of moods on evaluative judgment (Schwarz & Clore, 1983).
This finding establishes that the impact of moods on processing strategies
is indeed mediated by their informational value, as originally proposed. It
is less clear, however, what the general "cognitive tuning" assumption entails at a more specific level, as the contributions to this volume illustrate:
Do cognitive tuning effects primarily reflect differences in individuals'
willingness to engage in effortful processing strategies? Or do they reflect
differences in focus of attention? Or differences in the reliance on preexisting knowledge structures? I suppose that the most appropriate answer
is, all of the above. Central to the model is the idea that our moods inform
us about the benign or problematic nature of the current situation unless
their informational value is called into question. This assumption does not
entail that happy individuals are generally "cognitively lazy," whereas sad
individuals are generally "motivated."

If being in a bad mood signals a problematic situation, it would indeed
be adaptive to pay attention to details, much as we do when other information signals that something has gone wrong. In fact, failures to obtain a desired outcome have been found to elicit attention to one's actions at a
lower level of detail across a wide variety of tasks (e.g., Wegner &
Vallacher, 1986), and being in a negative affective state is associated with a
narrowed focus of attention (e.g., Broadbent, 1971; Bruner, Matter, &
Papanek, 1955; Easterbrook, 1959). Moreover, it would seem unwise to
rely on one's usual routines and preexisting general knowledge structures
without further consideration of the specifics, rendering data-driven proc-

essing more likely than theory-driven processing when one's mood signals a problematic situation (see Bless, chapter 1, this volume; Bless, Clore, et al., 1996; Bless & Schwarz, 1999; Bless, Schwarz, & Kemmelmeier, 1996). Data-driven processing and attention to detail, however, require more effort, and we are usually willing to expend it when needed. From this perspective, differences in processing effort are entailed by the processing requirements posed by a problematic situation and do not reflect some generic difference in motivation.

Benign situations, on the other hand, do not pose similar requirements. Hence we may pay less attention to detail and may be more likely to rely on our usual routines and general knowledge structures when we are in a good mood unless required otherwise by currently active goals. In contrast to cognitive-capacity accounts of reduced processing under happy moods (e.g., Mackie & Worth, 1989), this suggestion does not entail that happy individuals are somehow unable to engage in systematic processing. Nor does it entail that they are unwilling to engage in the effort required by systematic processing because they want to protect their good mood (e.g., Wegener & Petty, chapter 8, this volume). Rather, it only entails that the mood itself does not signal a situation that poses particular processing requirements. As a result, the spontaneously adopted heuristic-processing style and reliance on preexisting knowledge structures should be easy to override, rendering processing under happy moods more flexible than processing under sad moods.

Evidence and Issues

The bulk of the available data is consistent with the previous assumptions (see Clore et al., 1994; Schwarz & Clore, 1996, for detailed reviews). As already noted, being in a sad mood has been found to increase spontaneous message elaboration in persuasion experiments (for a review, see Schwarz, Bless, & Bohner, 1991), to decrease stereotyping and the reliance on category membership information in person perception experiments (for a review see Bless, Schwarz, & Kemmelmeier, 1996), to decrease the emergence of halo effects, and to improve performance on a variety of other cognitive tasks that require attention to detail (see Clore et al., 1994; Sinclair & Mark, 1992). In contrast, being in a happy mood has been found to decrease message elaboration, to increase stereotyping, and to increase the emergence of halo effects in person perception.

As the theoretical assumptions entail, however, these effects of mood on processing style are most likely to be observed in the absence of instructions or task demands that require a specific processing style. That is, the impact of moods on the spontaneous adoption of processing styles can be overridden by other variables. As noted previously, this is more likely for

happy than for sad moods, presumably reflecting that we hesitate to ignore a potential problem signal. Thus, instructing happy individuals to
pay attention to the quality of the arguments presented has been found to
override the otherwise observed lack of systematic processing in mood
and persuasion experiments (Bless et al., 1990). Similarly, happy individuals have been observed to pay attention to details when they encounter
information blatantly inconsistent with expectations (Bless, Schwarz, &
Wieland, 1996) and to perform well on concentration tests that explicitly
require detail-oriented processing (Bless, Clore, et al., 1996; see Bless,
chapter 1, this volume).

The latter finding is of particular interest because it illustrates the increased flexibility of processing under happy rather than sad moods. Specifically, Bless, Clore, et al. (1996) employed a dual-task-paradigm in
which happy and sad participants listened to a tape-recorded story about
having dinner at a restaurant that contained script-consistent as well as
script-inconsistent information. While listening to the story, participants
worked on a concentration test that required them to mark certain letters
on a work sheet. Note that the concentration test requires detail-oriented
processing, whereas the restaurant story lends itself to script-driven
top-down processing, as well as detail-oriented bottom-up processing.
Recognition tests revealed that happy participants processed the restaurant story in a top-down manner, whereas sad participants processed it in
a bottom-up manner. Specifically, happy participants were more likely to
recognize previously heard script-inconsistent information and showed
more erroneous recognition of previously unpresented script-consistent
information than sad participants. Thus mood affected participants' processing style on a task that lent itself to different strategies. Importantly,
however, happy individuals performed well on the concentration test, in
contrast to what a general "cognitive laziness" hypothesis would predict.
In fact, they outperformed sad individuals, reflecting that the top-down
processing style that they employed on the primary task was less taxing
than the bottom-up processing style used by sad participants, thus leaving
more cognitive capacity for the concentration test. In combination, these
findings indicate that moods influence the spontaneously adopted processing style under conditions in which different processing styles are compatible with the individual's goals and task demands. Under these conditions, sad individuals are likely to spontaneously adopt a systematic,
detail-oriented, bottom-up strategy that is usually adaptive in problematic
situations, whereas happy individuals rely on a less effortful top-down
strategy. Yet when task demands (as in the case of the concentration test;
Bless, Clore, et al., 1996) or explicit instructions (as in persuasion experiments; Bless et al., 1990) require detail-oriented processing, happy individuals are able and willing to engage in the effort.

Whereas the spontaneous processing style of happy individuals is easily overridden by task demands, it should be more difficult to override the systematic, bottom-up processing style observed under sad moods, given that ignoring a potentially problematic situation would be maladaptive. Data reported by Wegener, Petty, and Smith (1995) are consistent with this implication. These authors observed that happy individuals engaged in message elaboration when they were led to expect that this would make them feel happy, but not when they were led to expect that this would make them feel sad. In contrast, sad individuals engaged in message elaboration independent of expectations. In fact, they elaborated somewhat more on the message that would supposedly make them feel sad than on the message that would supposedly make them feel good (in contrast to the authors' predictions). In my reading, this asymmetry reflects that pursuing short-term hedonic goals is a luxury that we are less likely to afford in a situation characterized as problematic than in a situation characterized as benign.

In another conceptualization of mood effects on processing style, Clore et al. (chapter 2, this volume) suggest that positive affect serves as a generic "go" signal, whereas negative affect serves as a "stop" signal "for using whatever goal, strategy, information, or response is most accessible." In essence, individuals in happy moods are assumed to pursue whatever happens to come to mind, whereas individuals in sad moods are assumed to turn away from this information, pursuing alternative inputs or strategies. To derive predictions from this approach we need to know what is most accessible or which strategy is spontaneously used in the first place. In studies pertaining to the use of scripts or stereotypes, the most accessible information is presumably the general knowledge structure, resulting in greater reliance on this knowledge structure under happy than under sad moods. This, of course, is also what is predicted by the reasoning outlined herein (and consistent with the available data). Yet mood effects on processing style have also been observed under conditions in which relevant general knowledge structures are unlikely to be highly accessible. For example, Sinclair and Mark (1992) observed that sad participants were more accurate than happy participants in estimating correlation coefficients from scatterplots. On which basis are we to predict which differences in the accessibility of which information account for this finding? Unless questions of this type can be answered on a priori grounds, the "go/stop" signal proposal seems to lack the specificity required for empirical tests.

In addition, Clore et al.'s (chapter 2, this volume) assumption that sad moods serve as a stop signal for whatever strategy is initially used presumably entails that sad moods should decrease systematic processing under conditions in which systematic processing is the default. In contrast, happy moods should increase systematic processing under conditions in which systematic processing is the default. Empirically, this is not the case. In an early mood and persuasion experiment, Bless et al. (1990, Exp. 1) exposed happy or sad participants to strong or weak arguments. In one condition, the task was introduced as pertaining to language comprehension. In this case, sad participants spontaneously engaged in message elaboration and were influenced by strong but not by weak arguments, whereas happy participants did not engage in message elaboration and were equally influenced by both types of arguments. In another condition, participants were explicitly instructed to pay attention to the quality of the arguments, thus making message elaboration the default. Under this condition, happy as well as sad participants engaged in message elaboration, yet sad individuals did so to a significantly higher degree than happy individuals. Note that this latter finding is inconsistent with the stop-signal logic: According to this logic, sad participants should infer that the elaboration strategy evoked by the instructions is not working and should presumably "stop" pursuing it, whereas happy participants should give this strategy a "go." If so, the opposite pattern of findings should have been obtained, with happy participants showing greater message elaboration than sad ones. As these examples illustrate, the assumption that the information provided by our moods informs us primarily about the adequacy of the cognitive strategies we happen to employ falls short of providing a parsimonious account of the available data. In contrast, the available data are compatible with the assumption that moods influence processing styles by characterizing a situation as problematic or benign, resulting in processing strategies that are tuned to meet apparent situational requirements, unless different requirements are clearly specified or required by other goals.

In summary, the account of mood-induced differences in processing style suggested by Schwarz (1990) is based on two propositions. The first proposition holds that our feelings inform us about the nature of our current situation. In the case of global moods, positive moods indicate that the situation is benign, whereas negative moods indicate that the situation is problematic. Consistent with this assumption, the otherwise observed impact of moods on processing style is eliminated when the informational value of one's mood is called into question (Sinclair et al., 1994). Importantly, the information provided by global moods is relatively diffuse, reflecting that moods do not have a specific referent (see Clore et al., 1994, for a conceptual discussion of different affective states). Hence the information provided by one's mood may seem relevant to a wide range of different situations. The same logic, however, is also applicable to specific emotions, with the important distinction that the information provided by specific emotions is more constrained. Specific emotions have a specific referent, thus limiting their informational value to a narrower set of targets. Moreover, specific emotions entail a specific appraisal pattern and may therefore provide more specific information about the nature of the situation, resulting in more specific influences on processing style. This issue may be fruitfully addressed in future research.

The second proposition holds that our thought processes are tuned to meet the processing requirements entailed in the psychological situation signaled by one's feelings. The obvious weakness of this proposition is that we do not (yet) fully understand what these processing requirements are. Although we can specify the information provided by a given feeling by drawing on the characteristics entailed in the appraisal pattern that gives rise to the feeling in the first place (e.g., Keltner, Ellsworth, & Edwards, 1993), we know little about the mental procedures that individuals employ in dealing with different situations. For the time being, however, it is plausible to assume that individuals who face a situation characterized as problematic are likely to pay attention to detail, avoid reliance on their usual routines and general knowledge structures, and are willing to invest the mental effort required for doing so. As a result, being in a bad mood fosters what may be described as a systematic data-driven processing strategy. In contrast, benign situations do not signal any particular processing requirement. Unless prompted by other goals or situational demands (such as experimenter instructions; e.g., Martin, Ward, Achee, & Wyer, 1993), individuals in a happy mood are therefore likely to rely on default processing strategies and general knowledge structures, resulting in a processing style that may be characterized as heuristic.

Although similar predictions may be derived from different theoretical assumptions in some specific cases (see the other contributions to this volume), the feelings-as-information perspective offers a general framework that promises a coherent account for the impact of moods and emotions on evaluative judgments, as well as processing style, by paying attention to the information provided by a given feeling and the processing requirements entailed in the underlying appraisal pattern. To exploit the full conceptual potential of the model, future research will need to go beyond diffuse moods by addressing the impact of specific appraisal patterns on processing strategies.

Finally, it is worth noting that the logic developed in this section suggests a somewhat different account of the asymmetric misattribution effects observed by Schwarz and Clore (1983). Although it is certainly true that negative moods require more explanation than positive moods under most circumstances (with the obvious exception that feeling good in a sad situation requires explanation as well), it seems likely that the impact of moods on processing strategies contributes to asymmetric attribution effects. Specifically, sorting out the causes of one's feelings and employing the relevant discounting and augmentation logic requires a considerable degree of systematic processing, which individuals are more likely to engage in when in a sad mood. Accordingly, (mis)attribution effects should be more likely to be obtained under sad than under happy mood conditions, consistent with the general impact of moods on processing style.

MOOD AND CREATIVITY

The preceding discussion of mood effects on processing style bears in a relatively straightforward way on mood effects on creativity. Creative problem solving typically requires a playful combination of diverse elements and the exploration of novel solutions. These operations should be impeded by the detail-oriented, bottom-up processing style fostered by negative moods, a style that is associated with a narrow focus of attention. In contrast, these operations should be facilitated by the top-down processing style fostered by positive moods, which is not associated with a narrow focus on the details at hand. Moreover, the exploration of unusual solutions poses the risk of failure, which individuals may be more willing to accept in a situation that is characterized as benign rather than problematic. As a result, one may expect higher creativity under happy than under sad moods, consistent with the bulk of the evidence (see Clore et al., 1994; Schwarz & Clore, 1996, for reviews).

MOOD-CONGRUENT MEMORY

As noted in earlier presentations of the feelings-as-information model, the model is not intended to provide a comprehensive account of mood effects on the recall of valenced information from memory. It is worth noting, however, that the judgmental processes addressed earlier in this chapter may influence recall under some conditions. When asked to recall events from my kindergarten days (Bower, 1981), for example, I may first have an evaluative response, such as, "Gee, my kindergarten days. What were those like?" If so, I may arrive at a more positive assessment when in a good rather than a bad mood for the reasons discussed previously. Next, this global assessment may bias my search for relevant episodes, resulting in the recall of mood-congruent episodes. Importantly, however, this mood effect on recall would be mediated by a preceding mood effect on the evaluative assessment of the target. To address this possibility, Bless, Kocevar, Oberwallner, and Schwarz (reported in Bless, 1996, pp. 37–41) induced a happy or sad mood and asked participants to report events from their kindergarten days either before or after they provided a global evaluation of their time in kindergarten. Replicating numerous previous findings, happy participants evaluated their kindergarten days more positively than sad participants. More important, analyses of the reported events indicated that happy participants recalled more positive events than sad participants, but only when they had previously provided a global evaluative judgment. Obviously, this finding does not imply that all mood-congruent memory effects are mediated by mood-congruent judgment. It does, however, demonstrate that mood effects on evaluative judgments may facilitate subsequent mood-congruent recall, presumably because the global evaluation serves as a search cue. At the same time, the absence of mood-congruent recall under conditions in which no previous global judgment was elicited suggests that individuals do not always form such judgments spontaneously. This pattern of findings raises the possibility that mood-congruent recall may be particularly likely to be obtained under conditions that evoke spontaneous evaluative judgments. To what extent this conjecture can account for the inconsistent findings in the mood-congruent recall domain (see Clore et al., 1994; Schwarz & Clore, 1996, for reviews) is an open issue.

ADDRESSING CONTRIBUTORS' QUESTIONS

1. If the problem-solving mode induced by negative feelings is sufficiently general that it can influence processing in any number of subsequent tasks (e.g., scrutinizing persuasive messages, estimating the correlation in scatterplots), then by what mechanism does it become inapplicable when participants' attention is drawn to the mood induction? After all, the discounting cue does not change participants' moods (Schwarz & Clore, 1983), these moods presumably still signal a problematic environment, and this environment presumably still activates a general problem-solving mode. So exactly how does a discounting cue eliminate the effects of mood on processing?

In early discussions of mood effects on processing style (Schwarz, 1990), I speculated that one of several ways in which negative moods may facilitate systematic processing is through the activation of procedural knowledge relevant to the type of problem at hand. Note that such a process would not entail a generic problem-solving mode but preferential access to procedural knowledge relevant to the situation characterized as problematic by one's mood. I have not pursued this possibility, nor do the available data require the assumption that moods prime procedural knowledge.

To reiterate the key assumptions discussed herein, negative moods presumably signal that the current situation is problematic. In response to that signal, individuals employ a detail-oriented, bottom-up processing strategy with close attention to information that is relevant to the task at hand, from the content of persuasive messages to what is conveyed in a scatterplot. Attributing the negative mood to an unrelated cause (e.g., Sinclair et al., 1994) undermines its general informational value. In this case, the negative feelings still imply a problem, but the problem is identified (the event that gave rise to the mood) and the individual has little reason to respond to other tasks as if they were problematic. These assumptions do not imply that being in a bad mood induces a generic problem-solving mode.

2. The model suggests that moods influence judgments through a "How do I feel about it?" heuristic but that they influence processing by serving as a signal regarding the safety of the environment. The former is depicted as a kind of self-perception process, whereas the latter is depicted as a functional, evolutionary mechanism. Do moods provide information about the safety of the environment through a "How do I feel about it?" mechanism or do they provide this information through a more basic process? If the former, then why does the model make the assumption about evolutionarily basic processes? If the latter, then why are the effects of mood on processing easily overridden by discounting cues?

When we hear strange noises on a midnight stroll through the park, our fear reaction presumably prepares us for a flight-or-fight response—yet we do not follow through on this response when we realize that the source of the noise is a squirrel. In much the same way, negative moods may serve as an alert signal that we can choose to ignore once we realize that the feeling bears on something that is irrelevant to the task at hand. As the example of fear—often considered the prototype of adaptive emotional reactions (Frijda, 1999)—illustrates, the equation implied by the question (adaptive = automatic = impossible to override) is mistaken. Yet, in the absence of discreditation, individuals should be unlikely to ignore the problem signal provided by negative feelings, as discussed previously.

3. Your model suggests that positive moods signal a safe environment, which, in turn, allows people to maintain a generally low level of motivation with regard to processing (e.g., heuristic processing). How can you reconcile this heuristic–low motivation view of positive mood with findings (e.g., Bless) that although individuals in positive moods show reliance on scripts and stereotypes, they do not show any decrements in performance, and they may even perform better on secondary tasks than individuals in negative moods?

As discussed in some detail previously, the model does not imply that individuals in a good mood are cognitively lazy—it simply says that being in a good mood by itself does not signal any particular processing requirement. As the question correctly puts it, being in a good mood "allows people to maintain a generally low level of motivation with regard to processing"—but it does not force them to do so. If other currently active goals (including those provided by task instructions) require effortful processing, there is nothing that would impede it. But when the task allows for different strategies, individuals in good moods spontaneously prefer heuristic strategies, whereas individuals in negative moods prefer systematic strategies.

SUMMARY

In summary, the feelings-as-information model addresses the use of experiential information in judgment and reasoning. It treats moods as one of many different types of affective and nonaffective feelings, all of which share the quality that they can serve as a source of information. Mood effects on evaluative judgment are traced to the use of a "How do I feel about it?" heuristic, whereas mood effects on processing style are traced to the information that our feelings provide about the problematic or benign character of our current psychological situation. Both effects are eliminated when the informational value of the mood is called into question. Finally, the model is relatively silent on issues of mood-congruent memory, although the findings reviewed herein indicate that mood effects on evaluative judgments may affect subsequent recall. Importantly, any test of the model—and any attempt to rule out that an observed mood effect is not due to the informative functions of feelings—requires manipulations of the perceived informational value of the feeling under study. Unfortunately, the absence of such manipulations renders many findings in this area ambiguous with regard to the underlying processes.

REFERENCES

Bless, H. (1996). Die informative Funktion von Stimmungen: Auswirkungen auf evaluative Urteile, Verarbeitungsstil und Gedächtnis [The informative functions of moods: Effects on judgment, processing, and memory]. In E. H. Witte (Ed.), *Soziale Kognition und empirische Ethikforschung* (pp. 27–45). Lengerich, Germany: Pabst Science Publishers.

Bless, H., Bohner, G., Schwarz, N., & Strack, F. (1986, April). *Macht gute Stimmung denkfaul?* [Do positive moods induce cognitive laziness]. Fachtagung der Arbeitsgruppe Sozialpsychologie, Erlangen, Germany.

Bless, H., Bohner, G., Schwarz, N., & Strack, F. (1990). Mood and persuasion: A cognitive response analysis. *Personality and Social Psychology Bulletin, 16,* 331–345.

Bless, H., Clore, G. L., Schwarz, N., Golisano, V., Rabe, C., & Wölk, M. (1996). Mood and the use of scripts: Does being in a happy mood really lead to mindlessness? *Journal of Personality and Social Psychology, 71,* 665–679.

Bless, H., & Schwarz, N. (1999). Sufficient and necessary conditions in dual process models: The case of mood and processing style. In S. Chaiken & Y. Trope (Eds.), *Dual process theories in social psychology* (pp. 423–440). New York: Guilford.

Bless, H., Schwarz, N., & Kemmelmeier, M. (1996). Mood and stereotyping: The impact of moods on the use of general knowledge structures. *European Review of Social Psychology, 7,* 63–93.

Bless, H., Schwarz, N., & Wieland, R. (1996). Mood and stereotyping: The impact of category membership and individuating information. *European Journal of Social Psychology, 26,* 935–959.

Bohner, G., Bless, H., Schwarz, N., & Strack, F. (1988). What triggers causal attributions? The impact of valence and subjective probability. *European Journal of Social Psychology, 18,* 335–345.

Bower, G. H. (1981). Mood and memory. *American Psychologist, 36,* 129–148.

Broadbent, D. E. (1971). *Decision and stress.* London: Academic Press.

Bruner, J. S., Matter, J., & Papanek, M. L. (1955). Breadth of learning as a function of drive-level and maintenance. *Psychological Review, 62,* 1–10.

Clore, G. L. (1992). Cognitive phenomenology: Feelings and the construction of judgment. In L. L. Martin & A. Tesser (Eds.), *The construction of social judgment* (pp. 133–164). Hillsdale, NJ: Lawrence Erlbaum Associates.

Clore, G. L., Schwarz, N., & Conway, M. (1994). Affective causes and consequences of social information processing. In R. S. Wyer & T. K. Srull (Eds.), *Handbook of social cognition* (2nd ed., Vol. 1, pp. 323–418). Hillsdale, NJ: Lawrence Erlbaum Associates.

Easterbrook, J. A. (1959). The effect of emotion on cue utilization and the organization of behavior. *Psychological Review, 66,* 183–201.

Forgas, J. P. (1995). Emotion in social judgments: Review and a new affect infusion model (AIM). *Psychological Bulletin, 117,* 39–66.

Frijda, N. H. (1986). *The emotions.* New York: Cambridge University Press.

Frijda, N. H. (1988). The laws of emotion. *American Psychologist, 43,* 349–358.

Frijda, N. H. (1999). Emotions and hedonic experience. In D. Kahneman, E. Diener, & N. Schwarz (Eds.), *Well-being: Foundations of hedonic psychology* (pp. 190–210). New York: Russell Sage.

Grayson, C. E., & Schwarz, N. (1999). Beliefs influence information processing strategies: Declarative and experiential information in risk assessment. *Social Cognition, 17,* 1–18.

Higgins, E. T. (1998). The aboutness principle: A pervasive influence on human inference. *Social Cognition, 16,* 173–198.

Isen, A. M., Shalker, T. E., Clark, M. S., & Karp, L. (1978). Affect, accessibility of material in memory, and behavior: A cognitive loop? *Journal of Personality and Social Psychology, 36,* 1–12.

Keltner, D., Ellsworth, P., & Edwards, K. (1993). Beyond simple pessimism: Effects of sadness and anger on social perception. *Journal of Personality and Social Psychology, 64,* 740–752.

Keltner, D., Locke, K. D., & Audrain, P. C. (1993). The influence of attributions on the relevance of negative feelings to satisfaction. *Personality and Social Psychology Bulletin, 19,* 21–30.

Lombardi, W. J., Higgins, E. T., & Bargh, J. A. (1987). The role of consciousness in priming effects on categorization: Assimilation versus contrast as a function of awareness of the priming task. *Personality and Social Psychology Bulletin, 13,* 411–429.

Mackie, D. M., Asuncion, A. G., & Rosselli, F. (1992). The impact of affective states on persuasion processes. In M. Clark (Ed.), *Review of personality and social psychology* (Vol. 14, pp. 247–270). Beverly Hills, CA: Sage.

Mackie, D., & Worth, L. T. (1989). Processing deficits and the mediation of positive affect in persuasion. *Journal of Personality and Social Psychology, 57,* 27–40.

Martin, L. L., Abend, T., Sedikides, C., & Green, J. D. (1997). How would it feel if. . . ? Mood as input to a role fulfillment evaluation process. *Journal of Personality and Social Psychology, 73,* 242–253.

Martin, L. L., Ward, D. W., Achee, J. W., & Wyer, R. S. (1993). Mood as input: People have to interpret the motivational implications of their moods. *Journal of Personality and Social Psychology, 64,* 317–326.

Matlin, M. W., & Stang, D. (1979). *The Pollyanna Principle: Selectivity in language, memory, and thought.* Cambridge, MA: Shenkman.

Rothman, A. J., & Schwarz, N. (1998). Constructing perceptions of vulnerability: Personal relevance and the use of experiential information in health judgments. *Personality and Social Psychology Bulletin, 24,* 1053–1064.

Schwarz, N. (1987). *Stimmung als Information.* [Mood as information.] Heidelberg, Germany: Springer-Verlag.

Schwarz, N. (1990). Feelings as information: Informational and motivational functions of affective states. In E. T. Higgins & R. Sorrentino (Eds.), *Handbook of motivation and cognition: Foundations of social behavior* (Vol. 2, pp. 527–561). New York: Guilford.

Schwarz, N. (1998). Accessible content and accessibility experiences: The interplay of declarative and experiential information in judgment. *Personality and Social Psychology Review, 2,* 87–99.

Schwarz, N., & Bless, B. (1991). Happy and mindless, but sad and smart? The impact of affective states on analytic reasoning. In J. Forgas (Ed.), *Emotion and social judgment* (pp. 55–71). Oxford, England: Pergamon.

Schwarz, N., & Bless, H. (1992). Constructing reality and its alternatives: Assimilation and contrast effects in social judgment. In L. L. Martin & A. Tesser (Eds.), *The construction of social judgment* (pp. 217–245). Hillsdale, NJ: Lawrence Erlbaum Associates.

Schwarz, N., Bless, H., & Bohner, G. (1991). Mood and persuasion: Affective states influence the processing of persuasive communications. *Advances in Experimental Social Psychology, 24,* 161–199.

Schwarz, N., Bless, H., Strack, F., Klumpp, G., Rittenauer-Schatka, H., & Simons, A. (1991). Ease of retrieval as information: Another look at the availability heuristic. *Journal of Personality and Social Psychology, 61,* 195–202.

Schwarz, N., & Clore, G. L. (1983). Mood, misattribution, and judgments of well-being: Informative and directive functions of affective states. *Journal of Personality and Social Psychology, 45,* 513–523.

Schwarz, N., & Clore, G. L. (1988). How do I feel about it? Informative functions of affective states. In K. Fiedler & J. Forgas (Eds.), *Affect, cognition, and social behavior* (pp. 44–62). Toronto, Ontario, Canada: Hogrefe International.

Schwarz, N., & Clore, G. L. (1996). Feelings and phenomenal experiences. In E. T. Higgins & A. Kruglanski (Eds.), *Social psychology: Handbook of basic principles* (pp. 433–465). New York: Guilford.

Schwarz, N., Servay, W., & Kumpf, M. (1985). Attribution of arousal as a mediator of the effectiveness of fear-arousing communications. *Journal of Applied Social Psychology, 15,* 74–78.

Schwarz, N., Strack, F., Kommer, D., & Wagner, D. (1987). Soccer, rooms and the quality of your life: Mood effects on judgments of satisfaction with life in general and with specific life-domains. *European Journal of Social Psychology, 17,* 69–79.

Siemer, M., & Reisenzein, R. (1998). Effects of mood on evaluative judgments: Influence of reduced processing capacity and mood salience. *Cognition & Emotion, 12,* 783–805.

Sinclair, R. C. (1988). Mood, categorization breadth, and performance appraisal: The effects of order of information acquisition and affective state on halo, accuracy, information retrieval, and evaluations. *Organizational Behavior and Human Decision Processes, 42,* 22–46.

Sinclair, R. C., & Mark, M. M. (1992). The influence of mood states on judgment and action: Effects on persuasion, categorization, social justice, person perception, and judgmental accuracy. In L. L. Martin & A. Tesser (Eds.), *The construction of social judgment* (pp. 165–193). Hillsdale, NJ: Lawrence Erlbaum Associates.

Sinclair, R. C., Mark, M. M., & Clore, G. L. (1994). Mood-related persuasion depends on misattributions. *Social Cognition, 12,* 309–326.

Strack, F., Schwarz, N., Bless, H., Kübler, A., & Wänke, M. (1993). Awareness of the influence as a determinant of assimilation versus contrast. *European Journal of Social Psychology, 23,* 53–62.

Strack, F., Schwarz, N., & Gschneidinger, E. (1985). Happiness and reminiscing: The role of time perspective, mood, and mode of thinking. *Journal of Personality and Social Psychology, 49,* 1460–1469.

Wegener, D. T., Petty, R. E., & Smith, S. M. (1995). Positive mood can increase or decrease message scrutiny: The hedonic contingency view of mood and message elaboration. *Journal of Personality and Social Psychology, 69,* 5–15.

Wegner, D. M., & Vallacher, R. R. (1986). Action identification. In R. M. Sorrentino & E. T. Higgins (Eds.), *Handbook of motivation and cognition: Foundations of social behavior* (pp. 550–583). New York: Guilford.

Winkielman, P., Schwarz, N., & Belli, R. F. (1998). The role of ease of retrieval and attribution in memory judgments: Judging your memory as worse despite recalling more events. *Psychological Science, 9,* 124–126.

Wyer, R. S., & Carlston, D. (1979). *Social cognition, inference, and attribution.* Hillsdale, NJ: Lawrence Erlbaum Associates.

Zillman, D. (1978). Attribution and misattribution of excitatory reactions. In J. H. Harvey, W. I. Ickes, & R. F. Kidd (Eds.), *New directions in attribution research* (Vol. 2, pp. 335–368). Hillsdale, NJ: Lawrence Erlbaum Associates.

Chapter 8

Understanding Effects of Mood Through the Elaboration Likelihood and Flexible Correction Models

Duane T. Wegener
Purdue University

Richard E. Petty
Ohio State University

Our discussion uses the elaboration likelihood model (ELM; Petty & Cacioppo, 1986b) and the flexible correction model (FCM; Wegener & Petty, 1997) to understand various mood effects. These theoretical positions complement one another in that the ELM conceptually organizes effects of mood largely when the potential biasing effects of mood are not salient to the perceiver, whereas the FCM focuses on individuals' attempts to remove influences of mood that are perceived as inappropriate. After briefly describing the ELM and FCM, we explain how these perspectives can account for various effects of mood on judgment and information processing.

ELM: EFFECTS OF VARIABLES WHEN BIAS IS NOT SALIENT

According to the ELM, people generally want to hold reasonable views about the extent to which the various attitude objects in their environment (e.g., social issues, people, etc.) are good or bad. Yet across situations, individuals, and objects, there are likely to be differences in the extent to which people are willing and able to put a high level of cognitive effort into forming (and reforming) views of these attitude objects. To the extent that people are both motivated and able to put cognitive effort into forming or changing their views of an object, they are likely to carefully scrutinize information perceived as relevant to judging that object. That is, they are likely to effortfully assess the "central merits" of an object or advocacy in order to determine the extent to which it is good or bad (see Petty & Cacioppo, 1986a). Therefore, the ELM postulates an elaboration continuum corresponding to the amount of effortful scrutiny (elaboration) given to information perceived as relevant to the central merits (i.e., important characteristics) of various attitude objects.

The ELM is a "dual route" but multiprocess theory. The dual routes—central and peripheral—refer to changes in assessments of objects (or formation of assessments of objects) that are based on relatively different degrees of object-relevant information-processing activity. "Central route" assessments of objects are based on relatively extensive and effortful information-processing activity aimed at scrutinizing the central merits of the object (i.e., the central route anchors the high end of the elaboration continuum). "Peripheral route" assessments are based on one or more of a variety of lower effort shortcut processes (i.e., the peripheral route anchors the low end of the elaboration continuum). Some peripheral-route assessments are based on processes that differ primarily in quantitative ways from central-route processes (e.g., examining just the first few substantive pieces of information rather than all of them), but other peripheral-route changes result from processes that are both less effortful and qualitatively different (e.g., processing none of the arguments but using a "number of arguments" heuristic; see Petty, 1997; Petty & Wegener, 1998a). These low(er) effort processes are lumped together under the peripheral-route label because of the similarity in the consequences they are postulated to induce. That is, central-route attitude changes are postulated to be stronger than peripheral-route attitude changes (i.e., to be more enduring over time, more resistant to counterattack, and more predictive of behavior; see Petty, Haugtvedt, & Smith, 1995, for a review).

Importantly, as we explain in the following paragraphs, the ELM holds that at different points along the elaboration continuum, the same judgment-relevant variables can have an impact on judgment through different kinds of processes. When motivation and ability to process judgment-relevant information are high, all such information is effortfully scrutinized for its central merits relevant to the object. Therefore, one way for a variable to influence judgments is for the variable to represent a central merit of the object. For example, if the purpose of one's judgment is to rate the extent to which a particular restaurant has a good social image, then the physical or social attractiveness of the person endorsing the restaurant is likely to be central (important) to the merits of that claim. Thus, in such a case, variations in the attractiveness or social image of the endorser could influence evaluations through effortful consideration of the endorser's attractiveness, along with considerations of any other central merits, such as the extent to which the atmosphere of the restaurant is "trendy" and to which people are willing to stand in line for long hours to get a table (see Petty & Cacioppo, 1984b; Shavitt, Swan, Lowrey, & Wänke, 1994).

Another way for a variable to influence judgments when motivation and ability to think are high is to bias the processing of judgment-relevant information. That is, if multiple interpretations of judgment-relevant information are possible, a variable might make one interpretation more likely than other equally plausible interpretations.[1] For example, it has been repeatedly shown that people assume that attractive people possess other positive traits (e.g., Cooper, 1981; Thorndike, 1920). This halo effect could bias processing of information presented by an attractive person by making positive interpretations of ambiguous information more likely than if the source were not attractive. This could occur for a variety of reasons. For example, in some cases, the quality or qualities of the source might prime certain constructs that are used to disambiguate the information that is considered. In other cases, knowledge structures associated with the source characteristics (e.g., naive theories about what characteristics are possessed by attractive people) could be used to make inferences about information not presented or about the ambiguous implications of presented information. Biased processing should be less likely to the extent that judgment-relevant information is quite clear and unambiguous (e.g., see Chaiken & Maheswaran, 1994; Tesser & Cowan, 1975).

For some situations, people, or objects, however, motivation and/or ability to process judgment-relevant information is lacking. When this is the case, people devote less effort to assessing the central merits of an object. For example, they might consider fewer pieces of central evidence than individuals who are highly motivated and able to think (or they might consider the same pieces of evidence, but do so in a less thorough, more cursory way). In addition, when motivation or ability is low, people are more likely to use some kind of shortcut based on aspects of the message or setting that are peripheral to the central merits of the target. For example, people might come to an opinion of the object based solely on who presents information about the object, with little or no consideration of the central merits of the judgment-relevant information. Thus people might go along with an advocacy simply because the source is attractive, expert, or likable (Chaiken, 1980; Petty, Cacioppo, & Goldman, 1981; Petty, Cacioppo, & Schumann, 1983; see Petty & Wegener, 1998a, for additional discussion).

Thus, when either motivation or ability to process information is low, a variable might affect judgments if that variable can operate as part of a shortcut strategy for arriving at a reasonable view of the object (or if that

---

[1]Use of the word *bias* is not meant to imply a necessary inaccuracy or incorrectness. Rather, the term *bias* is used to denote a situation in which one of a number of equally plausible interpretations is consistently chosen based on the presence or absence of some other variable. Such bias effects could come about for either motivational or ability-based reasons (see Petty, Priester, & Wegener, 1994).

variable can be a salient but easy-to-process piece of relevant evidence). A wide variety of variables can be incorporated into simple decision rules regarding object perceptions. One common example of such a decision rule might be that "more is better" (e.g., Petty & Cacioppo, 1984a). Thus, if a large amount of information supporting a favorable view of an object is presented, people who are unwilling or unable to scrutinize the information might simply agree with the advocacy even if more careful scrutiny of the presented information might have led to a different view.

Finally, according to the ELM, variables can also affect judgments by influencing one's motivation and/or ability to think carefully about judgment-relevant information. Thus one might choose to think about information more fully if the source is attractive rather than unattractive (e.g., DeBono & Harnish, 1988; Puckett, Petty, Cacioppo, & Fisher, 1983). Of course, the likelihood of a variable influencing the amount of scrutiny is constrained by other variables in the judgment setting—factors both internal and external to the social perceiver. Thus, if the baseline likelihood of elaboration is already quite low (e.g., because distraction external to judgment-relevant information is at a high level; Kiesler & Mathog, 1968; Petty, Wells, & Brock, 1976) or quite high (e.g., because the judgment target is important or personally relevant [Leippe & Elkin, 1987; Petty et al., 1981; Petty et al., 1983] or because the people receiving judgment-relevant information are very high in "need for cognition" [Cacioppo & Petty, 1982b; Cacioppo, Petty, & Morris, 1983]), then impact of a variable on judgments is most likely to occur through the low- or high-elaboration roles outlined earlier. If background variables do not constrain elaboration to be particularly high or low and especially if a person is not sure whether or not effortful scrutiny of information about the target is merited, then the variable might affect judgments by helping to determine the level of thought given to the available judgment-relevant information.

In sum, according to the ELM, a variable can influence judgments (a) by serving as a central merit of a target, (b) by biasing processing of judgment-relevant information, (c) by serving as a peripheral cue to judging the target, and (d) by itself affecting the level of scrutiny given to judgment-relevant information. These different roles for variables are more or less likely depending on the overall baseline level of elaboration likelihood. Thus, the ELM is a model of moderated mediation (see Petty, Wegener, Fabrigar, Priester, & Cacioppo, 1993, for further discussion). Variables are most likely to bias processing of object-relevant information or to act as pieces of object-relevant information when extensive processing of information occurs (i.e., when motivation and ability are high; unless the variable can serve as a salient but very easily processed piece of information, which could also have an impact when minimal object-relevant scrutiny occurs). Impact of variables as peripheral cues is more likely when motivation or ability is low, and influences of variables on amount of information scrutiny are more likely when elaboration likelihood is moderate (e.g., when people are unsure whether scrutiny of relevant information is merited or not).

It is important to note that although the ELM outlines the various roles that variables can serve to influence judgments (e.g., central merit, bias processing, etc.) and indicates when variables are most likely to take on these different roles, there are a number of contextual features that are left unspecified (see Petty & Cacioppo, 1986a, for additional discussion). For example, the specific content that constitutes a central merit of an object can differ across objects, perceivers, and situations. A feature or attribute (e.g., weighing 300 pounds) can be quite favorable when processed as a merit for one attitude object (e.g., judging a football tackle), can be unfavorable for another (e.g., judging a horse jockey), and irrelevant for other objects (e.g., judging a college professor). Some features (e.g., social image associated with the judgment target) might be chronically considered as relevant to the merits of the target by some people (e.g., high self-monitors; Snyder, 1979) or in some situations (e.g., when the dimension is primed; Shavitt & Fazio, 1991) but not by other people (e.g., low self-monitors; see Petty & Wegener, 1998b; Snyder & DeBono, 1989) or in other situations.

In addition, just as the ELM itself does not specify what information serves as a central merit in any given context, it does not specify what variables serve as peripheral cues. These too can vary with objects, perceivers, and people. Thus, for some people who love the color green, it could serve as a favorable cue, but for those who hate it, it could serve as a negative cue. Similarly, the ELM does not specify which levels of variables lead to increases versus decreases in processing of judgment-relevant information under relatively moderate levels of elaboration likelihood and which interpretations of ambiguous information are made more likely by particular biasing agents when elaboration likelihood is high. Rather, the ELM specifies the conditions under which each of the "multiple roles" is most likely to be assumed by variables under study (see Petty & Cacioppo, 1986a; Petty & Wegener, 1998a).[2]

---

[2]For example, the ELM does not itself specify whether high levels of source expertise would lead to increases or decreases in scrutiny of judgment-relevant information at moderate baseline levels of elaboration. It could be that (at least in some circumstances) people would want to scrutinize what experts have to say more than what nonexperts do because experts are more likely to provide valid and valuable information or because recommendations by experts are more likely to be enacted (Heesacker, Petty, & Cacioppo, 1983; Petty & Cacioppo, 1986a). It could also be, however, that people would not need to scrutinize what experts say as much as what nonexperts say because they assume that an expert would not say something stupid, but a nonexpert's recommendations might be erroneous. Or each of these motivations could hold in different situations (see Petty & Cacioppo, 1981).

Finally, it is important to note that according to the ELM, the same overall judgment outcome can take place for very different reasons. Thus a high level of a variable (e.g., source attractiveness) can lead to increases in favorability of judgment (a) because elaboration was low, but the high level of the variable was used as a favorable peripheral cue or easy-to-process piece of information; (b) because elaboration was high, and the high level of the variable served as a favorable piece of judgment-relevant information; (c) because elaboration was high, and the high level of the variable biased scrutiny of judgment-relevant information in a favorable direction; (d) because the high level of the variable increased the amount of scrutiny of judgment-relevant information, and scrutiny of this information led to favorable thoughts because the information was cogent; or (e) because the high level of the variable decreased the amount of scrutiny of judgment-relevant information, and because of the decreased scrutiny people failed to realize the flaws in the information. Also, just as the same judgment outcome can occur for different reasons, the same information (e.g., attractive source) can assume different roles in different situations and therefore lead to different outcomes (see also Petty & Cacioppo, 1986b; Petty & Wegener, 1998a, 1999). Thus an overall judgment outcome alone often provides rather ambiguous evidence regarding processes that might underlie the judgment outcome. Yet according to the ELM, the process by which any outcome is achieved is important because of the consequences for the judgment.

In conclusion, although the ELM provides a useful organizing framework, additional theoretical and empirical developments complement the ELM by specifying which processes enable particular variables to affect judgments within each relative level of elaboration likelihood. Thus, although we use the ELM as the overarching framework from which to understand the multiple roles for mood, we also note theoretical and empirical developments that complement the ELM framework by identifying many of the more specific processes by which mood can affect judgments at different levels of elaboration likelihood.

FCM: PERCEPTIONS AND JUDGMENT
WHEN BIAS IS SALIENT

As we noted in the previous discussion, the ELM focuses on the effects of variables on judgment when issues of potential bias are not salient in the minds of perceivers. What happens, however, when people become aware that some aspects of themselves or the judgment setting might unduly or inappropriately influence judgments?[3] According to our flexible correction model (FCM; Wegener & Petty, 1997), attempts at correction (i.e., removal or avoidance of bias) are guided by perceivers' naive theories of the biases potentially at work (see also Petty & Wegener, 1993; Wegener & Petty, 1995; Wegener, Petty, & Dunn, 1998). The FCM assumes that there is variation in the default (i.e., uncorrected) effects of variables and that people must be motivated and able to identify potential biases and to correct for their perceived effects if correction is to occur. Both identification of potential biases and corrective efforts themselves are guided by people's naive theories of the potential biases that might operate in any setting. Consistent with these notions, when opposite theories of bias have been empirically identified, corrections in opposite directions have occurred. This has been the case regardless of whether the opposite theories of bias were of different effects for the same context operating on different targets (Wegener & Petty, 1995), different effects for different contexts operating on the same targets (Wegener et al., 1998), or different effects for the same contexts operating on the same targets but perceived by different people (Wegener & Petty, 1995). In addition, variations in the magnitude of the perceived bias have been shown to predict the magnitude of corrections (Wegener & Petty, 1995).

According to the FCM, a given theory-based correction is more likely to occur to the extent that the theory is accessible in memory, is applicable to the target and setting, and serves the goals of the perceiver. Thus, to the extent that a given theory of bias is inaccessible, inapplicable, or at odds with the perceiver's goals, that theory is unlikely to guide corrections. Theory-based corrections are considered generally to require greater cognitive effort than not attempting correction does, though repeated experience with a particular type of correction could lead that correction process to become less effortful or even routinized (cf. Smith, 1989). If routinization occurs, corrections might take place even with little or no explicit awareness of the potentially biasing factor(s). In most cases, however, before such extensive experience with a given correction occurs, the FCM conceptualizes corrections as following some awareness of a potentially biasing factor or factors.[4]

---

[3]Because the ELM assumes that, in the absence of other salient motives, the "default" motive in judgment settings is accuracy, it predicts that people would attempt to disregard perceived biasing influences if they were made salient. The ELM does not specify, however, the mechanism by which such avoidance of bias takes place, and here we rely on the FCM to complement the ELM. As described in subsequent sections, the FCM allows prediction of when "corrections" can produce reversed effects of some biasing factors.

[4]This is not to say that people are necessarily fully aware of the correction process, however. Even if people can sometimes state a theory of bias and even if such theories can predict

Although corrections guided by theories of bias are viewed as generally requiring some amount of cognitive effort, across people, situations, and targets there is variation in the amount of cognitive effort given to theory-based corrections (just as there is variation in cognitive effort given to judgments when corrections do not occur; see preceding section on the ELM). Therefore, similar to the ELM analysis of uncorrected judgments, corrected assessments based on greater cognitive effort are hypothesized to persist longer over time, to better resist future attempts at change, and to better predict additional judgments and behavior compared with corrected assessments based on lower levels of cognitive effort. Greater cognitive effort is hypothesized to lead to "stronger" (i.e., persistent, resistant, and predictive) assessments of targets because greater cognitive effort is likely to reflect judgments that have been related to and scrutinized in light of other related knowledge structures. Frequent activation of the assessment of the target during this scrutiny, along with links created between that assessment and other strongly held information in memory, should make that assessment relatively accessible in memory and should provide informational bases from which efforts at changing the assessment can be counterargued and resisted (see Petty & Cacioppo, 1986b; Petty & Wegener, 1998a, for further discussion).

Although in many natural settings effortful corrections might be most likely when a judgment target is important enough to also merit high levels of information scrutiny, corrections can also occur even if little judgment-relevant information was considered (e.g., if the perceived bias is created by a peripheral cue). That is, effort devoted to theory-guided corrections is conceptually distinct from the general effort aimed at scrutiny of information relevant to some judgment task. Evidence consistent with this notion was obtained by Petty, Wegener, and White (1998). Following presentation of judgment-relevant information, Petty et al. alerted college students to the possible bias associated with the likability of the source of information about a proposed school policy. In a first study, Petty et al. found that alerting students to the bias did not change the extent to which they scrutinized the presented information (i.e., the correction instruction left unaffected a manipulation of the quality of information presented about the target; see Petty & Cacioppo, 1986b; Petty et al., 1976), but it

---

the corrections in which people engage, we would not necessarily expect such people to be able to report which theory or theories of bias were used, how they were used, and so forth. That is, we do not regard theory-based correction as necessarily implying a fully conscious correction process. The extent of awareness of correction processes is likely to vary with such factors as the extent to which the correction process is invoked explicitly or implicitly, is highly practiced or not, and so forth. In many cases, however, regardless of whether or not people can report the correction process, it likely requires some amount of cognitive effort to engage in theory-guided attempts at correction (until such corrections become automatic).

did lead to corrections attempting to remove that bias (e.g., the dislikable source became more persuasive when the potential bias was pointed out than when the bias was not made salient). In a second study, the same correction instruction led to similar corrections, regardless of whether the information was initially scrutinized at high or low levels (Petty et al., 1998). Taken together, these studies suggest that corrections can be distinct from overall processing of judgment-relevant information and that high levels of processing do not necessarily include explicit efforts at bias correction (because the same amount of "instructed" correction occurred after high and low levels of scrutiny took place).[5]

EFFECTS OF MOOD WHEN BIAS IS NOT SALIENT: MULTIPLE ROLES FOR MOOD IN THE ELM

High Elaboration: Mood as Central Merit and Mood-Based Biases in Processing

According to the ELM, when motivation and ability to process judgment-relevant information are high, one way that mood can impact judgments is through its role as a central merit of the target (if mood is relevant to the merits of the object). For example, if one's judgment concerns whether or not a person would make a suitable spouse or significant other, the feelings associated with the presence of that person are a central dimension of the merits of that potential companion (Petty & Cacioppo, 1986a; Wegener & Petty, 1996). A recent set of studies presented by Martin, Abend, Sedikides, and Green (1997) can be interpreted as an example of this. In one experiment, people in either a happy or sad mood were given either a happy or sad story and were asked to evaluate the story and their liking for it. In such a case (in which the "target" story was obviously meant to bring about a particular feeling), the mood people felt when reading the story was likely to be perceived as a central merit of the story. Consistent with this notion, research participants' evaluations of and liking for the target stories were highest when the mood before the story (and presumably during the story) matched rather than mismatched the intended effect of the story. Interestingly, this study illustrates a situation in which mood as a central merit

---

[5]Future work might also show that correction instructions themselves (or variations in the type of correction instruction) might influence how much of a bias is identified. Although this might also have accounted for some of the difference between high-elaboration–no-instruction and high-elaboration–correction-instruction conditions in the Petty et al. (1998) research, there seem to be theoretical and some initial empirical reasons to conceptually distinguish between noncorrective and corrective effort (given that the same difference between no-correction and correction-instruction conditions existed for both high and low elaboration conditions).

can lead to mood-incongruent evaluations. When the purpose of the target story was to make people feel sad and people felt sad, the sad mood actually led to higher ratings of liking and of story quality than did a happy mood. Of course, our perspective also suggests that this effect could be reversed under different judgment circumstances (e.g., if processing level is low and mood is used as a peripheral cue or if people become aware of the effects of the prior mood induction and overcorrect for its perceived influence). Also, for many targets (e.g., the potential companion mentioned earlier), feeling good when encountering the target would constitute a positive (i.e., mood-congruent) central merit.

Perhaps more often, when people are actively evaluating information about the target (i.e., when elaboration likelihood is high), mood can bias the interpretations of that information, especially if the information is ambiguous (Chaiken & Maheswaran, 1994; Petty, Gleicher, & Baker, 1991). For example, positive moods might activate more positive interpretations than would negative moods (e.g., Bower, 1981; Breckler & Wiggins, 1991; Isen, Shalker, Clark, & Karp, 1978; Mathur & Chattopadhyay, 1991). Regardless of whether one conceptualizes such activation in terms of associative networks (e.g., Anderson & Bower, 1973; Bower, 1981) or connectionist models (e.g., McClelland, Rumelhart, & Hinton, 1986; Smith, 1996), happy moods have often been found to make events or objects seem more desirable and/or more likely than the same events or objects appear when people are in sad or neutral moods (e.g., see Erber, 1991; Forgas & Moylan, 1987; Johnson & Tversky, 1983; Mayer, Gaschke, Braverman, & Evans, 1992; Wegener & Petty, 1996; Wegener, Petty, & Klein, 1994).

Explicit evidence of mood biasing information processing was found by Petty, Schumann, Richman, and Strathman (1993). Under high-elaboration conditions in two experiments (i.e., when people were high in need for cognition [Cacioppo & Petty, 1982b] or encountered information about a self-relevant product [Petty, Cacioppo, & Schumann, 1983]), mood influenced judgments of the targets via cognitive responses to the information about the targets. That is, when effortful elaboration of judgment-relevant information was likely, positive mood produced positive thoughts about the information, which in turn influenced evaluations of the targets. Of course, mood would be less likely to exert a biasing impact on processing if there were salient and competing biasing factors operating—such as a strong prior attitude—or if the judgment-relevant information was completely unambiguous.

It is also important to note that when moods bias processing, the mood state does not invariably lead to mood-congruent biases in overall evaluation (Petty & Wegener, 1991; Wegener et al., 1994). For example, as noted earlier, mood can bias active assessments of targets, affecting assessments of the likelihood that the target possesses desirable versus undesirable characteristics. Using this expectancy (likelihood) × value (desirability) approach to judgments (e.g., Fishbein & Ajzen, 1975), Wegener et al. (1994) found that differential framing of information about target actions led to different biasing effects of mood on assessments of those actions. Specifically, when the arguments in a persuasive message were framed to say that adopting the recommended position was likely to make good things happen, a happy mood was associated with more favorable views of the advocacy than a sad mood. However, when the arguments were framed such that failing to adopt the advocacy was likely to make bad things happen, a sad mood was associated with more favorable views of the advocacy than a happy mood. The reason for this was that a happy mood made the positive consequences of adopting the advocacy seem more likely, and the sad mood made the negative consequences of not adopting the advocacy seem more likely. Consistent with the notion of this likelihood–desirability calculus being a relatively effortful activity, the likelihood mediation of mood effects on judgment only took place for people high in need for cognition. Of course, using this same likelihood–desirability view, one could also predict situations in which mood changes the perceived desirability of consequences of adopting the advocacy (thereby providing another means by which mood might bias the effortful assessment of the central merits of an advocacy; see Petty & Wegener, 1991, for additional discussion).

Low Elaboration: Mood as Peripheral Cue

When effortful elaboration of judgment-relevant information is unlikely (i.e., when motivation or ability is low), mood is likely to have an impact on judgments through relatively simple associations or heuristics (Petty, Schumann, et al., 1993; Wegener & Petty, 1996). Associating feelings with an object by classical conditioning would be one example of low-effort processes providing a link between mood and judgment (e.g., Griffitt, 1970; Zanna, Kiesler, & Pilkonis, 1970) in that classical conditioning does not rely on effortful scrutiny of information about the target (see also Cacioppo, Marshall-Goodell, Tassinary, & Petty, 1992). Mood might also affect judgment relatively directly if mood is consulted in a "How do I feel about it?" heuristic (Schwarz, 1990; see also Cacioppo & Petty, 1982a; Schwarz & Clore, 1983).[6] Petty, Schumann, et al. (1993) found evidence of

---

[6]A key difference between use of mood under low- and high-elaboration conditions is that under low-elaboration conditions, people would likely stop after inferring that "if I feel good, I must like it." Under high-elaboration conditions, people would also consider any other judgment-relevant information that was available and would assess whether current feelings were really informative about the attitude object (i.e., they would assess the central merit of mood for the judgment at hand).

this more direct (low-effort) effect of mood on judgments for people who were low in need for cognition or who encountered an irrelevant product. That is, in low-elaboration settings, positive mood induced more positive judgments than neutral mood, even though cognitive responses to the information about the targets were unaffected by mood (see Petty & Wegener, 1991; Wegener & Petty, 1996, for additional discussion). Of course, mood is less likely to serve in this simple cue role if competing alternative cues are salient.

Moderate Elaboration: Mood as a Determinant of Processing

When nonmood factors have not constrained elaboration likelihood to be either extremely high or low, then mood can affect the amount of processing of judgment-relevant information that takes place—especially if there are no other salient and competing factors present to influence the extent of processing. As noted previously, the ELM does not itself specify whether positive mood, for instance, should increase or decrease scrutiny of judgment-relevant information. In fact, a variety of processes might enable mood to influence amount of processing. For example, if certain moods are associated with decreased cognitive capacity (Ellis & Ashbrook, 1988; Mackie & Worth, 1989) or if certain moods inform people that effortful processing is unnecessary (Clore, Schwarz, & Conway, 1994; Schwarz, 1990), then processing of judgment-relevant information would tend to be low in those states.

In our own work on mood effects on processing, we have focused on the motivational consequences of pressures toward mood management across happy, neutral, and sad states. According to our hedonic-contingency view (Wegener & Petty, 1994), people in happy moods choose their activities based on the hedonic consequences of those activities more than do people in sad or neutral states. The rationale for this hypothesis is that for people in a happy mood, most behaviors in which that person could engage would make the person feel worse. Thus, if this person is to stay as happy or feel better than he or she currently does, activities must be chosen very carefully (i.e., hedonic rewards are highly dependent on the person considering the hedonic consequences of potential actions). For a sad person, however, the hedonic contingencies are quite different. Most potential behaviors would make the person feel better. Thus careful consideration of hedonic consequences is not as critical for sad people—they can reap hedonic rewards even if they act based on strategies that are unrelated to consideration of hedonic consequences (such as scrutinizing everything because there might be problems in the environment; cf. Clore et al., 1994; Schwarz, 1990). Because of these different hedonic contingencies, over time people might become more likely to consider the hedonic consequences of their actions when they are in a happy rather than a sad mood.[7]

In a direct use of this framework to study the effect of mood on the extent of scrutiny of judgment-relevant information, Wegener, Petty and Smith (1995) found that the hedonic qualities of the judgment-relevant information affected the amount of information processing for happy people more than for sad people. Wegener et al. (1995; Experiment 2) presented either strong (compelling) or weak (specious) arguments in support of "University Service" for college students. In addition, this strong or weak information was used either to support a proattitudinal (and uplifting) program in which students could reap the benefits of lowered tuition if they chose to enroll in the program or to support a counterattitudinal (and depressing) program in which students would be forced to enroll in the program or face tuition increases. No time frame was given for possible implementation of the university service plan in order to hold elaboration likelihood at a relatively moderate level. The strong and weak arguments supporting the University Service program were the same regardless of whether the introduction of the topic was up-

---

[7]Within this hedonic-contingency view, neutral moods might relate to mood management in various ways. Neutral moods might foster mood management in between the levels of happy and sad states because contingencies in neutral moods fall between those of happy and sad moods. There might also be circumstances in which mood management differs little between sad and neutral states. For example, if the neutral mood is not distinctive enough to serve as a salient signal for different reward contingencies, then neutral and sad moods might bring about similar levels of mood management (because hedonic rewards are relatively independent of considerations of hedonic consequences in sad moods and because current feelings—as well as motives to manage the feelings—might not be salient enough in the neutral mood). It is also possible, especially if there are any cues in the setting to make mood management salient, that at least some people in sad moods would engage in higher than usual levels of mood management (e.g., people high in negative mood regulation [Catanzaro & Mearns, 1990], self-esteem [Rosenberg, 1965; Smith & Petty, 1995] or on the mood-repair subscale of the Trait Meta-Mood Scale [Salovey, Mayer, Goldman, & Palfai, 1995]). Combining this increase in mood management for some sad people with the general contingency-based lower level of mood management for sad individuals might equalize the overall mood management of sad and neutral people (collapsed across any individual differences).

In fact, in research conducted within our hedonic-contingency framework, results have often shown similar levels of mood management for people in neutral and sad states, with higher levels of mood management found for happy people than for those in sad or neutral moods. Specifically, Wegener and Petty (1994) found that happy people based their choices of future activities on the affective qualities of those activities to a greater extent than did people in neutral or sad moods. Sad people and those in neutral states did not differ in their use of the information about affective qualities of activities (for additional data consistent with this view, see Carlson, Charlin, & Miller, 1988; Carlson & Miller, 1987; Miller & Carlson, 1990; Murray, Sujan, Hirt, & Sujan, 1990; see Wegener & Petty, 1994, 1996, for discussions).

lifting or depressing. Therefore, differences in information scrutiny by happy and sad people could not be due to differences in ability to scrutinize uplifting versus depressing information. Consistent with the hedonic-contingency framework, happy people showed greater attentiveness to the quality of the arguments in the message (i.e., were more persuaded by strong than weak arguments) when the introduction of the topic was uplifting rather than depressing. Sad people were equally affected by argument quality across the uplifting and depressing topic introductions. That is, information processing by happy people was more affected by the likely hedonic consequences of that processing than was information processing by sad people.

Another implication of the hedonic-contingency view is that happy moods can lead to either increased or decreased processing of judgment-relevant information when compared to neutral or sad moods, depending on the perceived hedonic consequences of information scrutiny or lack thereof. That is, if people in happy moods are more affected by the potential hedonic consequences of information processing, then happy people might avoid processing depressing information more often than people in sad or neutral moods but might process uplifting information more deeply than sad people or those in neutral moods. In fact, when one organizes the processing results from Wegener et al. (1995, Experiment 2) according to the hedonic quality of the information, the results indicate that happy mood led to greater processing than sad mood when the information framing was uplifting but led to less processing than sad mood when the information was framed as depressing (see also Howard & Barry, 1994). Given that most past research on the topic of mood and processing of persuasive communications has used counterattitudinal or depressing messages or topics (e.g., Bless, Bohner, Schwarz, & Strack, 1990; Kuykendall & Keating, 1990; Mackie & Worth, 1989; Worth & Mackie, 1987), the hedonic-contingency view seems capable of explaining why that research has generally found less processing in happy than in sad or neutral moods. At the same time, the hedonic contingency position also predicts that happy mood can lead to increases in processing when compared to neutral or sad states.

Future research will undoubtedly address the extent to which various processes in addition to hedonic contingency lead to effects of mood on scrutiny of judgment-relevant information. Consistent with the ELM organizing framework, we believe that such effects are most likely when elaboration likelihood is not constrained by nonmood factors to be extremely high or low. Although we believe that many such effects might be explained by a hedonic-contingency perspective, other processes (e.g., mood effects on cognitive capacity or perceptions of need for scrutiny of the environment) might also serve the role of complementing the ELM by specifying the specific motivational or ability processes involved.

CORRECTIONS FOR PERCEIVED MOOD-BASED BIASES

If people believe that a particular effect of mood is occurring (or will occur) and wish to remove that influence of mood (regardless of whether or not mood would actually have the anticipated effect), they might engage in corrective attempts guided by their theories of mood-based bias (see Wegener & Petty, 1997, for additional discussion). For example, if people believe that how they feel is unduly affecting (or will unduly affect) their perceptions of a target (and if people are motivated and able to correct for these perceived biases), they might be especially likely to adjust assessments of the target in a direction opposite to the perceived bias in an effort to characterize the target in an unbiased manner (see Petty & Wegener, 1993, for a measure of a perceived effect of mood; see also Wegener & Petty, 1995). In fact, in a recent series of studies (DeSteno, Petty, Wegener, & Rucker, 2000), we have obtained evidence of corrections reversing the uncorrected effects of mood. Specifically, students were placed in either a sad or an angry state and then instructed to estimate the likelihood of angry and sad events. When their mood state and accuracy concerns were not made salient, mood-congruency effects were observed (cf., Johnson & Tversky, 1983). That is, angering events were seen as more likely when people were angry rather than when they were sad, and sad events were seen as more likely when they were sad than when they were angry. However, when mood was made salient and people were reminded to be accurate in their judgments, individuals with high need for cognition showed the reverse pattern (with angering events rated as less likely in angry than in sad moods, and sad events rated as less likely in sad than in angry moods). These reversed mood effects are understandable if individuals with high need for cognition overcorrected their judgments for the expected effects of their emotional states. Measures of perceived bias (completed by a separate set of participants) were consistent with the observed corrections (for use of the FCM to explain corrections for general positive versus negative states, see Berkowitz, Jaffee, Jo, & Troccoli, 2000; Wegener & Petty, 1997).

Although corrections based on such naive theories of bias provide a potential means for lessening, removing, or reversing (if overcorrection occurs) the biasing effects of mood, a person's naive theories of bias could also introduce or augment existing mood-based biases. For example, if a person believes that a happy mood makes them too positive toward an advocacy, but in fact happy mood led to a less positive view of the advocacy than a sad mood (e.g., Wegener et al., 1994; see also Martin et al., 1997), then corrections aimed at removing an undue influence of mood might actually exacerbate the effect that would have occurred without the correction. People could become aware of potential effects of mood (and might become motivated to remove those perceived effects) regardless of whether elaboration of judgment-relevant information is high or low (e.g., regardless of whether the perceived effect of mood was to bias active information processing or to influence perceptions through use as a decision rule or heuristic; see also Petty et al., 1998). Although theories of bias could guide corrections in both cases, it might be more difficult to effectively correct for mood-based biases on interpretation of many pieces of judgment-relevant information. If such an effortful correction occurs, however, it should be more likely to last than would a simpler "overall" correction (see Wegener & Petty, 1997, for additional discussion of corrections for effects of mood).

ADDRESSING COMMON EFFECTS OF MOOD FROM THE ELM AND FCM PERSPECTIVES: JUDGMENT, RECALL, PROCESSING, AND CREATIVITY

Mood-Congruent Judgment

Mood-congruent judgment could occur for a variety of reasons. For instance, according to the ELM, if elaboration of judgment-relevant information is low, mood could serve as a peripheral cue, leading to more favorable judgments of targets when in a happy rather than a sad mood. As noted previously, possible peripheral processes responsible for such an effect could include classical conditioning (in which the feelings are paired with the presence of the target) or use of a "How do I feel about it?" heuristic or decision rule concerning the target. In addition to low elaboration likelihood and a relative absence of salient alternative peripheral cues as conditions encouraging use of feelings-based heuristics, it might also be necessary that people are not led to question the relevance of their feelings for such a judgment (see Clore et al., 1994; Schwarz, 1990). If people do question the legitimacy of their feelings as a basis for judgment, then there might be less of a judgment effect for mood because of use of nonmood bases (i.e., information) for the judgment (see the Schwarz & Clore, 1983, discussion of "discounting"). According to the FCM, there might be an attenuated or even a reversed mood effect if questioning the legitimacy of mood leads to theory-based corrections away from a perceived mood-congruent effect (Berkowitz et al., 2000; DeSteno et al., 2000; Ottati & Isbell, 1996; Petty & Wegener, 1993; see also Wegener & Petty, 1997). As noted earlier, mood-congruent judgment could also be the result of "overcorrecting" for a perceived mood-incongruent bias. If people were to believe erroneously that a mood-incongruent effect was occurring, then theory-based corrections could actually enhance an existing mood-congruent effect (or create one if it did not already exist). Judgments unaffected by mood could occur if adequate "discounting" or correction processes take place or if salient nonmood peripheral cues dominate the uncorrected "cue" effects of mood.

According to the ELM, the primary uncorrected influence of mood under high-elaboration conditions (i.e., when nonmood factors make motivation and ability to process judgment-relevant information quite high) would be to affect the nature of thoughts that come to mind concerning the judgment-relevant information. As discussed earlier, mood-congruent or mood-incongruent outcomes could occur depending on what thoughts mood is influencing (e.g., thinking about the likelihood of good things being associated with adopting the advocacy, or thinking about the likelihood of bad things being associated with rejecting the advocacy; see Petty & Wegener, 1991; Wegener et al., 1994). Biasing effects of mood are less likely if other salient biasing factors overwhelm effects of mood in directing the interpretation of judgment-relevant information or if judgment-relevant information is not open to multiple interpretations (i.e., the information is unambiguous).

Mood-congruent or mood-incongruent outcomes could also occur if people perceive their feelings as central merits of the judgment target. As noted earlier, in some instances, the positive or negative feelings people experience when they encounter the target are viewed as directly relevant to determining the extent to which the target is good or bad. In many cases, "good" feelings lead to the mood-congruent outcome of favorable judgments (e.g., when considering a potential dating partner, that person might be viewed more positively if one experiences positive rather than negative feelings when in the person's presence). However, as in the case presented earlier, if people are judging the quality of a "sad" story, then a story that actually makes people feel sad might be viewed more positively (i.e., as higher in quality) than a story that is aimed at making people sad but fails to do so (Martin et al., 1997). Similarly, one could find that a "scary" movie is judged more positively if the person actually experiences fear than if only amusement is experienced during the movie. Also as noted previously, in high-elaboration settings people could question the legitimacy of using mood as a basis for judgment (either in biasing processing of information or in considering one's mood as a central merit of the object). In such cases, flexible correction processes could lessen the judgment effect of mood, remove that effect, reverse that effect, or even exacerbate the original effect, depending on the direction and magnitude of the perceived effect of the mood (see Wegener & Petty, 1997).[8]

When elaboration likelihood is not constrained to be either high or low, the effects of mood on judgment will depend on the direction of effects of mood on scrutiny of judgment-relevant information and on the content of the judgment-relevant information considered. If the judgment-relevant information is largely supportive of a favorable view of the target (e.g., as when "strong" arguments are included in a persuasive message; see Petty & Cacioppo, 1986b; Petty, Wegener, et al., 1993), then increases in scrutiny of that information by people in happy moods (e.g., when thinking about that information seems potentially uplifting; Wegener et al., 1995) could lead to a mood-congruent judgment outcome. However, decreases in scrutiny of the same favorable information by people in happy moods (e.g., when thinking about that information seems potentially depressing; Wegener et al., 1995) could lead to a mood-incongruent judgment outcome (see also Schwarz, Bless, & Bohner, 1991). Just the reverse might occur if the judgment-relevant information actually supports an unfavorable view of the target (as when "weak" arguments are presented for an advocacy). In such cases, increases of information scrutiny by happy people could lead to mood-incongruent judgments, but decreases of scrutiny could lead to mood-congruent judgments.

Mood-Congruent Recall

Although the ELM and FCM are models of judgment and not of recall, mood-congruent memory could potentially play a role in some of the processes discussed thus far. For example, if mood leads people to engage

---

[8]That is, the same "feelings-as-information" and correction mechanisms outlined for low-elaboration conditions exist when people question the legitimacy of their mood under high-elaboration conditions (e.g., when feelings are perceived as relevant to the central merits of the target, but the person's current feelings are questioned because of the existence of additional—or recent—mood-influencing stimuli or events that might be unduly influencing perceptions of the target). For example, even if a person views his or her feelings when with a potential dating partner as relevant to the "merits" of the partner, the legitimacy of using those feelings might be questioned if the person realizes that he or she just experienced an unrelated extremely depressing (or uplifting) event. In such circumstances, ignoring mood and basing judgments on non-mood-based information might lead to lack of an effect of mood. Also, engaging in theory-based corrections of a perceived mood-congruent influence might lead to less mood-congruent effect, to no effect of mood, or even to a reversed (mood-incongruent) effect, depending on the nature of the person's naive theory of mood (and the person's motivation and ability to invoke the theory-based correction).

in biased processing under high-elaboration conditions, this could enhance the likelihood of mood-congruent recall (e.g., if a person in a positive mood elaborates the favorable information in a message more fully than the unfavorable information, this should increase the likelihood of later recalling the favorable information; Craik & Lockhart, 1972). Also, if mood-congruent material comes to mind when encountering a target, this information might be used in constructing a standard of comparison to which the target might be either assimilated or contrasted along the judgment dimension (see Petty & Wegener, 1991; Sherif & Hovland, 1961). To the extent that mood-congruent memory could influence perceptions of desirability or likelihood (see McGuire & McGuire, 1991, for one discussion of such effects), this impact should become evident under conditions of biased processing (e.g., high elaboration likelihood with relatively ambiguous judgment-relevant information).

It could also be that some (at least implicit) activation of mood-congruent material might influence ability to think about information that matches or mismatches one's current feeling state. Thus, under some circumstances (e.g., with relatively complex information about the target and some constraints on time to deal with the information), one might find higher levels of processing when mood matches rather than mismatches the valence of the judgment-relevant information (cf., Forgas & Bower, 1987; Mackie & Worth, 1989). Although such an effect has not been a factor in some relevant research (e.g., in Wegener et al., 1995, the same judgment-relevant information was introduced in such a way as to make it support either an uplifting or a depressing target), future research might investigate whether or when such ability effects of matching mood with information exist.

One interesting possibility based on our hedonic-contingency work (Wegener & Petty, 1994; Wegener et al., 1995) is that some mood-congruent recall effects might be due to mood management rather than to structural properties of cognitive representations. As noted by a variety of researchers, mood-congruent memory effects have typically been stronger for happy as opposed to sad moods, perhaps because people in sad moods attempt to engage in mood repair (e.g., Blaney, 1986; Isen, 1984; Singer & Salovey, 1988). Although much of the focus in this work has been on the resulting cognitive structure differences between positive and negative material, observed recall differences could often also occur because of attempts at mood management in that recall situation. That is, mood-congruent recall in happy states could be due to happy people seeking uplifting material in memory. Some conditions have produced mood-incongruent recall for sad individuals, perhaps in attempts to repair negative feelings (see Parrott & Sabini, 1990; Smith & Petty, 1995), but it might also be the case that happy people often engage in mood management to a greater degree than sad people do (Wegener & Petty, 1994). If so, motivations to seek positive material would often be stronger in happy than in sad moods, and thus motivational pressures toward mood-congruent recall in happy moods would be stronger than motivational pressures toward mood-incongruent recall in sad states. Of course, if people believe that mood-congruent (or mood-incongruent) recall is unduly influencing their views of a target, they might attempt to change this outcome by altering their recall tendencies and searching out additional countervailing information (or by making adjustments to the perceived "biased" implications of the mood-congruent or -incongruent material).

Processing of Judgment-Relevant Information

As noted earlier, within the ELM perspective, effects of mood on amount of processing of judgment-relevant information should be most likely when elaboration likelihood is not constrained by nonmood factors to be either very high or very low. Given that nonmood factors can influence amount of information processing independent of mood effects on processing, such nonmood factors (such as external distraction [Petty et al., 1976] or high personal relevance [Petty & Cacioppo, 1979; 1990]) can also constrain any opportunity for mood effects on processing to be observed.

In our work on mood and processing, we have found that the typical effect of happy moods leading to less processing than sad or neutral moods (e.g., Bless et al., 1990; Mackie & Worth, 1989) might often be confined to situations in which people view the processing of judgment-relevant information as relatively mood threatening (i.e., depressing) or at least not mood enhancing. According to our hedonic-contingency view, because happy moods increase attention to the hedonic consequences of potential activities, happy people might avoid processing material thought to be depressing more often than would people in neutral or sad moods. When the same information supports a more enjoyable target, however, happy people can actually scrutinize that information more fully than people in sad moods (Wegener & Petty, 1996; Wegener et al., 1995). Consistent with this perspective, it might also be that happy people could process some potentially negative material more fully than people in sad or neutral moods if processing that information would allow the person to better serve mood-management goals (e.g., if the negative material discusses actions that a person could take to keep an undesirable event from occurring; see Wegener et al., 1995). This does not mean that all effects of mood on processing would necessarily be guided by differential mood management across affective states, but much of the current literature is consistent with such a mood-management perspective.

Consistent with the FCM, if people form theories about how mood influences amount of processing of information, then people might also attempt to change how much they scrutinize information if they believe that mood might be influencing thought in an undesired way (e.g., "I usually don't like to think when I'm happy, but I really should think about this, so I'd better concentrate especially intently"). Depending on the form of such theories and the nature of the information to be considered, such attempts at correcting the processing effects of mood could diminish or enhance mood-based processing differences and might even create additional processing patterns that were not originally present in the judgment setting. Although no research has directly investigated this type of naive theory, this presents a potentially interesting avenue for new research.

Mood and Creativity

Across a variety of settings, a happy mood has been shown to increase the creative nature of responses to tasks and problems (e.g., Hirt, Melton, McDonald, & Harackiewicz, 1996; Isen & Daubman, 1984; Isen, Daubman, & Nowicki, 1987; Murray et al., 1990). Although the ELM and FCM are not models of creativity, one might apply some aspects of our hedonic-contingency work to this domain. For example, in recent research, Hirt et al. (1996) showed that creative responses led to greater posttask interest in the activity (i.e., greater enjoyment of the activity). If, consistent with our hedonic-contingency perspective, happy people are more spontaneously concerned with feeling good during and after the task, they might be more likely to engage in the task in a manner that makes the task more enjoyable. Thus it could be that happy people generate more creative responses (in part) as an attempt to enjoy the task more. Such a view is also consistent with the fact that people in neutral and sad moods often do not differ in the level of their creativity (e.g., Hirt et al., 1996; Isen et al., 1987). Of course, creativity might also be spawned by other processes (e.g., the amount and nature of information cued by that feeling state; Isen et al., 1987). Even so, a mood-management interpretation also seems quite compatible with much of the evidence.

SUMMARY

The ELM (Petty & Cacioppo, 1986b) and FCM (Wegener & Petty, 1997) provide fruitful frameworks within which to organize the myriad uncorrected and corrected effects of mood (see also Petty, Cacioppo, & Kasmer, 1988; Petty et al., 1991; Wegener & Petty, 1996). The ELM focuses on the effects of mood through its multiple roles when people are not attempting to remove influences of mood on judgment (though mood could be discounted or counterargued if perceived as a weak argument). Within this perspective, mood can influence judgment through either high- or low-effort processes or by influencing the amount of effort given to scrutiny of judgment-relevant information (depending on the baseline level of elaboration likelihood created by nonmood factors). Effects of mood associated with high-effort processes should be stronger (e.g., more long lasting) than effects of mood relying on lower effort processes.

According to the FCM, when mood-based biases become salient, people can engage in corrective efforts if mood is seen as unduly biasing or inappropriate. Corrections are guided by individuals' naive theories of how mood influences perceptions of the target. Although these corrections generally entail greater cognitive effort than not making corrections, variation in effort aimed at correction corresponds to the strength of the corrected assessments (i.e., their persistence over time, resistance to change, and likelihood of the corrected assessments directing other judgments and behavior—similar to the ELM predictions dealing with uncorrected assessments of targets). Corrective effort is postulated to be conceptually distinct from effort given to general scrutiny of judgment-relevant information (i.e., although circumstances that encourage either one of these processes might also at times tend to encourage the other, circumstances also exist in which one but not the other type of effort is exerted). Important aspects of both the ELM and FCM approaches include the contextual nature of mood effects and the importance of acknowledging (and studying) the multiple processes that potentially bring about the same outcome of mood on perceptions and judgment.

ADDRESSING CONTRIBUTORS' QUESTIONS

1. The model attempts to be very general and account for a wide range of mood effects in a wide range of conditions. One can ask whether this generality comes at the expense of precision. How would you address the criticism that your model has too few constraints and too many degrees of freedom? Are there findings that could disconfirm the model?

Social psychological theories come in a variety of shapes and sizes. Some theories are quite limited in scope, focusing on a small number of potential independent variables, explanatory constructs, processes, and effects. For instance, a classical-conditioning view of mood effects on judgment might be applicable to a number of potential independent variables (mood inductions) and dependent variables (judgment targets), but the basic tenets of the view are that feelings (the unconditioned stimulus) become paired with a new target (the conditioned stimulus) such that the target comes to bring about a response that is similar to that produced by the unconditioned stimulus (the conditioned response). Such a view leads to the straightforward, but limited, hypothesis of mood-congruent judgments.

Other theories are somewhat more complex and make use of explanatory constructs that might themselves be considered more flexible. For example, in the mood-as-input view (Martin, Ward, Achee, & Wyer, 1993), positive moods can lead to either greater or less persistence on a processing task compared with negative moods. In this view, the result depends on whether people are told to focus on whether or not they enjoy the task or on whether or not they have "done enough" on the task to be satisfied with their performance. Theories at this "moderate" level of complexity are becoming common in social psychology. Some of these theories are applicable to a wide variety of phenomena, despite the use of only a small number of critical explanatory concepts. One might consider the flexible correction model (FCM; Wegener & Petty, 1997) that forms a substantial part of our view as one such theory. Though the FCM specifies a number of conditions that encourage or discourage corrections, the hypothesized corrections are predicted to be guided by stored or generated naive theories of bias or both. As reviewed elsewhere, the FCM is applicable to a wide variety of contexts in which people might become aware of potential biases, including person impression, persuasion, courtroom judgment, and other social judgment domains (see Wegener & Petty, 1997), but the set of explanatory constructs is relatively small (as in most social psychological theories).

The elaboration likelihood model (ELM; Petty, 1977; Petty & Cacioppo, 1986a) differs from most theories in this regard. In a number of senses, the ELM is a metatheory—a model that organizes and makes use of other existing theories in addition to making certain predictions of its own, such as specifying when various processes influence judgments. Consider, for example, the way in which the ELM would deal with mood effects based on classical conditioning. According to the ELM, classical-conditioning effects should be most likely when motivation or ability to engage in extensive thought about a judgment target is relatively low. That is, classical-conditioning effects do not depend on scrutiny of the qualities of targets—they are the result of a simple pairing of the emotion with, typically, a previously neutral stimulus. In fact, such low-effort effects might generally be overwhelmed by thoughts occurring in response to more high-effort scrutiny of judgment-relevant information. Thus, the ELM would limit the impact of classical conditioning on judgments to settings in which elaboration likelihood is relatively low (e.g., see Cacioppo et al., 1992). Thus some existing theories of mood effects on judgment would be viewed from an ELM perspective as focusing on relatively low-elaboration processes (e.g., classical conditioning [Staats & Staats, 1958], use of a "how do I feel about it" heuristic [Schwarz, 1990]), others on relatively high-elaboration processes (e.g., mood priming influencing thoughts; cf. Bower, 1981; Isen et al., 1978; Petty, Schumann, et al., 1993; Wegener et al., 1994), and yet others on factors that influence the amount of processing (e.g., cognitive capacity [Mackie & Worth, 1989], hedonic contingency [Wegener, Petty, & Smith, 1995]).

So, in part, some of the "constraints" come from the set of existing (complementary) theories that focus on processes involving different levels of elaboration. In this regard, however, it is important to note that a test of one (or between two) of these complementary theories is not necessarily a test of the ELM view. For example, if a series of critical tests comparing the classical-conditioning versus the mood-as-information view comes to favor one theory over another, this would not be considered a test of the ELM. The critical ELM prediction is that to the extent that these theories operate, they should work better when the elaboration likelihood is low rather than high.

This is not to say that the ELM itself is lacking constraints (for a discussion of similar concerns voiced by Mongeau & Stiff, 1993, outside the mood domain, see Petty, Wegener, et al., 1993). To be sure, if the ELM were simply to say that mood congruency can come about for many reasons (i.e., mood acting as cue, biasing processing, influencing amount of processing, acting as an argument) without specifying when each of these is most likely, the model might well be unfalsifiable. This is not what the ELM does, however. The ELM organizes all theories and processes along the elaboration continuum, stating for example that processes such as biased processing should be most likely to have an impact when elaboration likelihood is high but that other processes such as mood-based heuristics or conditioning should be most likely to have an impact when elaboration likelihood is low (e.g., see Petty, Schumann, et al., 1993; Wegener et al., 1994). Furthermore, the ELM specifies both situational and individual, as well as motivational and ability, variables that influence the elaboration likelihood. In experiments testing the ELM, it certainly would have been possible, for example, for the impact of argument-quality manipulations on judgment to be unaffected by motivational (e.g., personal relevance; Petty & Cacioppo, 1979) or ability (e.g., distraction; Petty et al., 1976) variables or for such variables to exert only strong main effects on persuasion (as in social judgment theory; Sherif & Hovland, 1961; see Petty, Cacioppo, & Haugtvedt, 1992; Petty, Wegener, et al., 1993, for additional discussion). Likewise, it would be difficult for the ELM to account for classical-conditioning (and other cue-based) effects occurring primarily under conditions of high elaboration or for biased-processing effects occurring primarily under conditions of low elaboration, though this has not been the pattern of data so far (e.g., Petty, Schumann, et al., 1993). Thus, in our view, the ELM is disconfirmable, though the data to this point have been quite supportive.

Some researchers might yearn for times when there was a single primary explanation for mood-congruency effects, and mood-incongruent outcomes signaled a specific challenge to the accepted point of view. Work using such "single-effect" and "single-process" assumptions (Petty, 1997), however, is clearly no longer tenable in the mood literature. One of the strengths of the ELM and FCM frameworks, we believe, is that both approaches explicitly dissociate outcome from process. For example, according to the ELM, mood-congruent judgment (a judgment outcome) could come about from positive mood (a) serving as a peripheral cue or easily processed piece of information, (b) biasing processing in a mood-congruent direction, (c) increasing processing when favorable (strong) judgment-relevant information is available, (d) decreasing processing when unfavorable (weak) judgment-relevant information is available, or (e) serving as a piece of favorable judgment-relevant information. Importantly, each of these possibilities is postulated to occur under specified conditions (e.g., see Petty & Cacioppo, 1986a; Petty, Cacioppo, Sedikides, & Strathman, 1988; Petty et al., 1991; Wegener & Petty, 1996). Similarly, within the FCM, a mood-congruent outcome could be the result of lack of correction for a mood-congruent bias or of a correction for a perceived mood-incongruent bias, again under specified conditions (see Wegener & Petty, 1997). The fact that many processes are acknowledged as capable of bringing about the same judgment outcome reflects a maturity in the literature and associated theory (Petty, 1997) and does not threaten the utility of the ELM and FCM. Rather, the acknowledgment of multiple processes underlying judgments improves the predictive utility of the models by enabling them to predict which of many possible mood-congruent outcomes, for example, are likely to persist over time and which are not.

2. How does the model explain the findings, over a number of experiments, that tasks that require more extensive, constructive, and substantive processing are more likely to show mood effects (e.g., Forgas, 1992)? Wouldn't your model predict mood effects as a function of priming in conditions of high substantive processing but as a function of heuristic and peripheral processes in conditions of low substantive processing? Is there some reason to assume that the affective influences produced through the heuristic mechanism are smaller than those produced through the priming mechanism?

The question correctly notes that our framework provides for mood effects under conditions of both high and low levels of information processing. We assume that mood effects, like the effects of many other variables, can occur under both high- and low-processing conditions but that the mechanisms are different.[9] For example, consider a manipulation of the number of arguments in a message. According to the ELM, increasing the number of arguments in a message from three to nine could induce more persuasion under low-elaboration conditions because the number of arguments can invoke the heuristic, "the more the better." Under high-elaboration conditions, however, increasing the number of arguments can also increase persuasion if substantive processing of the arguments leads people to generate more favorable thoughts (see Petty & Cacioppo, 1984a).

Which effect will be bigger, the cue-based (peripheral) effect under low-elaboration conditions or the substantive-processing (central) effect under high-elaboration conditions? The answer to this question should depend on a number of factors. For example, what is the size of the argument number manipulation? Perhaps comparing five versus seven arguments would produce a very small cue effect because five does not seem very different from seven as a cue to validity. However, adding two strong arguments might have a noticeable effect when processing is high. In contrast, comparing three versus nine arguments might produce a much larger cue effect that is equivalent in magnitude to the substantive-processing effect. Of course, the substantive-processing effect itself should depend on the nature of the arguments presented. If the arguments presented are not particularly persuasive, then adding arguments under high-elaboration conditions might not be helpful (and may even backfire), whereas adding them under low-elaboration conditions would be helpful because the merits of the arguments are not processed here (Petty & Cacioppo, 1984a). Thus the cue effect under low-elaboration conditions could exceed the substantive-processing effect under high-elaboration conditions. In sum, according to the ELM, the cue effect of a variable can be smaller than, equivalent to, or larger than the substantive-processing effect of the same variable. The key is to understand the nature of the cue process under investigation (e.g., the nature of the heuristic involved) and the nature of the central process under investigation (e.g., whether the arguments produce favorable, unfavorable, or mixed thoughts when processed).

---

[9]The ELM also holds that mood and other variables can work by low-effort versions of the high-effort processes that operate under high elaboration (e.g., biasing the processing of just one of the many arguments presented rather than all of them; see Petty, 1997; Petty & Wegener, 1999, for further discussion).

A similar analysis leads to the conclusion that the mood effects under high-elaboration conditions can be larger than, equivalent to, or smaller than the effects observed under low-elaboration conditions. Consider, for example, how the effects of mood might vary as a function of the number of arguments in a message. As the number of arguments in a message increases, the biasing effect of mood on thoughts might increase because there is more information that can be processed in a biased fashion. However, as the number of arguments in a message decreases, there might be fewer biased thoughts produced. Similar predictions could be made concerning the number of arguments that are ambiguous rather than unambiguous, with larger numbers of ambiguous arguments leading to increases in biased processing. If this would occur, the fewer the (ambiguous) arguments in a message, the greater the likelihood that the mood-as-cue effect would be equal to or exceed the biased-processing effect of mood. Similarly, consider a case in which positive mood is paired with a message containing positively framed arguments (e.g., if you buy this satellite dish, you will enjoy viewing all of the weekend sporting events) that are already perceived by individuals as the maximum in desirability and likelihood (i.e., enjoying all the weekend sporting events is seen as maximally good and maximally likely if the satellite dish is purchased). Here, mood is unlikely to have an effect under substantive processing because the desirability or likelihood of the consequence cannot be improved further (Petty & Wegener, 1991). The substantive-processing effect of positive mood on these positively framed arguments could be increased, however, by using arguments that were more moderate in desirability and likelihood.

Thus our framework suggests that social psychological studies of mood and judgment could produce larger mood effects under high- than under low-elaboration conditions because of the information available concerning the judgment target (e.g., numerous pieces of relatively ambiguous information). Alternatively, if mood is not the only relevant heuristic or decision rule available (e.g., if the person has an existing stereotype or category that could be used instead of mood), cue effects of mood could be small or nonexistent, especially if the alternative cues are more salient than mood. However, if other materials had been routinely selected (e.g., containing few pieces of unambiguous information or using targets for which no alternative heuristics are available), the difference in size between cue and biased-processing effects could be attenuated or reversed. We have already demonstrated in empirical research that mood effects on judgment need not be greater under high- than low-elaboration conditions (e.g., see Petty, Schumann, et al., 1993). More important, as our earlier discussion indicates, the ELM suggests variables that would moderate whether mood effects are greater or lesser under high- compared with low-elaboration conditions.

3. The model suggests that individuals in an analytic mode attend to the attributes of an object, whereas individuals in a less analytic mode attend to the object as a whole. The model further assumes that the effects of mood at these two levels of focus reflect different processes (i.e., mood-congruent retrieval versus affect as information). No data are included, however, to support the idea that more than one process is involved or that either of them is mood-congruent retrieval or affect as information. Can the assumption about different processes be supported?

This question, like the previous one, is applicable to more variables than just mood. The essence of the question appears to be this: When a variable produces the same effects under high- and low-elaboration conditions, how can you know that different processes are involved? For example, when people are shown to be influenced by the number of arguments or by mood under both high- and low-elaboration conditions, what is the evidence that the process is different?

ELM researchers have provided evidence of different processes for the same variables in a number of ways. For example, reconsider the work on number of message arguments described previously (Petty & Cacioppo, 1984a). In this work, students were presented with either three or nine arguments that were strong or weak in favor of senior comprehensive exams. The exam policy was presented as either relevant to the students (fostering high-elaboration conditions) or irrelevant (fostering low-elaboration conditions). When all of the arguments presented were strong, people were more persuaded by the nine- than the three-argument messages under both high- and low-elaboration conditions. Based on these conditions alone, it is not clear that the processes induced under high- and low-elaboration conditions were different. When the arguments were weak, nine arguments also produced more persuasion than three under low-elaboration conditions (the same result as was obtained with strong arguments). Under high-elaboration conditions with weak arguments, however, nine arguments produced less persuasion than three arguments (the opposite result to that obtained with strong arguments). The fact that the number-of-arguments manipulation had a main effect under low-elaboration conditions (i.e., more arguments increased persuasion with both strong and weak arguments) but interacted with argument quality under high-elaboration conditions (i.e, more arguments increased persuasion with strong arguments but decreased persuasion with weak arguments) suggests that the process by which argument number influences attitudes is different in high- versus low-elaboration settings.

In our research on mood effects, we have provided more direct evidence for the view that mood works differently under high- and low-elaboration conditions. Recall that in a study cited previously (Petty, Schumann, et al., 1993), the data showed that positive mood increased persuasion over neutral mood under both high- and low-elaboration conditions. However, positive mood only increased positive thoughts under high-elaboration conditions, and controlling for positive thoughts eliminated the effect of mood on attitudes in these settings. This again suggests that the effect of mood can be the same on judgments even though the mediating process differs across conditions.

Finally, it is important to reiterate what the ELM does and does not specify. The ELM holds that different types of processes can mediate the effects of mood (and other variables) under low- and high-elaboration conditions (i.e., cue-based processes versus cognitive responses in reaction to scrutiny of central merits). The ELM does not specify one particular cue-based process for low-elaboration effects of mood or one particular process by which mood affects cognitive responses in high-elaboration settings. Thus, as noted in response to the first question, the ELM does not specify whether classical conditioning, mood as information, or some other low-effort process is the one that accounts for mood effects under low-elaboration conditions. Each of these relatively simple processes might account for mood effects in some low-elaboration settings. Similarly, ELM hypotheses regarding high-elaboration effects of mood do not depend on those effects being mediated by mood-congruent retrieval per se. We have engaged in initial research to uncover mechanisms by which mood has an impact in high-elaboration settings (e.g., Wegener et al., 1994). However, the key ELM prediction is that low-effort processes (such as classical conditioning) should be responsible for mood effects when the elaboration likelihood is low, but high-effort processes (such as those postulated by expectancy-value theories) should be responsible for mood effects when the elaboration likelihood is high (Petty & Wegener, 1991; Wegener & Petty, 1996). Still other processes (e.g., hedonic-contingency mechanisms; Wegener & Petty, 1994) are more likely to come into play when the elaboration likelihood is more moderate.

ACKNOWLEDGMENTS

Work on this chapter and the research described therein was supported by a grant to Duane T. Wegener from the Yale University Social Science Research Fund and by a National Science Foundation grant (SBR-9520854.) to Richard E. Petty.

REFERENCES

Anderson, J. R., & Bower, G. H. (1973). *Human associative memory*. Washington, DC: Winston.
Berkowitz, L., Jaffee, S., Jo, E., & Troccoli, B. (2000). On the correction of feeling-induced judgmental biases. In J. P. Forgas (Ed.), *Feeling and thinking: The role of affect in social cogni-*

tion: Studies in emotion and social interaction (Second Series, pp. 131–152). New York: Cambridge University Press.

Blaney, P. H. (1986). Affect and memory: A review. Psychological Bulletin, 99, 229–246.

Bless, H., Bohner, G., Schwarz, N., & Strack, F. (1990). Mood and persuasion: A cognitive response analysis. Personality and Social Psychology Bulletin, 16, 331–345.

Bower, G. (1981). Mood and memory. American Psychologist, 36, 129–148.

Breckler, S. J., & Wiggins, E. C. (1991). Cognitive responses in persuasion: Affective and evaluative determinants. Journal of Experimental Social Psychology, 27, 180–200.

Cacioppo, J. T., Marshall-Goodell, B. S., Tassinary, L. G., & Petty, R. E. (1992). Rudimentary determinants of attitudes: Classical conditioning is more effective when prior knowledge about the attitude stimulus is low than high. Journal of Experimental Social Psychology, 28, 207–233.

Cacioppo, J. T., & Petty, R. E. (1982a). A biosocial model of attitude change. In J. T. Cacioppo & R. E. Petty (Eds.), Perspectives in cardiovascular psychophysiology (pp. 151–188). New York: Guilford.

Cacioppo, J. T., & Petty, R. E. (1982b). The need for cognition. Journal of Personality and Social Psychology, 42, 116–131.

Cacioppo, J. T., Petty, R. E., & Morris, K. (1983). Effects of need for cognition on message evaluation, recall, and persuasion. Journal of Personality and Social Psychology, 45, 805–818.

Carlson, M., Charlin, V., & Miller, N. (1988). Positive mood and helping behavior: A test of six hypotheses. Journal of Personality and Social Psychology, 55, 211–229.

Carlson, M., & Miller, N. (1987). Explanation of the relationship between negative mood and helping. Psychological Bulletin, 102, 91–108.

Catanzaro, S. J., & Mearns, J. (1990). Measuring generalized expectancies for negative mood regulation: Initial scale development and implications. Journal of Personality Assessment, 54, 546–563.

Chaiken, S. (1980). Heuristic versus systematic information processing and the use of source versus message cues in persuasion. Journal of Personality and Social Psychology, 39, 752–766.

Chaiken, S., & Maheswaran, D. (1994). Heuristic processing can bias systematic processing: Effects of source credibility, argument ambiguity, and task importance on attitude judgment. Journal of Personality and Social Psychology, 66, 460–473.

Clore, G. L., Schwarz, N., & Conway, M. (1994). Affective causes and consequences of social information processing. In R. S. Wyer & T. K. Srull (Eds.), Handbook of social cognition: Vol. 1. Basic processes (pp. 323–417). Hillsdale, NJ: Lawrence Erlbaum Associates.

Cooper, W. H. (1981). Ubiquitous halo. Psychological Bulletin, 90, 218–224.

Craik, F. I. M, & Lockhart, R. S. (1972). Levels of processing: A framework for memory research. Journal of Verbal Learning and Verbal Behavior, 11, 671–684.

DeBono, K. G., & Harnish, R. J. (1988). Source expertise, source attractiveness, and the processing of persuasive information: A functional approach. Journal of Personality and Social Psychology, 55, 541–546.

DeSteno, D., Petty, R. E., Wegener, D. T., & Rucker, D. D. (2000). Beyond valence in the perception of likelihood: The role of emotion specificity. Journal of Personality and Social Psychology, 78, 397–416.

Ellis, H. C., & Ashbrook, P. W. (1988). Resource allocation model of the effects of depressed mood states on memory. In K. Fiedler & J. Forgas (Eds.), Affect, cognition, and social behavior (pp. 25–43). Toronto, Ontario, Canada: Hogrefe.

Erber, R. (1991). Affective and semantic priming: Effects of mood on category accessibility and inference. Journal of Experimental Social Psychology, 27, 480–498.

Fishbein, M., & Ajzen, I. (1975). Belief, attitude, intention, and behavior: An introduction to theory and research. Reading, MA: Addison-Wesley.

Forgas, J. P. (1992). On bad mood and peculiar people: Affect and person typicality in impression formation. Journal of Personality and Social Psychology, 62, 863–875.

Forgas, J. P., & Bower, G. H. (1987). Mood effects on person perception judgments. *Journal of Personality and Social Psychology, 53,* 53–60.

Forgas, J. P., & Moylan, S. (1987). After the movies: The effects of mood on social judgments. *Personality and Social Psychology Bulletin, 13,* 467–477.

Griffitt, W. B. (1970). Environmental effects on interpersonal affective behavior: Ambient effective temperature and attraction. *Journal of Personality and Social Psychology, 15,* 240–244.

Heesacker, M. H., Petty, R. E., & Cacioppo, J. T. (1983). Field dependence and attitude change: Source credibility can alter persuasion by affecting message-relevant thinking. *Journal of Personality, 51,* 653–666.

Hirt, E. R., Melton, R. J., McDonald, H. E., & Harackiewicz, J. M. (1996). Processing goals, task interest, and the mood-performance relationship: A mediational analysis. *Journal of Personality and Social Psychology, 71,* 245–261.

Howard, D. J., & Barry, T. E. (1994). The role of thematic congruence between a mood-inducing event and an advertised product in determining the effects of mood on brand attitudes. *Journal of Consumer Psychology, 3,* 1–27.

Isen, A. M. (1984). Toward understanding the role of affect in cognition. In R. S. Wyer & T. K. Srull (Eds.), *Handbook of social cognition: Vol. 3* (pp. 179–236). Hillsdale, NJ: Lawrence Erlbaum Associates.

Isen, A. M., & Daubman, K. A. (1984). The influence of affect on categorization. *Journal of Personality and Social Psychology, 47,* 1206–1217.

Isen, A. M., Daubman, K. A., & Nowicki, G. P. (1987). Positive affect facilitates creative problem solving. *Journal of Personality and Social Psychology, 52,* 1122–1131.

Isen, A. M., Shalker, T., Clark, M. S., & Karp, L. (1978). Affect, accessibility of material in memory, and behavior: A cognitive loop? *Journal of Personality and Social Psychology, 36,* 1–12.

Johnson, E., & Tversky, A. (1983). Affect, generalization, and the perception of risk. *Journal of Personality and Social Psychology, 45,* 20–31.

Kiesler, C. A., & Mathog, R. (1968). The distraction hypothesis in attitude change. *Psychological Reports, 23,* 1123–1133.

Kuykendall, D., & Keating, J. (1990). Mood and persuasion: Evidence for the differential influence of positive and negative states. *Psychology and Marketing, 7,* 1–9.

Leippe, M. R., & Elkin, R. A. (1987). When motives clash: Issue involvement and response involvement as determinants of persuasion. *Journal of Personality and Social Psychology, 52,* 269–278.

Mackie, D. M., & Worth, L. T. (1989). Processing deficits and the mediation of positive affect in persuasion. *Journal of Personality and Social Psychology, 57,* 27–40.

Martin, L. L., Abend, T. A., Sedikides, C., & Green, J. (1997). How would I feel if . . . ? Mood as input to a role fulfillment evaluation process. *Journal of Personality and Social Psychology, 73,* 242–253.

Martin, L. L., Ward, D. W., Achee, J. W., & Wyer, R. S., Jr. (1993). Mood as input: People have to interpret the motivational implications of their moods. *Journal of Personality and Social Psychology, 64,* 317–326.

Mathur, M., & Chattopadhyay, A. (1991). The impact of moods generated by television programs on responses to advertising. *Psychology and Marketing, 8,* 59–77.

Mayer, J., Gaschke, Y., Braverman, D., & Evans, T. (1992). Mood-congruent judgment is a general effect. *Journal of Personality and Social Psychology, 63,* 119–132.

McClelland, J. L., Rumelhart, D. E., & Hinton, G. E. (1986). The appeal of parallel distributed processing. In D. E. Rumelhart, J. L. McClelland, & The PDP Research Group (Eds.), *Parallel distributed processing* (Vol. 1, pp. 3–44). Cambridge, MA: MIT Press.

McGuire, W. J., & McGuire, C. V. (1991). The content, structure, and operation of thought systems. In R. S. Wyer, Jr., & T. Srull (Eds.), *Advances in social cognition* (Vol. 4, pp. 1–78). Hillsdale, NJ: Lawrence Erlbaum Associates.

Miller, N., & Carlson, M. (1990). Valid theory-testing meta-analyses further question negative state relief model of helping. *Psychological Bulletin, 107*, 215–225.

Mongeau, P. A., & Stiff, J. B. (1993). Specifying causal relationships in the elaboration likelihood model. *Communication Theory, 3*, 65–72.

Murray, N., Sujan, H., Hirt, E. R., & Sujan, M. (1990). The influence of mood on categorization: A cognitive flexibility interpretation. *Journal of Personality and Social Psychology, 59*, 411–425.

Ottati, V. C., & Isbell, L. M. (1996). Effects of mood during exposure to target information on subsequently reported judgments: An on-line model of misattribution and correction. *Journal of Personality and Social Psychology, 71*, 39–53.

Parrott, W. G., & Sabini, J. (1990). Mood and memory under natural conditions: Evidence for mood incongruent recall. *Journal of Personality and Social Psychology, 59*, 321–336.

Petty, R. E. (1997). The evolution of theory and research in social psychology: From single to multiple effect and process models. In C. McGarty & S. A. Haslam (Eds.), *The message of social psychology: Perspectives on mind in society* (pp. 268–290). Oxford, England: Blackwell.

Petty, R. E., & Cacioppo, J. T. (1979). Issue involvement can increase or decrease persuasion by enhancing message-relevant cognitive responses. *Journal of Personality and Social Psychology, 37*, 1915–1926.

Petty, R. E., & Cacioppo, J. T. (1981). *Attitudes and persuasion: Classic and contemporary approaches.* Dubuque, IA: Brown.

Petty, R. E., & Cacioppo, J. T. (1984a). The effects of involvement on responses to argument quantity and quality: Central and peripheral routes to persuasion. *Journal of Personality and Social Psychology, 46*, 69–81.

Petty, R. E., & Cacioppo, J. T. (1984b). Source factors and the elaboration likelihood model of persuasion. *Advances in Consumer Research, 11*, 668–672.

Petty, R. E., & Cacioppo, J. T. (1986a). *Communication and persuasion: Central and peripheral routes to attitude change.* New York: Springer-Verlag.

Petty, R. E., & Cacioppo, J. T. (1986b). The elaboration likelihood model of persuasion. In L. Berkowitz (Ed.), *Advances in experimental social psychology* (Vol. 19, pp. 123–205). New York: Academic Press.

Petty, R. E., & Cacioppo, J. T. (1990). Involvement and persuasion: Tradition versus integration. *Psychological Bulletin, 107*, 367–374.

Petty, R. E., Cacioppo, J. T., & Goldman, R. (1981). Personal involvement as a determinant of argument-based persuasion. *Journal of Personality and Social Psychology, 41*, 847–855.

Petty, R. E., Cacioppo, J. T., & Haugtvedt, C. (1992). Involvement and persuasion: An appreciative look at the Sherifs' contribution to the study of self-relevance and attitude change. In D. Granberg, & G. Sarup (Ed.), *A Social judgment and intergroup relations: Essays in honor of Muzifer Sherif* (pp. 147–175). New York: Springer-Verlag.

Petty, R. E., Cacioppo, J. T., & Kasmer, J. (1988). The role of affect in the elaboration likelihood model of persuasion. In L. Donohew, H. Sypher, & E. T. Higgins (Eds.), *Communication, social cognition, and affect* (pp. 117–146). Hillsdale, NJ: Lawrence Erlbaum Associates.

Petty, R. E., Cacioppo, J. T., & Schumann, D. (1983). Central and peripheral routes to advertising effectiveness: The moderating role of involvement. *Journal of Consumer Research, 10*, 134–148.

Petty, R. E., Cacioppo, J. T., Sedikides, C., & Strathman, A. (1988). Affect and persuasion: A contemporary perspective. *American Behavioral Scientist, 31*, 355–371.

Petty, R. E, Gleicher, F., & Baker, S. (1991). Multiple roles for affect in persuasion. In J. Forgas (Ed.), *Emotion and social judgments* (pp. 181–200). Oxford, England: Pergamon.

Petty, R. E., Haugtvedt, C., & Smith, S. M. (1995). Elaboration as a determinant of attitude strength: Creating attitudes that are persistent, resistant, and predictive of behavior. In

R. E. Petty & J. A. Krosnick (Eds.), *Attitude strength: Antecedents and consequences* (pp. 93–130). Mahway, NJ: Lawrence Erlbaum Associates.

Petty, R. E., Priester, J. R., & Wegener, D. T. (1994). Cognitive processes in attitude change. In R. S. Wyer & T. K. Srull (Eds.), *Handbook of social cognition: Vol. 2. Applications* (2nd ed., pp. 69–142). Hillsdale, NJ: Lawrence Erlbaum Associates.

Petty, R. E., Schumann, D., Richman, S., & Strathman, A. (1993). Positive mood and persuasion: Different roles for affect under high and low elaboration conditions. *Journal of Personality and Social Psychology, 64,* 5–20.

Petty, R. E., & Wegener, D. T. (1991). Thought systems, argument quality, and persuasion. In R. S. Wyer & T. K. Srull (Eds.), *Advances in social cognition* (Vol. 4, pp. 143–161). Hillsdale, NJ: Lawrence Erlbaum Associates.

Petty, R. E., & Wegener, D. T. (1993). Flexible correction processes in social judgment: Correcting for context-induced contrast. *Journal of Experimental Social Psychology, 29,* 137–165.

Petty, R. E., & Wegener, D. T. (1998a). Attitude change. In D. Gilbert, S. Fiske, & G. Lindzey (Eds.), *The handbook of social psychology* (4th ed., Vol. 1, pp. 323–390). New York: McGraw-Hill.

Petty, R. E., & Wegener, D. T. (1998b). Match versus mismatch of persuasive appeals to functional bases of attitudes: Effects on processing of message content. *Personality and Social Psychology Bulletin, 24,* 227–240.

Petty, R. E., & Wegener, D. T. (1999). The elaboration likelihood model: Current status and controversies. In S. Chaiken & Y. Trope (Eds.), *Dual process theories in social psychology* (pp. 41–72). New York: Guilford.

Petty, R. E., Wegener, D. T., Fabrigar, L. R., Priester, J. R., & Cacioppo, J. T. (1993). Conceptual and methodological issues in the elaboration likelihood model of persuasion: A reply to the Michigan State critics. *Communication Theory, 3,* 336–363.

Petty, R. E., Wegener, D. T., & White, P. (1998). Flexible correction processes in social judgment: Implications for persuasion. *Social Cognition, 16,* 93–113.

Petty, R. E., Wells, G. L., & Brock, T. C. (1976). Distraction can enhance or reduce yielding to propaganda: Thought disruption versus effort justification. *Journal of Personality and Social Psychology, 34,* 874–884.

Puckett, J. M., Petty, R. E., Cacioppo, J. T., & Fisher, D. L. (1983). The relative impact of age and attractiveness stereotypes on persuasion. *Journal of Gerontology, 38,* 340–343.

Rosenberg, M. (1965). *Society and the adolescent self-image.* Princeton, NJ: Princeton University Press.

Salovey, P., Mayer, J. D., Goldman, S. L., & Palfai, T. P. (1995). Emotional attention, clarity, and repair: Exploring emotional intelligence using the trait meta-mood scale. In J. Pennebaker (Ed.), *Emotion, disclosure, and health* (pp. 125–154). Washington, DC: American Psychological Association.

Schwarz, N. (1990). Feelings as information: Informational and motivational functions of affective states. In R. M. Sorrentino & E. T. Higgins (Eds.), *Handbook of motivation and cognition: Foundations of social behavior* (Vol. 2, pp. 527–561). New York: Guilford.

Schwarz, N., Bless, H., & Bohner, G. (1991). Mood and persuasion: Affective states influence the processing of persuasive communications. In M. P. Zanna (Ed.), *Advances in experimental social psychology* (Vol. 24, pp. 161–201). San Diego, CA: Academic Press.

Schwarz, N., & Clore, G. L. (1983). Mood, misattribution, and judgments of well-being: Informative and directive functions of affective states. *Journal of Personality and Social Psychology, 45,* 513–523.

Shavitt, S., & Fazio, R. H. (1991). Effects of attribute salience on the consistency between attitudes and behavior predictions. *Personality and Social Psychology Bulletin, 17,* 507–516.

Shavitt, S., Swan, S., Lowrey, T. M., & Wänke, M. (1994). The interaction of endorser attractiveness and involvement in persuasion depends on the goal that guides message processing. *Journal of Consumer Psychology, 3,* 137–162.

Sherif, M., & Hovland, C. I. (1961). *Social judgment: Assimilation and contrast effects in communication and attitude change*. New Haven, CT: Yale University Press.

Singer, J. A., & Salovey, P. (1988). Mood and memory: Evaluating the network theory of affect. *Clinical Psychology Review, 8*, 211–251.

Smith, E. R. (1989). Procedural efficiency: General and specific components and effects on social judgment. *Journal of Experimental Social Psychology, 25*, 500–523.

Smith, E. R. (1996). What do connectionism and social psychology offer each other? *Journal of Personality and Social Psychology, 70*, 893–912.

Smith, S. M., & Petty, R. E. (1995). Personality moderators of mood congruency effects on cognition: The role of self-esteem and negative mood regulation. *Journal of Personality and Social Psychology, 68*, 1092–1107.

Snyder, M. (1979). Self-monitoring processes. In L. Berkowitz (Ed.), *Advances in experimental social psychology* (Vol. 12, pp. 86–128). New York: Academic Press.

Snyder, M., & DeBono, K. G. (1989). Understanding the functions of attitudes: Lessons from personality and social behavior. In S. J. Pratkanis, S. J. Breckler, & A. G. Greenwald (Ed.), *Attitude structure and function* (pp. 339–359). Hillsdale, NJ: Lawrence Erlbaum Associates.

Staats, A. W., & Staats, C. K. (1958). Attitudes established by classical conditioning. *Journal of Abnormal and Social Psychology, 57*, 37–40.

Tesser, A., & Cowan, C. (1975). Some effects of thought and number of cognitions on attitude change. *Social Behavior and Personality, 3*, 165–173.

Thorndike, E. L. (1920). A constant error in psychological ratings. *Journal of Applied Psychology, 4*, 25–29.

Wegener, D. T., & Petty, R. E. (1994). Mood-management across affective states: The hedonic contingency hypothesis. *Journal of Personality and Social Psychology, 66*, 1034–1048.

Wegener, D. T., & Petty, R. E. (1995). Flexible correction processes in social judgment: The role of naive theories in corrections for perceived bias. *Journal of Personality and Social Psychology, 68*, 36–51.

Wegener, D. T., & Petty, R. E. (1996). Effects of mood on persuasion processes: Enhancing, reducing, and biasing scrutiny of attitude-relevant information. In L. L. Martin and A. Tesser (Eds.), *Striving and feeling: Interactions among goals, affect, and self-regulation* (pp. 329–362). Mahwah, NJ: Lawrence Erlbaum Associates.

Wegener, D. T., & Petty, R. E. (1997). The flexible correction model: The role of naive theories of bias in bias correction. In M. P. Zanna (Ed.), *Advances in experimental social psychology* (Vol. 29, pp. 141–208). New York: Academic Press.

Wegener, D. T., Petty, R. E., & Dunn, M. (1998). The metacognition of bias correction: Naive theories of bias and the flexible correction model. In V. Yzerbyt, G. Lories, & B. Dardenne (Eds.), *Metacognition: Cognitive and social dimensions* (pp. 202–227). London: Sage.

Wegener, D. T., Petty, R. E., & Klein, D. J. (1994). Effects of mood on high elaboration attitude change: The mediating role of likelihood judgments. *European Journal of Social Psychology, 24*, 25–44.

Wegener, D. T., Petty, R. E., & Smith, S. M. (1995). Positive mood can increase or decrease message scrutiny: The hedonic contingency view of mood and message processing. *Journal of Personality and Social Psychology, 69*, 5–15.

Worth, L. T., & Mackie, D. M. (1987). Cognitive mediation of positive mood in persuasion. *Social Cognition, 5*, 76–94.

Zanna, M. P., Kiesler, C. A., & Pilkonis, P. A. (1970). Positive and negative attitudinal affect established by classical conditioning. *Journal of Personality and Social Psychology, 14*, 321–328.

Author Index

Subject Index